LETTERS TO GIL

LETTERS
TO GIL

A MEMOIR

MALIK AL NASIR

With a Foreword by Lemn Sissay

WILLIAM
COLLINS

William Collins
An imprint of HarperCollins*Publishers*
1 London Bridge Street
London SE1 9GF

WilliamCollinsBooks.com

HarperCollins*Publishers*
1st Floor, Watermarque Building, Ringsend Road
Dublin 4, Ireland

First published in Great Britain in 2021 by William Collins

1

A catalogue record for this book is available from the British Library

ISBN 978-0-00-846443-1

Typeset in Dante MT Std
Printed and bound in the UK using 100% renewable electricity at CPI Group (UK) Ltd

MIX
Paper from
responsible sources
FSC
www.fsc.org   FSC™ C007454

This book is produced from independently certified FSC™ paper
to ensure responsible forest management.

For more information visit: www.harpercollins.co.uk/green

This book is dedicated to the woman from whom
I derived my strength, my resilience and who gave me life –
my mother – Sonia Parry.

FOREWORD

Like the Mariner in Samuel Taylor Coleridge's ballad *The Rime of the Ancient Mariner*, Malik Al Nasir has an incredible story to tell. His book *Letters to Gil* is part of a surge of literature from writers who have been fostered, adopted, orphaned or in children's homes, who have been treated atrociously and who have lived to tell epic tales of betrayal and redemption. With *Letters to Gil*, Malik has joined this illustrious company of creative explorers of the universe: writers like Sally Bayley, Oscar nominee Samantha Morton, Jenni Fagan and the legendary Jeanette Winterson. Regardless of their personal biographies they are all storytellers. Commanders of the written word. Ciphers of the spoken word. They are fuelled by wild imagination, by hard-won facts and attention to detail.

Memory can be a haunting phantasm until the writer coaxes it onto the page. It's no surprise writers who have not experienced such dislocation as Malik employ the fostered, adopted or orphaned child in their 'fiction'. Homer did it: Oedipus was a foundling. J.K. Rowling did it with Harry Potter. He was a foster child. The list is long: think of *Jane Eyre*, *David Copperfield*, *Lord of the Rings*, *Wuthering Heights*. These all-star fostered, adopted or orphaned characters. Superman spent time in children's homes and he was adopted!

There is something about the child who has spent time in 'care' that fiction writers love, because without the classic family structure the child and adult digs deep to become the hero of their own story, be they Oliver Twist or Lyra Belacqua. These characters don't need a shocking back story for propulsion. They overcome adversity by becoming more of who they already are.

Enough of fiction. Malik's relationship with Gil Scott-Heron is magical, and his story of perseverance against all odds is real. What a life this man has had. And what a read you have ahead of you. The moment I finished the manuscript I called Malik on the phone to tell him how transfixed I had been by *Letters to Gil*, by the intimacy of the time he and Gil spent together and by his incredible life. Full disclosure: I have been a fan of Gil Scott-Heron for thirty-five years and I have known Malik for twenty-nine. This book was kind of made just for me ... which is how every book should feel.

My own connection with Malik, of which I am increasingly proud, began the day I encouraged him on to the stage. He recalls the moment in 2018, in the Edge Hill University magazine *Degree*.

[Malik] was coaxed into the arena by another North West poet, Lemn Sissay, who was performing with Jalal Nuriddin. Lemn asked to hear one of Malik's poems, told him it was good, and invited him to perform at the open mic event which followed the show.

'I remember standing up there with my head bowed, and all these people staring at me,' says Malik. 'And I was really self-conscious. Introducing myself saying "I'm Malik Al Nasir, I'm not a poet. I am just an ordinary guy who happened to write some poetry." And then I launched into my poem and I got a standing ovation and that changed everything for me, that was the point that I realised that I could actually do this.'

I feel proud to have played a small part in a great life. In our phone conversation, Malik said, 'I put the poems in my mother's cupboard and published them in December 2004.' That debut collection was called *Ordinary Guy* by Mark T. Watson, as author, and Malik Al Nasir, as illustrator, with a 'Fore-Word' by Jalal Nuriddin of the Last Poets, Harlem's original protest poets.

Given that I have known Malik for so long, given that just a few years ago he helped me in my quest to sue the government for stealing my childhood, something he himself had done as part of a class action some years before, given all *that* … how little I knew about his heroic life until I read *Letters to Gil*. Wow!

Like the Ancient Mariner, Malik found himself out at sea, literally and metaphorically. Like the Ancient Mariner, the crew turned against him. Like the Ancient Mariner, he was challenged and changed by the experience, in his case from Mark Watson to

Malik Al Nasir; and like the Ancient Mariner, he was tested, traumatised and eventually transformed.

At a certain part of his mind-boggling life story, the spirit of Gil Scott-Heron filled Malik's sails. In *Letters to Gil*, you will be spirited away too, as I have been. You will learn much about Gil Scott-Heron, but it is Malik's story that transfixes me in its glittering eye. I love Gil Scott-Heron, as a fan. Malik's relationship with him is more than fandom. In *Letters to Gil*, I see Malik emerge from under the wing of *the* Gil Scott-Heron. And I think to myself, How did he do it? This miraculous man, one of us, this complex and beautiful hero.

Lemn Sissay, June 2021

PROLOGUE

It's June 2nd, 2011, and I am sitting in a church on the East Side Highway in Harlem, New York, watching Kanye West perform his hit 'Lost in the World'. West is the most successful rapper in the world and he doesn't normally arrive at events without fanfare and a huge entourage. But today, he's come with just his manager. I don't usually sit in a church these days, but this time, I've made an exception.

Kanye's here to pay tribute to the poet, musician and civil rights activist Gil Scott-Heron – a man who inspired his own career and many others. 'Lost in the World' contains a poem entitled 'Comment #1' from Gil Scott-Heron's debut album, which had launched the radical black poet onto the world stage back in 1970. Kanye, famous for sampling the great masters, had decided to take the whole poem and wrap his rap around it.

Alongside members of Gil's family and friends sitting in Harlem's Riverside Church, watching Kanye perform, are a host of music industry heads and famous musicians, some of whom have played in Gil's bands over his forty-year recording career. Gil's ex-wife, the actress Brenda Sykes, is here to deliver the eulogy.

Like all funerals, it's a time for reflection. Everyone present is taking stock of how Gil's death has left a huge hole in their lives.

You might ask who I am and what I was doing sitting there, in that grand neo-Gothic church in Upper Manhattan? Like everyone else, I was paying homage to one of the greats of American black music. But for me, it was much more than that, which compelled me to fly 3,000 miles to pay my respects.

This is the story of my life's journey, which had culminated at this juncture. In these moments of reflection, a journey – which had shaped the man that I became and would forever shape the man that I would become – had been brought to an abrupt end ...

BLACK & BLUE

(A POEM FOR GIL)

Life can be so sad,
when you're black & blue.
Running 'round in circles,
you don't know what to do.
With all the worries in the world
beating down on you.
Is it little wonder why you cry,
when you're black & blue?

Every day's a bad-old-day,
when you're black & blue.
The good times only memories
or dreams that might come true.
Night and day you ponder
what the world is coming to.
But still you're left to wonder why,
when black, you're always blue?

It doesn't seem to matter,
what you say or do.
Close your ears and close your eyes
but still it gets to you.
To stand and fight. To run and hide.
To turn and face the truth.
That sweetness flowed from lions' bones
but first came black & blue.

No one says you have to cry,
because you're black & blue.
So wipe the teardrops from your eye
and view the world anew.
Turn your worries into rhythm,
troubles into song.
'Cause black and blue are as beautiful
as night and day are long.

Let it be, just what it is,
and keep your mind intact.
Like summer sun and autumn rain,
it's just a natural fact.
As long as you can bring about
the melody in you.
You'll soon find out,
there's more to being black
than feeling blue.

CHAPTER 1

THE MEETING

The air was thick with cigarette smoke and expectation. It was 1984, and Liverpool's Royal Court Theatre was packed.

My name is Malik Al Nasir, but that wasn't always so. In 1984, I was called Mark Watson. I was homeless, bereft of hope, and searching for some inspiration.

I'd heard that Gil Scott-Heron was performing in Liverpool. Everybody in our community – the city's black community, that is – had turned out to see him. The show was the latest in a world-wide tour in opposition to Ronald Reagan's re-election campaign. Gil's music was politically charged and talked of social struggles; this struck a chord with the thousands of fans who had turned out to see him, especially the Toxteth community groups, such as the Liverpool Black Caucus, which formed during the Toxteth riots of 1981. I'd turned up at the show with no ticket and no cash, just a determination to get in. As I approached the stage door, I saw Penny Potter in the line, and I called out to her and asked if she could get me in. Penny was my brother's mate's girlfriend, and she was also a photographer. Thankfully she had a backstage pass, and she told the doorman that I was her assistant. It worked. We entered the backstage area while everyone else was queuing up. Throngs of people were corralled outside the main entrance. We passed through the security cordon and into the theatre's main hall from the stage side, which put us in the press pit, just below the stage, between the crowd barriers and the stage itself. It was a prime vantage point, allowing me to watch the whole show from the front row.

I was utterly mesmerised throughout. Gil was a captivating, luminous figure, with his signature 1970s black-power afro hair bulging out of the sides of his rimmed denim bucket hat. Tellingly, Gil was wearing a Black Caucus T-shirt on the night of the gig. This tall, thin man, with a light brown complexion – derived of his Jamaican ancestry, no doubt mixed with a few colonial European genes – had walked out on stage to rapturous applause. You could hardly hear yourself think. Then, like a world leader, he raised his hand and the crowd fell silent. You could hear a pin drop.

'How's everybody doing?' he asked, raising the roof once again. It was as if he'd already played the show and won over the crowd, but he hadn't even stroked the keys on his piano.

There was something in the atmosphere that night, a sense of anticipation, and I could tell that this was special. We were a generation looking for something, though I honestly couldn't say what that was. We wanted change, but we didn't know where it would come from. Gil represented much more than simply an artist coming to do a show; people expected something more from him. He was a symbol of their resistance: people wanted him to know that, and he did.

Gil came on stage alone, and started the show by cracking a few jokes, mostly at the expense of then prime minister, Margaret Thatcher. Thatcher was regarded with utter contempt in the city of Liverpool, where no Conservative had won a seat in Parliament, or on the City Council, in decades. This contempt wasn't confined to the Militant Labour Council led by Derek Hatton (whom we referred to as 'Degsy') and the unions. Everyone despised Thatcher and her government's plans to put Liverpool into what was termed 'managed decline'. Liverpool's grand if somewhat run-down architecture in the city centre pointed to its prosperous past, but that was long behind it, and the region's shipbuilding and other industries were collapsing. Just as Thatcher had shown no pity for the destruction her policies were wreaking on the rest of the industrial North, she showed no sympathy at all for this city's plight.

Thatcher's friendship with the US Republican president, Ronald Reagan, was another source of rancour. Gil's satirical mockery of Reagan's career on his new single, 'Re-Ron', provided a soundtrack for political rebellion that many people in Britain could relate to. The two leaders were seen to have taken their respective nations' 'special relationship' beyond its stated purpose as 'strategic allies' to form a right-wing ideological alignment between the British Conservatives and the US Republicans, and furthermore, to take that relationship into the realms of the absurd.

As Gil continued to enthral the local crowd with his quick-witted repartee, his band emerged onto the stage and began plugging in. For this tour, Gil had brought over a new band. His collaboration with jazz pianist and flautist Brian Jackson was now over, and his former group – The Midnight Band – was replaced with a drummer, bass player, guitarist, tenor saxophonist and percussionist. They operated under the name Amere Facade.

The band's definitive sound came from Gil's 1960s analogue Fender Rhodes electric piano, on which he produced a haunting whirlwind of diminished jazz and blues chords. You got a sense that he was taking you out of your musical comfort zone as your ears tried to render the melody into something familiar. When the band kicked in, you resigned yourself to the reality that you'd never heard anything like this music before. You found yourself submitting to its evocative ambience and allowed it to take you to wherever Gil wanted it to go.

It was hard to describe Gil's performance – he rapped, he played jazz piano, he sang and he recited poetry. In between songs, you could have mistaken him for a stand-up comedian; his jokes, however, had a very serious side – they would make you laugh and pause for thought at the same time. He might have been just singing a song, but it was as if he was part of a collective soul that existed in the room. You could almost feel it in the atmosphere surrounding you. Gil had a name for it – 'The Vibosphere'.

On the night of the show, I was eighteen years old. I'd had a traumatic childhood in local authority care, from which I'd just recently emerged. I had no prospects. A year or so before, my older brother Reynold had introduced me to one of Gil's albums, *Moving Target*. It had a picture of Gil running through the streets but seen through the telescopic lens of a gun sight.

Reynold was politically engaged and well-read, unlike me. I didn't take life too seriously, partly because I couldn't face up to what had happened to me. Reynold, on the other hand, was 'deep' – a sort of ghetto philosopher. He could see through the veneer of life and cut through all the bullshit to get to the kernels of truth that lay within. Some people were unnerved by this, as he had no problem working you out in about two seconds flat and then telling you exactly what you were, and he'd always be spot on. It was like being stripped in public; suddenly you'd feel like your inner self was somehow exposed, he could disarm you with words and would deliver them with the poise of a cobra, gazing attentively before spitting venom in a deadly strike. We'd often joke about the fact that in Chinese astrology, he was born in the year of the snake.

I looked up to Reynold. He was not only clever but artistic. He could see an object and just draw it and it would look exactly like the real thing. He used to create crazy cartoon characters and then bring them to life on the page. It was Reynold who shaped my musical tastes in my late teens, I just tended to follow his lead.

One day, he had sat me down and started to pick me apart, as he was apt to do. As we spoke, we listened to Gil Scott-Heron's song 'Washington D.C.', from *Moving Target*, on Reynold's stack system.

In those days, you either had a 'stack' or a 'rack' system to play music. Most working-class kids had racks – cheap, all-in-one hi-fi units pioneered by Alan Sugar's Amstrad company, in which everything – the amplifier, speakers, tape deck and turntable – was integrated. With a stack system, you bought all the individual components and stacked them on top of each other. An amplifier alone could cost you the same or more than a whole rack system.

Black kids were obsessed with having a proper stack system, and you'd save every penny you had just to buy one component.

'Washington D.C.' sounded amazing on Reynold's stack. I was so consumed by the music – its heavy funky bassline filled with 'slapping' and 'popping', a style of bass-playing made famous around that time by musicians such as Stanley Clarke and Funkadelic's Bootsy Collins – that I barely listened to the lyrics at first.

But then I listened intently. At the end of the song, Reynold asked me: 'What did that mean to you?' I looked up at him from my perch on the couch, as he lifted the arm on the turntable to select another track on the record. I felt like I should say something profound, but in truth, because I was concentrating on that bassline, the words and their meanings had gone over my head. 'I really don't know,' I replied.

'Gil is talking about the urban ghettos that surround the White House, the bits the tourists don't see, the reality of the city's ghetto life.' My brother explained what the song really meant. He drew a parallel between what Gil was talking about in America and what we were facing in post-riot Toxteth in Liverpool. We were the invisible minority here; poor black people, living on the doorsteps of the rich whites. Reynold was trying to wake me up politically by relating the lyrics to the life I was then living. He was also concerned about my future. I had already got in with the wrong crowd, and he was concerned that if I didn't dissociate myself from them, it would only be a matter of time before I would be incarcerated again – and this time not in a care home.

So when Reynold heard Gil Scott-Heron was performing in Liverpool, he encouraged me to go to the show. He figured, I guess, that I might get a little positive inspiration. Little did he or I know the extent to which that very encounter with Gil Scott-Heron was about to change my life.

After the gig, I went backstage with Penny. Gil was standing there with loads of people around him; photographers snapping away, reporters stuffing mics under his nose, promoters carrying bags of cash, the band members waiting to get paid. I stood by the door feeling very unsure of myself, and then the promoter decided there were too many people backstage and shuffled everyone out.

I'll never forget how a security guard, a friend of mine called John 'Robbo', helped me out in that moment. Robbo, with his clean-shaven head, hobnailed boots, white T-shirt and black braces with half-mast trousers, had a classic skinhead look – and as any black person knew in the 1970s and 1980s, if you saw a

Gil's 1984 performance at Liverpool's Royal Court Theatre. © Penny Potter

skinhead, you had two choices: fight or run. But while Robbo may have looked like a racist thug, he was the total opposite. He recognised me. 'Mark, wha'ppen, man?' he said. 'Wha'ppen, Robbo, what are you doing here?' I asked.

'Working security for the theatre.' A light went on in my head. 'Listen, Robbo, I've got to see Gil. Help me out, man?'

'Look,' said Robbo, 'go and wait on the top of that spiral staircase, when all these guys have cleared out, come back down and I'll let you in.'

I ran up to the top of the black wrought-iron spiral stairs and waited. I could see a guy in a long trenchcoat, his jet-black hair neatly gelled and slicked back meticulously into a ponytail, as he waved everybody out of the backstage area, except for Gil, the band and a few girls who were with their entourage. I remember sitting there on those cold, cast-iron stairs for what seemed an eternity, but in reality was just a few short minutes. My sense of anticipation and excitement was almost overwhelming.

I was still intoxicated with the magic of the performance I'd witnessed. It was like nothing I'd ever seen or heard. I'd been to a few concerts before, but the bands playing usually sounded better on their records. This was different. The songs that Reynold had played me on the album were amazing, but the live experience was nothing short of spectacular. Soon enough, I heard a whistling sound, looked below and saw Robbo's bald head. He was motioning me to come down. Robbo swung open the dressing-room door and there was Gil.

Gil exuded a kind of presence that can't easily be put into words, like he was shrouded in a sort of invisible aura that connected to the souls of those who came into contact with him.

It's one of those things you can't quite put your finger on, but everybody feels it.

I'd tried to meet artists before at the Empire Theatre, people like the Moody Blues and AC/DC, but they always pushed past the crowd on their way to their tour bus. But here there were still people buzzing round. Everybody seemed to want something from Gil. I remember feeling a slight unease at this, that the man had just given his all and people still wanted more from him. I decided that I didn't want anything from him. I wanted to give him something, a compliment. I walked purposefully across the room, apparently unnoticed by his entourage. Gil, who was sitting down, looked up at me and cast a heart-warming smile, which immediately put me at ease and made me feel welcome. I reached out, shook his hand and said: 'Thank you, man, you really moved me and that was a great performance, I appreciate it.'

As I turned around to leave, I heard his deep distinctive baritone voice call out, 'Hold on a minute, brother.' He got up and walked towards me. 'What's going on round here?' he asked. 'I heard y'all had some riots?'

I started to tell him about Toxteth, then the heart of Liverpool's black community, and how people here – and across black communities in England – had rioted, in what the newspapers came to refer to as 'the long hot summer of 1981'.

Gil said: 'Yeah, we had some riots back in DC.' He wanted to know about our struggles. I was thrilled to be in conversation with him. It felt surreal. Imagine, my whole community – and what seemed like the whole city – had turned out to see this guy; and there I was, seemingly the most insignificant person there, or so I felt at that time, homeless, broke, unemployed, traumatised, having a one-to-one with this titan of the US black protest movement. It has taken me years to come to terms with the gravity of what was happening in that moment to this eighteen-year-old kid. In some ways, I'm still coming to terms with it.

When it came time to leave the venue, we were deep in conversation. Gil said, 'C'mon with us, brother. Pick up some drums or something.' So I grabbed a set of drums, carried them out of the stage door and packed them into the back of the tour bus. Gil motioned for me to jump in. He said, 'Get on the bus and come with us.'

We drove to the Atlantic Towers Hotel on Liverpool's waterfront.

The band was buzzing after a great show, and there were some journalists hanging around in the lobby, chatting with members of the band. Gil said to me, 'Hey, brother, we have a day off tomorrow, why don't you come on down?' I happily agreed.

Gil's road manager was a guy called Phil Rainford. He was the figure I'd seen looming backstage in a long trenchcoat and with hair slicked back into a ponytail.

Gil and the band, I was to discover, called him 'Count Rainford' or else just 'the Count'. Despite his vampiric look, he was actually a really nice guy, polite and courteous. I'm sure he was wondering who I was, to be getting so much of Gil's attention, but he didn't say anything. Phil passed pleasantries with me, until Gil announced, 'Count! This here is brother Mark.' I was shocked that he'd remembered my name. 'He's been telling me about Toxteth and the riots. I wanna see for myself. Can you drive us?' 'Sure,' replied the Count.

We left the band at the hotel and a few minutes later we were back on the tour bus, just Gil, the Count and me. I gave them a guided tour of the riot zone. By now it was late and the roads were deserted, so we had a run of the streets, unencumbered by the daytime hustle and bustle. I took Gil to Parliament Street and Lodge Lane, where there were still a lot of burnt-out buildings among other evidence of the unrest. I gave him a running commentary of the week-long chaos and the aftermath of the uprising of 1981.

I explained to Gil that this hadn't been the first racially charged riot in Liverpool's history. There'd been one in 1919, in the same area, after white soldiers had returned from the First World War to a decimated local economy. I told Gil this was history people in the black community had learned about through local research, and from knowledge that had been passed down through generations via oral history.

I told him how black people, drafted in from the Empire's colonies, had fought for the British in the trenches of the First World War. They were known as 'Black Tommies'. There had been a Black Tommy called Walter Tull, a footballer who had played for several British teams before the war, including Tottenham Hotspur. He was killed in the war but was only really known for his football career, as black soldiers were rarely memorialised.

The Black Tommies who returned to Britain after the war were persecuted, as were their black comrades from Africa and the Caribbean, who'd been drafted in to work on the docks and in the factories. Rather than being honoured for their considerable contribution to the war effort, they were maligned for having jobs that white servicemen felt they deserved. Returning white soldiers had started to push to get the local government to 'send the Ethiopians back'.

All black people were referred to as Ethiopians in those days, regardless of where they actually came from. The lord mayor had requested funds to 'repatriate the Ethiopians' but the government refused this, so they were stuck here. The clamour to throw them out of the factories and the docks to make way for returning white servicemen grew and eventually erupted. A mob of white locals chased a 24-year-old black man from Bermuda called Charles Wootton along Parliament Street and down to the river. They beat and stoned him to death and threw him in the Mersey. That was the spark that ignited the 1919 Liverpool race riots.

After the more recent riots of 1981, local activists had acquired a building on Parliament Street and named it the Charles Wootton College of Further Education. I had attended a drama class there run by Michelle Charters, a local black woman who was one of the Liverpool Black Sisters, a group of politicised and vocal black women from Toxteth who were engaged in community development. Michelle had us pitch a play about Charles Wootton to Channel 4 TV. I only had a minor part with a few lines – which I memorised – but the producers didn't go for it. As the Count drove past the Charles Wootton building, I explained the whole backstory to Gil.

When we arrived back at the hotel about an hour later, I was still telling Gil the history of Liverpool's black community. I asked him if I could cook a meal for the band, since they had the next day off. I was astounded by how humble and accommodating he was. He asked how many people he could bring? 'Bring everyone,' I replied.

I'd learned how to cook in the children's homes whilst in local authority care. The trouble was, I didn't have a place to cook a meal. I was staying in a hostel for homeless black youths in Toxteth, called Ujamaa House. I couldn't accommodate the band there, I needed a bigger place. So, I asked my friend Dobbo if I could borrow his flat, cashed my £16 giro cheque (which was how the government paid benefits via the post office in those days) and spent my two weeks' money on food. The next day, Gil bought his entire seventeen-strong entourage to Dobbo's flat on Devonshire Road in Toxteth and I fed them all. I cooked Jamaican-style snapper fish, with peas and rice for the entrées, as well as starters, enthusiastically served with a host of soft drinks like mango juice: I gave them the full works.

For music, I played a cassette tape of the best radio show in the region at that time. We had almost no black music on the radio in Liverpool, so if we wanted to hear good soul music we had to tune in to neighbouring Manchester's stations. And in Manchester, the main man for black music then was Mike Shaft. We used to record his weekly show so we'd have something to listen to throughout the week, as there was really nothing else regionally or nationally. The following year the Ranking Miss P started a reggae show – once a week, for an hour on Sundays on BBC Radio 1 – but that was it.

The band seemed happy with everything, and I was relieved that I'd managed to pull it off. I felt really privileged to have this group of people in my presence but had to keep it a secret to avoid a crowd gathering outside. Word of the gig and Gil's patronage of local causes, such as the Black Caucus, had raised his profile even further. Details of the meal never got out, so it all went off without a hitch. I was just glad that the band had actually been kind enough to accept my invitation. I suppose Gil could see that I'd spent some money putting everything together, so as he was leaving he drew out two £50 notes and passed them to me. I refused to accept them. He tried again, and once again I refused. He stuffed them in my shirt. Determined not to be outdone, I took out the ruffled notes and stuffed them back into his coat pocket, making it abundantly clear that I did not want his money. What he'd given me by gracing me with his presence was payment enough, and I wanted to say thanks from my heart. I just wanted to give him something.

He could see that I had holes in my shoes and ragged trousers. I wasn't the most well-turned-out person, but I was making an effort.

He said: 'We're going to Europe for a couple of weeks and when we come back, we're going to be doing a tour of the UK and I'd like you to come with us. Would you be willing to do that?'

'To do what,' I asked?

'Whatever the fuck you wanna do, carry some drums, whatever you want,' came his response. 'Count!' Gil called out. 'Give him the dates and the details of where we're staying when we get back to London from Europe, and take his number. We'll be in touch, brother.'

Sure enough, two weeks later I got a call at the hostel. 'Mark?'

'Yes.'

'This is the Count – from Gil's tour. Gil asked me to call you and arrange for you to come to London for the tour, we'll be staying at the Norfolk Plaza Hotel in Norfolk Square in Paddington. Can you make it down tomorrow?'

'I'll be there. Thanks, man.'

'OK, here's the number. Call when you arrive.'

I had never been to London before, but I knew there was a National Express coach that went from Skelhorne Street bus station in Liverpool. So I went to the post office, cashed my giro, packed a small bag and bought a single ticket, as I had no idea when I'd be coming back.

When I arrived at London Victoria, I was amazed at how big the city looked. I got on the Tube to Paddington station: Norfolk Square was right there, and the Norfolk Plaza Hotel, with a row of flags waving over the entrance.

At this point, the only hotels I'd visited were the Atlantic Towers two weeks before and the Alicia Hotel in Sefton Park, where I had worked as a kitchen porter, washing dishes.

It all felt so surreal, considering how my life had been up to that point. Looking back now, I'd say ninety per cent of my peers in the care system ended up as junkies, alcoholics or criminals, with many of them now dead or in jail. Had I not met Gil that night, I probably would have followed the same path. It was hard to comprehend then, but in hindsight, meeting Gil backstage at that concert had already begun to change my life in ways unimaginable to my younger self.

CHAPTER 2

BLACK TO WHITE

I was born in 1966, the year that England won the World Cup and the year before the Biafran War broke out in Nigeria.

Before all our lives were thrown into disarray, we lived at 53 Upper Warwick Street in Toxteth, an inner-city area of Liverpool which many locals referred to as Liverpool 8, L8 or simply 'the 8'. My earliest childhood memories are of this happy and cosmopolitan place, where my father regularly held parties and was an integral part of the local Guyanese and West Indian community.

Toxteth was full of clubs back then. On Parliament Street there was Jamaica House (where they held weekend shebeens, unlicensed club nights, which the Jamaicans called 'blues'), the Nigeria Club, Dutch Eddie's and the Gladray (named after its patrons – two black women called Gladys and Rachel). Nearby, on the outskirts of Toxteth where it bordered the town centre, Somali seamen had started the Casa (the Casablanca Club). Then there was the Rialto Ballroom, the Sierra Leone Club and the

Silver Sands. An old redbrick church building with an ornate rotunda had been converted into the Ibo Social Club. A huge detached white mansion was the Yoruba Social Club.

Black seamen had developed their own clubs because the colour bar that had existed in Liverpool for generations meant they were not allowed into most clubs in the city centre. All the nightclubs in the city centre closed at 2 a.m. but the black clubs in Toxteth were almost always unregulated, and most went on till 6 a.m.

No one bothered them, generally. I suspect the reason for this was that if the police or the council closed them down black people would simply flood into the city centre, and they didn't want that, so there was a tacit agreement between the club owners, the city council and the police that so long as there was no trouble, they could pretty much do what they liked.

My father was born in Grove, East Bank Demerara, in 1918, in what was then British Guiana (now Guyana). On his birth certificate, he is called Reginald Wilcox July – he took the family name of his mother, Olivia July, as she was not married to my grandfather, George Edward Watson, a man of African and Scottish descent. Sometime after his birth, my father adopted his father's family name to become Watson.

Olivia, who was an Amerindian from an indigenous Guyanese tribe, lived in a town called Meadowbank on the east side of the Demerara River, in western Guyana. My grandfather George Edward Watson was a schoolmaster, who taught in a Scottish-named town called Belladrum, next to the Dutch-named village of Weldaad, on the eastern side of what was formerly Dutch Guiana in the province of Berbice.

Before he left British Guiana in the late 1930s to become a merchant seaman, my father lived with a woman and a child in a village called Kitty. I have never discovered much about this woman and child, but according to the people of Meadowbank, they lived with my grandmother Olivia until she died. I never found out if the child was a girl or a boy, but the woman was obviously my father's partner and I assume the child was his. Olivia had owned several properties, but rumour had it she'd been cheated out of them by a corrupt lawyer called Llewelyn John who was formerly a government minister.

My mum – Sonia Parry – is the daughter of Elsie Knight, who was from Chorlton-cum-Hardy in Manchester, and Elvin Parry, from Holywell in north Wales. Elsie died in 1953 when my mum was just nine; and Sonia grew up in a small village called Dyserth, near the popular seaside town of Rhyl. My mother had three children with my dad: my older brother, Reynold Anthony, then me and my younger sister, Michelle Olivia (named after our grandmother). There was also our older sister, Jacqueline Ann, who my mum had with a man called Kermit Lewis. He was a Jamaican living in Toxteth in the 1960s, but we never met him.

My father had arrived in the UK from Guyana before the war, working on British supply ships until 1942, when he joined the Royal Navy in Greece, seeing action in the Atlantic during the war. In 1945, when the war ended, he settled in the UK for good.

Seamen were considered well-off in those days. The effects of the war were still being felt in Liverpool, even in the 1960s. The local economy was crumbling, and people had become accustomed to scrimping and scraping for even the most rudimentary things like food and clothing. Much of the city was still bombed-out and the docks were an economic lifeline. Seamen were a valuable resource. These men went on long trips for months at a time, spending no wages on the ships, so all that money came home with them. Many bought houses in the city with cash.

My dad lived in London for a time and in Tiger Bay, Cardiff, south Wales, before buying his house in Liverpool. It was a big Georgian townhouse, so he began to rent out rooms. My mother came to Liverpool and fell pregnant with my sister Jacqueline. She became a tenant in my father's house shortly after Jacqueline was born. They got acquainted, as they say, and three children later, we were a family. Also living there was a woman we called our 'Nan', Florence Mary Watson, known to everyone else as Flo'.

We lived in relative comfort. I guess we were an upper-working-class family in that we owned our house outright, and there were two salaries coming in as my father and Flo' both worked in Dunlop's. There was also the rental income from the rooms my father let. Our house was close to the seaport and the people who stayed came from all corners of the world, but most were Guyanese or West Indian. Toxteth also had Arabs, Somalis, Nigerians, Chinese, mostly seamen, and also American GIs from the US Air Force base at Burtonwood, just outside Liverpool.

We were relatively happy, but in 1969 everything changed.

I was only three years old at the time, but I can still recall packing all our stuff into colonial tea chests – plywood boxes with aluminium frames, which had black emblems with the name of the tea stamped on one side. We nailed the chests shut, then prised them open with crowbars when we got to our new home in a recently built council housing estate in Netherley, five or so miles east of Toxteth, in south Liverpool.

The city council had seized my father's property in Upper Warwick Street under a compulsory purchase order. This was done at a vastly reduced price to what the property was really worth. We had a four-storey townhouse, which would perhaps fetch half a million pounds today. The council took it then for just £68, and demolished it to build a sports centre.

What we didn't know at the time was that the sale was part of a policy the local government had adopted to 'dilute and disperse' inner-city black communities around Liverpool. The council wanted to assimilate the black seamen into the wider white community. They felt that having them all together as a homogenous group gave them a certain amount of political power. They wanted to break them up, and used housing policy as a means to achieve this. So, where black people were concentrated in high numbers, the local government would decide they wanted to 'regenerate' the area and would move people out, dispersing black neighbours far away from each other and destroying any sense of a cohesive black community.

Back then, we didn't know what was happening behind the scenes. All we knew was that we were swapping our lovely, spacious home in Toxteth for a little four-bedroom rental in the far-flung white working-class estate of Netherley. It was winter when we left Upper Warwick Street. Snow was on the ground and it was bitterly cold.

This sense of a nasty chill was to linger with us. We were a mixed-race family, marooned on a concrete island with more than 100,000 white families, many of them either deliberately or unwittingly racist – as was the norm back then. We were one of just five black families decanted from Toxteth. There was us, the Springers, the Coles, the Gills and the Amoos.

People from other areas had different names for Toxteth. In the mainly white neighbourhood of Netherley, for example, they'd say 'going down Granby', meaning Granby Street, the main thoroughfare running through the heart of the black community, where all the international food shops sold their wares, or 'down Parly' meaning Parliament Street, where many of the black clubs were. If a white woman was said to be 'going down Parly' it meant, to the whites, that she went to black clubs, or that she slept with black men. 'Going down Granby' was generally short for buying weed off the Jamaicans.

In Netherley, my parents were far away from good jobs, the docks and our communities. We couldn't even find a barber who could cut afro hair. That's when the problems started for us.

That first winter was spent exploring our new home. My dad took the master bedroom, with my nan. My sisters, Jacqueline and Michelle, shared the bedroom at the back, which looked out over the garden; and my mum was in what we called 'the tunnel room', as it was positioned above the alleyway that separated these terraced houses, leading through to another square of houses, what we called 'the back square'. At that time, I never stopped to think why my mum would have a separate room to my dad, or why my dad shared a room with my nan. It would be years before that would become clear. But as children, we never knew any different and we never asked. Reynold and I shared a room at the front of the house, overlooking the front yard.

In Netherley, kids played out in streets, regardless of their ages. I often used to go to the farmers' fields, beyond the council estate's boundary. There were trees and a pond and a stream where I'd hunt for newts and tadpoles. If only there'd been a similar escape hatch at my school, Cross Farm County Primary. My siblings and I were treated with contempt, because we were among the few black children enrolled there. They used to have a big reel-to-reel tape recorder at the school, where they would play recordings of 'The Story of Little Black Sambo' during assemblies. They would make us sit cross-legged on the wooden floor and listen to it. Afterwards, all the kids would call us 'Black Sambo' and 'nigger boys' and we'd get into fights. The teachers would ask what all the fuss was about. They never saw the harm done to us but the trouble caused was always our fault.

In Netherley, my siblings and I were often attacked. I remember being chased across a field near the woods and thrown down the banks of a shallow stream by a group of three young men from the far-right National Front, who were an active presence on the estate. I was eight years old. My mum would also regularly visit Cross Farm to complain about racial abuse, and she'd be ignored by the headmaster, Mr Talbot.

There was constant conflict between my family and the school. It wasn't long before social services got involved; the school told them that we were 'trouble', that we were 'always fighting' and our mother was 'always complaining to the school'.

Sadly, the social workers only reinforced what the teachers were saying. They dismissed our views, because they didn't understand why we got upset when someone called us 'niggers'. 'Sticks and stones may break your bones ...' they would say. But they were expressing their own racist ideologies, as were the teachers and the people on the streets. There was a general consensus that the problem was we were black, and any racial abuse that came our way, we just had to accept it. But my father was a black nationalist. He respected Malcolm X, Marcus Garvey and Muhammad Ali. He didn't take no shit. He'd tell us: 'Fight them!' And if we were beaten up, he'd take his belt off and beat us for getting beaten. It got so bad that we were being attacked almost every day coming home from school.

One of the worst incidents, I remember, was when about fifty kids surrounded Reynold. They were kicking him while he was fighting with this kid. Jacqueline jumped in to try and get them off him and she ended up in the middle of it too. I ran home and got my father. There were so many kids, he had to throw bricks to disperse the crowd, to get them off his children. We had to face the teachers and parents the next day. The only question they raised was why my father threw bricks. They didn't see the fact that there were fifty white kids kicking this guy's son and daughter. They didn't care about that.

Despite the hostile environment and our relocation taking us far away from good jobs, my father still had to provide for his family. He was a hard worker, and by Christmas 1974 he was employed as a Netherley property guard, patrolling the warehouses on the Liverpool docks. I have a clear memory of him in his brown uniform with a peaked hat. He'd been given a guard dog, which he brought home with him. It was a Chinese Chow, which looked like a wolf but seemed friendly enough to us.

It was a horribly cold winter that year and would prove a fateful one for our family. On Christmas Day, Dad left the house at 5 a.m. to wait for the bus to take him to work. It didn't come. He waited until 10 a.m., the snow up to his knees by then, before at last trudging home defeated. That was the only time I saw this big, strong seaman cry. He didn't open his Christmas presents. He just went straight to bed.

That night, he had a stroke in his sleep; and when he woke up, he was a quadriplegic, paralysed from the neck down.

Dad's ill health took away what little cheer and warmth we could muster in our new home. We had to care for him ourselves. There was a lot of pressure on my mum. She was a white woman with four black children. One social worker openly suggested that she would be better off if she gave all her black kids to social services and went and found herself a nice white man and started a new family. There was also a lot of tension brewing between my mum and my nan, Flo'.

Flo' was a white Englishwoman of similar age to my father. Theirs had been an unusual living arrangement since back in Warwick Street, when my mum had been lodging in my father's house. It became especially complicated after Mum fell pregnant with my brother Reynold.

The most problematic angle when we moved to Netherley was that it involved race. You had this black man living with two white women. It may have worked OK on Upper Warwick Street in diverse Toxteth and among seamen, but not in Netherley. A story was contrived that Flo' was actually our grandmother, which was conceivable. Born in 1920, she was so much older than our mum, who was born in 1944, and so we innocently grew up calling her Nan.

Nan blamed Mum for everything that had gone wrong, and we became the reason for all her woes. I was accused of stealing £10 from her little black money box, where she kept her Christmas hamper money that she collected from the community. She'd become an agent for the hamper company, and she'd take orders from people and collect money weekly, then deliver them an expensive Christmas hamper right before the holiday started. It wasn't me who'd taken the money, but I was the one who got the blame. It seemed like out of all the kids, whatever one of us did, I was always to blame.

Surrounded by racists on our estate and with my dad now a quadriplegic, I felt less protected than ever. Fed up with the drama in the house and at school, at eight years old I decided to join a gang.

There were gangs everywhere in the 1970s. The one I found was led by a guy called Bryan 'Budgie' Burges. Budgie was older than us and nobody messed with him. My fellow gang members were all white but, the funny thing is, the issue of my skin colour never came up. They protected me. If anybody called me a name, the whole gang would retaliate. From the moment I joined the gang, I never got touched. I was safer in the short term, but I didn't realise all this only fuelled the case that was secretly being built against me to the social services, by Flo'.

I'd heard about social workers and how they came and 'took children away'. The day I heard that they'd been at our home and would be returning, I used my secret route – out the bathroom window, onto the bin shed and down the ladder – to get out of the house and across the field. I went over to my favourite newt pond. It had a huge tree with branches overhanging the pond, one of which had a rope attached to it that kids used as a swing. I climbed up the tree and hid. I must have stayed there for a few hours, but it felt like an eternity. I remember feeling hungry and cold and aware that it was starting to get dark. I realised that I couldn't stay in that tree forever. When I got back home, the social worker was waiting for me.

Her name was Vivienne Chell and though she looked like a hippy, wore Sixties-style clothes, had long brown hair and was quite young herself, she scared me. My mum was crying. She told me I had to go with Vivienne, that they were going to take me someplace but that she would come and see me soon.

I was totally confused. Were they going to take me away forever? Would I ever see my mum again? What would happen next, and would I have any control over it? I was terrified, but there was nothing I could do. If I'd known what I'd done to deserve this, I would have said sorry so that we could all be one family again. But my pleas fell on deaf ears. I was being taken away and there was nothing anyone could do. I was nine then. Vivienne bundled me into her car. I still remember it – a tiny dark-green Hillman Imp with a cream interior, not much bigger than a bumper car at the funfair. She got into the car and spoke politely to me, but she was taking me away from my family, away from everyone I knew and loved. She was taking me to a place that was anything but polite, and she knew it. Since that day, I have never trusted a social worker again.

CHAPTER 3

WARD OF THE STATE

On the night Vivienne Chell took me into care, I sat in her little green car with a sense that the world that I knew was over. She asked me if I'd stolen £10 from my nan. I had no idea what she was talking about.

I asked if I would go to my school the next day.

She hesitated, then told me Cross Farm wasn't my school anymore.

'When can I see my mum?' I asked.

Again, there was a long pause, then she said, with something of a nervous quiver in her voice, 'S-soon, yes, very soon.'

I squirmed in my seat and stared out of the window. Somehow I didn't believe her. I was trying to see where I was, trying to spot something familiar, anything that would give me a reference point to where she was taking me so that I could find my way home. I noticed that she'd turned left at the fire station on Childwall Valley Road. I knew this area because when we'd first moved to Netherley, there were no school or nursery places available in our vicinity and my mum had taken me with her on the bus to a nursery provision at Belle Vale Primary.

I felt a chill when we passed the school. It was the last bastion of familiarity as we progressed up Belle Vale Road onto Gateacre Brow. I recognised one other landmark on the way: the detached white house at the top of Gateacre Brow, which was the home of Ken Dodd, the Liverpudlian comedian famous throughout the UK for his TV puppet show *Ken Dodd & the Diddy Men*. All the kids knew who he was – and his distinctive house, alone at the top of the brow, elevated about twenty feet above the pavement, wasn't something you'd forget.

Vivienne turned left at Ken Dodd's house, and then halfway down the road, eventually, she slowed down and turned right into the driveway of a mansion. It looked like the haunted house from *The Addams Family*.

We parked up and approached what seemed like a huge wooden door. Vivienne rang the white porcelain bell. The door creaked open and a tall figure appeared in the half-light. I couldn't make out his features, but I could see he was a big man and I felt very, very small. He was a haunting figure who showed little emotion; and when we entered the hallway and could see his face, it was expressionless. His presence petrified me.

He introduced himself as Mr Greaves, but to me he looked like Gomez Addams. To add to the macabre experience of this terrifying trip, Mr Greaves had a black talking mynah bird in his office.

This was the Liverpool Children's Admission Unit, which was previously a children's home called Aymestrey Court. Many years

Liverpool Children's Admission Unit, Acrefield Road, Woolton c.1969.

later, I learned that the house had been built in 1881 by the sugar baron Henry Tate, of Tate & Lyle fame, as a wedding gift to his daughter. Perhaps its forbidding, almost Gothic, style was fashionable back then, but it's difficult to grasp how anyone could see such a building as suitable for children in care. Maybe it was bequeathed to the local authority by a descendant of Mr Tate? Whatever the truth of this, I was now in an appointment with a fear that would haunt me for the rest of my life.

After the social worker handed me over to the haunting figure of a man, she left without saying a word. Another man took me to a bathroom and told me to get undressed and take a shower; I was hesitant. He stripped me and directed me to the shower, then left the room. I showered then wrapped myself in the towel he'd provided me with; I realised that he'd taken my clothes. He soon returned with some striped pyjamas. He instructed me to put them on, then left again, and I did as I was told.

Sometime later he led me down a dark corridor in total silence. I could hear children's voices in the background, but I couldn't see anyone else. He swung open the door to a large bedroom and indicated for me to go inside. I was petrified but compliant. Then he slammed the door shut. I heard the lock click behind me, and his heels clapping on the wooden floor as he disappeared down the corridor. There was a gap under the door of about three or four inches; I dropped to the floor but couldn't see anything. I was trapped in this terrifying mansion with Gomez from the Addams family and his talking crow.

I ran to the window to look out, to see if I could open it and escape, like I could out of the window at home, but the windows had bars on them and wouldn't open. I was imprisoned. I wanted my mum: 'Mummy! Mummy! I'm sorry, please tell them to let me out?' But nobody came. I cried myself to sleep.

I was locked in that room for fourteen days and nights. This was standard practice in the 1970s. The room had a double bed with some toys strewn on it, some more dotted around the floor. There was also a toilet, but nothing else. I was in solitary confinement; and for a nine-year-old just separated from his family, it couldn't get much worse.

The staff wouldn't talk to me or answer my questions. They'd bring food and push it under the door, then they'd return some time later, collect the empty plate and leave, locking the door behind them without uttering a word. It was all part of their method of acclimatising new children to the care system. Apparently, it was borrowed from methods used to train homing pigeons. It was hoped that the children would, when released, always 'fly back' to the loft, or in this case the institution, having grown accustomed to the limited space and regular supply of food. It was also a means to sever the ties between a child and their family.

But I wasn't having any of that. After two weeks of crying, screaming, banging on the door and the barred windows, they took me out of isolation. As soon they let me into the 'unsecured' dilapidated communal areas of the Children's Admission Unit, I absconded.

I was only nine, but I figured out that the place wasn't too far from my real home and I was able to find my way there. The day they released me from solitary confinement, I jumped over the exterior wall and ran down towards Ken Dodd's house. I thought about knocking on his door and asking him if he knew what they did to children when they took them away. I was sure Ken would be on my side but I didn't have the nerve. What would I say if he answered the door? Would Ken believe what had just happened? I headed home instead, sure that every time I looked back, the people from social services would be pursuing me. I didn't see anyone coming, so I kept on going. Nobody noticed me. I thought the whole of Liverpool would be out looking for me; but in truth, nobody cared.

When I arrived at my mum's house, about an hour after my escape, she answered the door and burst into tears. 'Where have you been?' she asked, but I could hardly speak and didn't know where to begin. We went inside, and to my surprise there were two white men sitting in our living room. My siblings were all out playing and I didn't see any of them on that occasion. The men were off-duty policemen – hired by the social services to escort me back to the Admission Unit. For a brief moment, I'd thought I was free. Now my hopes had been dispelled by total despair, it was a miserable anti climax for a nine-year-old! This was another way of acclimatising me to my new reality, as one of the officers told me: 'You can't beat the system!' Something I'd hear repeatedly throughout my time in care. It didn't deter me though, since now I knew the way back home. During my six-week assessment period at the Admission Unit, I ran away every chance I got. But it was always the same routine – escape and capture.

After the initial six-week assessment, social services made the separation permanent. I was taken to juvenile court where an application had been made under the Child Care Act of 1969 to formalise care proceedings.

The care order was granted. The judge used the Latin term 'in loco parentis' to place me in care. I had no idea what it meant at the time, but with a stroke of his pen and the utterance of those foreign-sounding words, I ceased to be my mother's son and became a ward of the state. My mother had no clue how to contest what had just happened. In those days, she wouldn't have known how to even get a lawyer. There was no real understanding of how these things were done. Social services were targeting troubled families in poor neighbourhoods, where people would put up the least resistance. Before the families knew it, their children were gone. Once the paperwork was finalised, it would be too late to stop what was happening.

At the initial case conference, at the Admission Unit, they decided to place me in Mossfield Children's Home in Picton, Liverpool. I was to attend Northway County Primary School. A

Mr and Mrs Moreland ran Mossfield. They were an elderly couple, and they seemed like decent people. Mossfield was a huge Victorian mansion on the corner of Thingwall Road and Childwall Valley Road, with large grounds and a big tree in the front garden that I used to climb. There was a dumb waiter that linked the upper floors to the basement kitchens, reminiscent of the olden days where servants cooked downstairs and sent the food to the butler on the upper floors to serve the distinguished guests. It was just big enough for me to climb into, so it made a good hiding place when things got rough. At Mossfield, children were allowed to travel home to see their families on weekends.

Northway County Primary had received a report from my previous school that identified me as a troublemaker. I realised this upon my arrival. There was a reluctance to accept me, or even to talk to me. The teachers adopted a sort of ambivalence to my presence, acknowledging me and then ignoring me. They'd taken me on a 'trial basis', but it was clear after a short space of time that it wasn't going to work out. Why should it have? To begin with, I didn't understand why I had to be there in the first place. I was without my siblings, in an unfamiliar environment, and in a home without my parents. Because Mossfield wasn't secure, I began to regularly board a bus and return to my mum's. It was a straight run on the 79 down the Valley Road. The escort officers would always come looking for me.

After a while, instead of going to school, I started slipping off to Netherley during the day. The area's large network of corporation flats had workmen's offices on the ground floor and a group of maintenance workers had their base there. One smoky office was occupied by some local guys. They spent more time sipping tea, reading the paper and talking about football than they did working. They didn't mind me hanging around; and when they did eventually go out and do some work, I'd help by pushing the wheelbarrow and brushing up leaves. They even showed me how to use the lawnmower and lawn-edging iron.

The school would then report my absence to social services. This happened enough times within my first three months at Mossfield that they reconsidered my placement. It was no good putting me somewhere I could get out. It was decided I would be sent to the Woolton Vale Assessment Centre, also known as Menlove as it was situated on Menlove Avenue. It was 1975 and I was still only nine years old.

Woolton Vale's status had been legally changed in 1972 from that of a 'remand centre' to a 'children's assessment and observation centre', but until about 1977, it was still used as an overspill for the local prison at Risley in Warrington. It was erroneously operating under remand home rules, which permitted locking children behind doors. When I was taken there in 1975, they were mixing children who were there for 'assessment and observation' – that is, being considered for the care system due to familial breakdown, truancy and other non-criminal matters – with remand prisoners, often violent young offenders up to eighteen years old.

I was the second-youngest person ever sent there, and the youngest during my three-month stint. It was a secure facility all right. There were bars on the windows, and doors were locked behind you. I had to be escorted to the toilet for my own pro-tection.

Menlove was a children's prison in everything but name. It was a mansion that had once belonged to Victorian prime minister William Gladstone. Adjoining the main house stood an incongruous 1970s square concrete-block extension built on stilts.

There was a long and winding tree-lined driveway from the front gates up to the mansion house. On entering the secure reception area, you couldn't help but notice the isolation cell on your left. This had concrete walls, a prison-style grey metal door with a spyhole and a hatch in it, and a green and red indicator light outside just above the door.

The child 'inmates' all slept in dormitories. There were eight dorms, some with more beds than others, all with locked doors and bars on the windows. I think there were about twelve of us in the one I was in. At the end of the dorm, there was a metal prison-style doorway, with a spyhole that connected to the warden's residence. The message was clear: they were always watching us, even in our sleep.

The warden was a brutal man called Ivor Buckley and his deputy was equally sadistic.

There were a few other black kids in Menlove whom I recall, in particular, Ray Maxfield and Carl Moore. Carl had a major afro, was very cool and was an expert at table tennis. They were both from Toxteth, but they didn't know me, as we'd left Toxteth six years before in 1969. They stuck together and I remained an outsider. We used to eat meals in a giant central dining hall with ceilings that were so high you'd need a window cleaner's ladder to change a light bulb. There were trestle tables lining the hall, enough for about a hundred children to sit and eat at. We'd be marched through in form groups to collect our meals on a tray and were then seated according to our class groupings. They had Portakabins in the yard being used as classrooms and I was in Mr Neal's class. Mr Neal was a cockney, and his favourite punishment was to paddle your behind with a cricket bat that he kept beside his table.

One day when Mr Neal brought us into the dining hall, I sat down at our class's trestle table opposite Keith Coleman. He was about eighteen and effeminate, which led the other kids to skit him and call him a 'queer'. I had no idea what the word meant at that time. As I started to eat my food, Keith reached over and tried to take my plate. 'What the fuck are you doing?' I pushed his hand away and defended my food. He lifted himself up to reach further across the wooden trestle to get to my plate and I put my arms around it. He sat back down, and I thought that was the end of it. Then he leant across, snorted up whatever snot his big nose could muster and spat right in my meal.

My response was immediate. 'Fuck off, you queer!' I lifted my plate and smashed the whole meal into his face.

He lost it, jumping up on the table even while wiping the mashed potatoes and snot out of his eyes. He came for me. He was about six feet tall and clumsy at the best of times. I was smaller and quicker. I dashed like a rabbit under the first trestle, then over the next one, sprinting along the rows with this six-foot bully in pursuit, covered in food. Looking back, it was funny as hell, but at the time it was anything but. Mealtimes here were executed with military-style discipline and our chase had caused the room to erupt in mayhem. There were kids egging us on, shouting and jeering. When I was eventually caught by a teacher, they frogmarched us both to Alan Scales' office.

We sat in dread outside that office. Keith was opposite me, still covered in my dinner and still snarling about how he was going to kill me after this was over. I was more worried about the punishment. Keith went in first and in a quick minute was dismissed. Then it was my turn. Scales had already made up his mind that it was my fault and didn't want to hear anything. He removed a cane from behind his desk and told me pull my pants down and bend over. I was terrified but there was no option other than to comply. Whack! I screamed, but before I could get a word out – Whack! Whack! Whack! Whack! Whack! I was in tears.

'Pull your pants up and get out of my sight,' he said.

I'd had the cane in school before. When my siblings and I were infants at Netherley Comp, one kid had decided to throw bricks onto the flat roof of the kitchens from the elevated schoolyard opposite the building known as A-Block. I had joined in, but instead of hitting the roof, my brick soared through the window and hit a dinner lady.

'A-Block' at Netherley Comprehensive School.

I was so sorry. It was technically an accident, but I'd been sent to Mr Blaire, the headmaster, anyway and he'd caned me on the hands. That was traumatic, but this was on a whole new level. I couldn't sit down. Mr Neal also believed single-mindedly that I deserved it and assured me that next time 'it would be the cricket bat, not the cane'. I'd already been on the receiving end of his cricket bat for getting some glue on his new tables when we were doing craft. He was a ruthless man, and everyone hated him. I wondered if all cockneys were like him, since he was the first one I had ever met.

I spent eight weeks in Menlove leading up to the winter of 1975. Whenever people would ask me what I was in for, I'd say: 'Stealing £10 off me nan. But it wasn't me.' I recall other inmates either laughing at the absurdity of it, or being amused by the triviality of the supposed crime. The staff on the other hand would say things like: 'Yeah, that's what they all say.' Or 'Oh so you're another innocent victim of a miscarriage of justice then?' Or words to that effect. The point was, not only was I not guilty of the 'crime', but even if I had been, it would be a travesty of justice to rip a nine-year-old child away from his mother for the sake of £10. But that's when I started to really think about who my nan, Flo', actually was, and why she had so much bitterness towards me that she'd get me taken away.

The institution was cruel, but somewhat bizarrely they gave us all a Christmas present. I got a watch, my first ever.

After six weeks, I had a case conference where they decided what to do with me next. I was assessed as needing a 'community home with education on the premises'. I was to be moved to Greystone Heath Community Home in Great Sankey, Warrington, but they couldn't take me immediately so the hippy social worker, Vivienne Chell, arranged for me to go home for Christmas. It marked a year since my dad's stroke had changed our fortunes entirely. In less than two years there would be calls for a public inquiry into allegations of abuse at Menlove.

Vivienne came to pick me up in her green Hillman Imp and I can't begin to express the relief I felt as they processed me out the door. I was free! At least for Christmas.

When I got home, everyone was pleased to see me but strangely no one talked about what had happened. It was like I'd gone out to play and come home for tea. But months had passed. Traumas and terrible experiences had occurred. I was not the same happy-go-lucky kid who'd left in the summer.

The watch didn't last long. My brother Reynold had a mind for fixing things that weren't broken. He loved taking things apart and then putting them back together when he'd discovered how they worked. I guess my watch – with its sophisticated 17-jewel mechanism and coil spring – was a bit beyond his understanding.

I remember that an ambulance turned up at the door during my stay, and my father was wheeled into the house for his home visit. At that time, he was in the geriatric ward at Broadgreen Hospital. He stayed at the hospital all week, only coming home on weekends. There was a hospital bed in the living room and we'd transfer him manually from the wheelchair, as he was unable to get up at all. He had limited mobility in his right hand and could scribble with some help. He could move his head and talk but since the stroke the rest of his body was immobile and we had to do everything for him. I'm not sure what he knew about my circumstances, but it was never discussed.

After Christmas, Vivienne arrived in her little green car that ferried me from one traumatic experience to another. When she started driving through farmlands, I knew we were leaving Liverpool.

We drove for about forty-five minutes before we reached a massive complex. Greystone Heath looked like a cross between a council estate and a school. It had seven, soulless 1970s-style, flat-roofed housing units, built in brick, with bitumen lining the rooftops, and a Victorian administrative building next to the entranceway. What struck me after Menlove was that there were no bars on the windows here and no barbed wire – only a waist-high ranch-style wooden fence. There was an orchard that covered about half an acre, a farm, a small block of seven class-rooms, some workshops, a gymnasium, and a massive sports field with football goalposts and a running track marked out on the grass with lime. The house units were all named after trees. There was 'Poplars A' and 'Poplars B', 'Willows A' and 'Willows B', 'Pines A' and 'Pines B', and the last one – the odd one – at the top on the right, overlooking Liverpool Road, was 'Rowans'.

Vivienne handed over my file to a man who introduced himself as the headmaster, Mr Charles Wells. I couldn't work out what his problem was. It was as if he didn't want to be there but was going through the motions. His mouth drooped on one side, something I'd seen before on the geriatric ward when I'd visited my father at Broadgreen Hospital. He processed me like I was a horse entering a stable.

I thought I'd only be there for six weeks, perhaps then they'd let me go home. But that was not to be. I was placed in Poplars A, which was the assessment unit, and after my six-week assessment, I had the case conference. Vivienne turned up with another woman who would be my new social worker. Her name was Michelle Elliot.

'Can I go home to my mum now, please?' I asked.

'No, you've now been assigned to Pines A and this is your new house father, Mr Morris.'

Bill Morris looked at me with a smirk. I had a sinking feeling in my stomach. I knew somehow that this wasn't going to be good.

There were up to fourteen kids in a unit at Greystone, and the dormitories were named according to how many beds were in them. We called them 'dorm 7', 'dorm 5', '3 dorm' and '1 dorm'. It was considered the ultimate privilege to be assigned to 1 dorm, because you didn't need to share. 'A privilege you had to earn.'

Bill Morris took no time at all to let me know what he thought of me. 'You're on my unit now and you'll do as I say. If I get any trouble from you, you'll feel the back of my hand.' I didn't have to wait long. The first day, Mike Farnworth, a kid from Bolton who was almost sixteen years old and due for release soon, approached me after school. Farnworth was in 1 dorm and was considered 'Morris's favourite'.

Every night after school, we were expected to clean our shoes on the bench outside the unit and place them in the boot room, just inside, to the right of the main entrance. As I was polishing my shoes, Farnworth, who had a beard and the physique of a rugby player, approached me and demanded: 'Clean my shoes.' 'Fuck off!' was my immediate response. He then spat in my face; I threw my shoes at him and he chased me into the unit, shouting, 'I'm gonna fuckin' banjo you!' I had no idea what he was talking about, but I guess in Bolton, getting 'banjo'd' meant getting a beating. I didn't stick around to find out. It was the Menlove dining hall all over again. Morris caught me, said nothing at all to Mike Farnworth and proceeded to smack me repeatedly, shouting profanities that I can't even recall, such was the ferocity of the assault. I was still only nine years old.

That was to be the first of many brutal beatings that I would receive at the hands of Bill Morris, who became my nemesis for the next two and a half years. I only escaped him by campaigning relentlessly, finally being moved back to Poplars. Poplars B had a Welshman called Glynn Williams as the house father. Mr Williams was kind to me; and more so after he met my Welsh mother, and disclosed that he used to deliver the mail in her home village of Dyserth and likely knew my mother's family.

But Morris wasn't done with me. He'd managed to convince the Poplars warden – a wicked and cruel man called Ivor Warmington – to pick up where he'd left off; and so, the persecution continued. My only reprieve was that the house father was on duty more than the warden. The kids called Warmington 'Popeye' or 'Pop Warmington', which he hated, and we all hated him. He was a military man who professed to have been an officer in the army during the war. He ran the cadet squadron at Greystone and conducted everything, including dinner, like a military operation. We had to have inspections in the morning. We had to strip our beds and fold the sheets and blankets into a perfectly square pile in the centre of the foot of the bed. The bedding had to be placed on top of a folded bedcover, which was then used to wrap the whole bundle; then the edges were turned back over diagonally to look like a page curl on either side of a parcel. Popeye would make you stand by your bed and have your bedding inspected. If it wasn't neat enough, he'd scrag it and demand you to do it again and again until it was perfect. He'd also examine our fingernails before we sat for dinner and would stand and watch us in the shower. Popeye told me that if I thought I'd escaped Morris, I had another thing coming, and the intimidation continued.

Although they were 'wards of the state', children in care – whatever their initial assessment – were entitled to a case conference every six months, which could potentially lead to a home release. But these were often delayed or postponed altogether, dashing any hope. I was at Greystone Heath between 1975 and 1979, despite being told when I went there that it would only be for six weeks. I had to wait for the next case conference, then the next one ... After a while I gave up. Bill Morris had written consistently terrible reports about me, and despite glowing assessments from most of the teachers for the first two and a half years, it was clear that Morris had no intention of letting me go home. It was the same with Popeye.

In all that time, I barely saw the social worker assigned to my case. For the first two years of my internment, I saw her perhaps once. When I came to sue the system several years later, part of my evidence was the negligence of the second social worker, Michelle Elliot (later known as Shelley Lewis). I had four case conferences over two years, only one of which she attended but left halfway through (I was told she had to dash off to Manchester so no case conclusion could be reached). It was like having an indeterminate sentence, for having committed no crime. My chances of being released were severely affected by her absence. The staff at Greystone kept telling me: 'Your social worker didn't come, so we couldn't make a decision.' On one occasion, the social workers were 'on strike'.

I was getting increasingly distressed. My mother came and saw me occasionally on a Saturday, when you were allowed a visit on the premises from your parents or family from 2–4 p.m. They could bring you cakes and sweets if they could afford them. I knew my mum couldn't afford them but she always brought some whenever she came. After the first three months, home visits were allowed. Things were dire for my mum. She was weighed down with having to support my siblings, and was also fighting eviction from our home in Netherley.

Hatred and tensions were building between my mum and Flo' but since my dad was in hospital there was no arbiter to keep the peace and it started to get out of hand. Flo' was involved with the local councillor, Margret Delany, and was also a member of the pensioners union. I'd heard her say on a few occasions that she was 'going to tell Margret Delaney' this or that, but I just assumed she was another one of the pensioners. I didn't find out she was a councillor until years later.

Flo' was also friends with the local police constable, Liam Lynch. Before I'd been taken into care, she'd told me more than once that she'd report me to Liam Lynch 'cause she'd heard I'd been running with a gang. Once Constable Lynch had come to the house and had taken me for a ride in the 'panda car' for a talking-to. In those days police cars were little sky-blue and white minis, which everyone referred to as pandas. I was petrified; I'd never been in a police car up until that point, and this so-called 'friendly chat' was to be a warning of things to come. He drove me by the school and pulled over and started telling me what happened if you got in trouble with the law. I really didn't know why I was there. He said, 'Your nan's asked me to have a word with you.' What I hadn't realised at the time, was that this was part of a wider campaign to get at my mum by threatening her kids. What Flo' really wanted was to get us all out of what she regarded as her house.

In the care homes people were asking questions like: 'Why would your nan put you in care?' Social workers were trying to understand the family dynamic and asked me who was who in the household. For me, it was straightforward, 'me mum me dad an' me nan'. But somehow the social workers were confused, assuming that Flo' must be my mum's mum. If she wasn't, then who was she? She was three years younger than my dad, so she couldn't be his mum. But I really didn't give it much thought. By this time I was deep inside the care system and the only thing on my mind was how to get out.

Michelle Elliot was the key to getting me back home to my family. After your initial case conference and the six-week assessment, the residential social workers would schedule any home leave. Mine was to start at about three months in, with what the social workers referred to as a '1–7 accompanied'. This meant you could get picked up at 1 p.m. by your social worker or family on a Saturday and get dropped off back to Greystone by 7 p.m. the same day, as long as your parents gave consent. This allowed me to go home finally, albeit for a few hours.

After the next case conference, it was customary to award enhanced home leave, allowing you to leave at 9 a.m. on Saturday morning and return at 7 p.m. that evening unaccompanied. Overnight weekend leave from Saturday to Sunday or Friday to

Sunday was also possible, but that was reserved for older children who were close to leaving.

My mum and siblings were still in Netherley, and Flo' had become increasingly hostile to them. Flo' was working at the Blue Cap frozen food factory in Belle Vale. My mum worked at Plessey's Telecommunications. We'd had a babysitter who would meet us from school and look after us until either my mum or Flo' got home. This carried on with my siblings after I'd been taken away. Flo' always brought tinned food home from Blue Cap and had now decided that she needed a place to store it. She forced my mum out of the tunnel room and put a lock on the door. From then on my mum shared a room with my two sisters and Flo' proceeded to fill the tunnel room with food from Blue Cap and alcohol for the Christmas parties that my dad had always hosted, ever since we were in Warwick Street. Flo' wanted to continue with the parties when my dad came home for Christmas from the hospital, and that was one of the very few occasions when all the Guyanese would come from Toxteth and my dad would sit in a wheelchair watching everyone drink and dance to his old calypso reggae records. My sister had worked out how to pick the lock on the tunnel room with a pair of scissors, and we'd go in and open cans of peaches and pineapples and drink the sweet juice. Flo' would go mad when she opened them at Christmas and find the rotten mouldy fruit inside. That one I did do.

Dad lived in the hospital, so he had no idea what went on through the week. I came home one weekend and found everyone in the house freezing cold, with no electricity or heating. I was shocked that there was a chain with a padlock on the fridge. I asked my mum what was happening and she said, 'Flo' locks the fridge when she's out and doesn't open it 'til she gets back.' I asked: 'Why is the heating off, it's freezing?' She said, 'Flo' takes the fuses out of the leccy, so when she's out, we can't use any electricity.' 'What's the fuses?' I asked. My mum took me to the leccy cupboard, where the meter was, and there was a fuse board with some big plug-like fuses in, but about four of them were missing. I was fuming at this point.

I left the house and went over to the flats by my old mate Steph Taylors' house, on Brittarge Brow. Steph had been one of our gang before I was taken into care. I was looking for an empty flat. You could always tell which ones were empty, because either the windows were broken or they were boarded up. I saw some windows broken on a flat on the first floor, so I ran up the stair-well, onto the long landings that extended from one end of the huge tenements to the other. I walked along until I found one with the window on the door boarded up. This was it. I literally booted the door in. The leccy cupboard was right next to the door. I opened it and removed all the fuses. I was barely ten years old but I couldn't see my family in this state. I had to do something, so I did.

I got back to the house and told my mum I'd got the fuses. She looked startled. 'Where did you get them?' she asked. 'From an empty flat,' I replied. My mum never said a word, she went to the leccy cupboard with a torch. Each of the fuses was colour-coded. She matched the colours and as if by magic the telly and the lights kicked in. Weirdly, that turned out to be a happy day. I was so caught up in my own misery up till that point that it hadn't occurred to me what the rest of my family might be going through. My mum told everyone to say nothing to Flo' and no one did. She would come home every day like clockwork and five minutes or so before she was due, someone would take the fuses out. It was absurd, but it was how we survived.

My mum and I had a relatively good relationship during my childhood. Coming from a small Welsh village, inner-city life in Liverpool must have been a culture shock for her. After moving to Netherley, she used to organise day trips for the local community to the nearby towns of Freshfield, Southport, New Brighton, or the Welsh seaside towns of Rhyl and Ffrith Beach. These trips took place during the summer holidays, before I was taken into care, and remain some of my happiest childhood memories.

I wanted all that back. Michelle Elliot was now responsible for actively trying to solve my issues, for administering my case and integrating me back into society. She failed me. Years later, when she was subpoenaed to respond to my statement on her negligence, her account basically read: 'I have no recollection of this child, although it would appear from the file that I was his social worker for two and a half years.' Of course she wouldn't remember me, because she met me only twice out of the three occasions she'd acted on my case; firstly the day I was handed over to her from Vivienne Chell, then at the case conference when she left early, and finally when she showed up at Greystone Heath to hand me over to a new social worker, Colin Derby, two and half years later.

Before that, I was a just a two-year-old case file on her desk that she probably never even read. Her replacement, Colin Derby, was a former police and probation officer turned social worker.

When he saw how my case had been mismanaged, he felt that a degree of injustice had been done. He vowed to make things better but only if I continued doing for the next six months what I'd been doing for the last two years: being a 'good boy'. But it had been three years since I'd entered the care system and I was angry. I told him: 'You do what you're going to do, and I'll do what I'm going to do.' I fiercely rebelled and when he came to my next case conference, Colin received the worst possible reports from all quarters at Greystone.

He was perplexed at the change that had come over this otherwise 'well-behaved child' whose only reason for not going home before now was ostensibly because the social worker didn't come to represent him. The school reports were the most important ones and despite the negative house reports from Bill Morris, all of the others had been good up until this point. I told Colin that I had 'no trust whatsoever' in either him 'or the system'. As far as I was concerned, everyone was a liar. I was almost twelve years old. He'd organised for me to get out of Pines A and into Poplars B, as it had become clear that Bill Morris was biased, and his reports were contrary to everyone else's. But it was too little too late. By the next case conference he attended, I had turned into a revolutionary and uttered the words that chilled the Greystone staff to the bone.

I swore that if I ever got out, I would 'go to the newspapers and expose everything' they did in there. From the moment I said this their attitudes changed. It was an empty threat because I didn't know the first thing about making such a report. What I didn't know then was there was indeed something far more sinister going on at Greystone that needed to be reported, of which I was at that time totally unaware.

The panel at the next case conference authorised my release – extremely reluctantly – on a 'home on trial' basis. Basically, they just saw me as a liability and wanted me out. The staff at Greystone had reckoned that I shouldn't be going home but rather to a worse institution called Mobberley Hall in Knutsford, just outside Manchester. All the children in Greystone knew about that place. It was vicious and dangerous. If you were from Liverpool and went there, you'd be targeted. Greystone took kids up to sixteen years old but Mobberley took kids up to the age of eighteen, many of whom had been involved in all manner of crimes – gun possession, robbery, arson, even rape and murder.

Colin didn't like that I had embarrassed him by having him advocate for my release against a background of such bad reports. He would have to look for a school for me, despite my recent poor record and dire reports over the past six months. However, he warned me that if I made 'one single mistake, got into one little fight, got reported for one bit of trouble', he would take me 'straight to Mobberley Hall'. Later on, Colin denied that threat in his witness statement in my court case with LCC. It was like having the sword of Damocles hanging over your head but in truth anything was better than staying in a care home; and I just needed to get free of them.

So I was finally released or, more accurately, 'thrown out' – and I was going back to my mother, albeit with the wrong mentality, having convinced myself that the only strategy that worked was to fight!

By then the situation at home wasn't rosy.

At the time of my temporary 'home on trial' release, Flo' had finally succeeded in kicking my mother out of the four-bedroom council house in Netherley. My mum and my siblings had moved to a new home in Belle Vale, Liverpool 25 – an empty maisonette at the foot of the sprawling blocks of council flats. It was around then that I came to know who Flo' actually was. It turns out that Flo' Watson was my father's wife. She couldn't have kids, so when my mum fell pregnant to my dad with Reynold, apparently Flo' was OK with it, even two kids later. We also had no reason to think otherwise, at least until my father had the stroke. That's when she blamed us for his illness, became fully hostile and asserted her rights as my father's wife to have us all evicted.

I still couldn't wrap my head around it, but to be honest I had bigger fish to fry at that time. I was just glad my family were out of there, despite the fact that she kept everything and they left with barely the clothes on their backs and we had to start again from scratch.

In Belle Vale, there were hardly any shops on the estate, so a couple had devised a way to make a living with a mobile shop in a van. It parked right outside our door and sold most of what you'd need on a day-to-day basis. Milk, bread, sweets, cigarettes, domestic cleaning products, newspapers and so on. It also provided credit or 'tick'. We lived on tick and then when money came in, we'd settle our balance. We couldn't get tick in the main shops, so we relied mainly on the mobile.

When I first came home, we had literally nothing. Since there was a provision that I had to at least have a bed in order for Greystone Heath to release me, Colin Derby organised for us to collect furniture that had recently been donated to social services. He took me to the house of an old lady who'd died, and we picked up furniture such as beds, headboards, wardrobes, sideboards, kitchen utensils and cutlery.

We had no money. My mother had previously been working at the Meccano factory in Huyton but had lost her job. Colin had enrolled me at Gateacre, a comprehensive school with 1,200 pupils. This was a huge change for me. There had only been about a hundred kids at Greystone Heath's so-called 'educational facility', where we were taught very little, and I hadn't received any support or counselling when I left the children's home.

At the new school, it was decided that because my academic development had been severely interrupted, I'd be enrolled in the year below my age group. The image of us queuing up for dinner at lunchtime on my first day was hilarious. A row of little white children, then this big black kid, followed by another row of little white kids. Naturally, the bullies singled me out. Someone came up to me and said, 'See that guy over there? He wants to fight you.' That boy had no idea of the implications that challenge had for me.

Thankfully, there was a guy in the school, Arthur Jones, who was an old friend from Cross Farm. Arthur, who was now in the year above me at Gateacre, asked where I'd 'disappeared to' and I told him about my time in the care system. Arthur identified my challenger as a kid called Clegsy and promised to handle it. Together with his friend, Peter Roberts, Arthur effectively squashed that beef on my behalf. No one messed with me after that for a while.

I was soon struggling at Gateacre. While I was considered bright, I'd had scant education and couldn't cope with the structures and demands of schooling. Despite this and for reasons unbeknownst to me, halfway through the year, the school decided to move me to the year above. The subjects were totally unfamiliar – French, technical drawing, physics, chemistry. I'd had no experience of these topics in the care homes. I had barely grasped the lessons in the year below and was now faced with even more complex work, and finding it even harder. As a result, I became disruptive.

At that time, two subcultures had emerged in the school and the wider community, dividing adolescents and young people into two main social and cultural groups: 'Mods' and 'Rockers'. Even though the mods listened to black music like ska and soul, they were still often very racist.

I found myself gravitating towards the rockers. I had a friend at the school called Tim Hemmings. Tim and his brother Paul were both rockers. They invited me to a few concerts and even paid for my tickets. There was a rumour that their dad owned a refrigeration company and drove the kids to school in a Rolls-Royce. I don't know if that was true – all I know is that they were good to me and I appreciated their kindness.

They took me to various shows to see AC/DC, Def Leppard, Sammy Hagar and Deep Purple's Ian Gillan, but the most memorable gig I went to with them was Thin Lizzy at the Liverpool Empire in May 1979.

My brother Reynold was also listening to rock music and he introduced me to Thin Lizzy's *Jailbreak* album; we loved the track 'The Boys Are Back in Town'. But what floated my boat most about Thin Lizzy was that even though they were a white Irish rock band, their frontman – Phil Lynott – was black.

Music aside, I found that the rockers at the school were more accepting of me to. All except for one of them: Floyd. Floyd came to school dressed like a Hell's Angel in a black leather jacket, with a sleeveless denim jacket over the top, which we rockers used to call 'a cut-off Wrangler'. One night, I was walking home from school and I caught him staring at me intently.

'What are you looking at?'

He looked away, and that, I thought, was the end of it. But a few days later, I found out word had gone round the school that Floyd and I were to fight.

I knew nothing about this. I was fully aware of Colin Derby's warning – but I'd grown sick of living in dread, and perhaps testosterone had also kicked in because, foolishly, I decided to take Floyd on.

Peter Roberts and I came out of the assembly hall and walked around the corner. It seemed like the whole school was in the yard and on the embankment surrounding it, waiting for this spectacle to take place. I had been off ill for a few days before and a friend told me that Floyd had looking forward to this.

'He told everyone that you hadn't been in because you were shitting yourself and he's been wearing his hobnailed boots for three days waiting for you,' he said.

'I've had enough of this shit,' I said. As I marched round the corner, Floyd was standing there in his smelly cut-off Wrangler. He was overweight, and his long ringleted black hair was greasy.

I walked calmly past the crowds but then started running at him. I smashed my fist into his face. Soon it was an all-out brawl. The teachers separated us, and we were summoned to the head-master's office. He asked for both our school reports. Floyd was a model student, but with my appalling record and feedback from Greystone Heath, my fate was sealed. Floyd went scot-free, while I received a caning. The teachers also told me that they'd 'informed the social worker'. I was filled with trepidation. I knew for sure what would happen next: I'd be expelled, and Colin Derby would put me in the dreaded Mobberley Hall Approved School. I went home and my brother Reynold confronted me when I arrived. I was wearing his shirt, and he had been looking for it. He hit me and we fought. He had no idea of what had just happened in school.

After all this, I didn't want to live anymore, so I went upstairs to my mum's bedside cabinet and took out her tablets. They were her antidepressants, the packet said 'Bolvidon'. Inside were two full strips of about twenty tablets. I took the lot. I then crawled into my bed, ready and waiting to die. My sister Jacqueline must have seen the pill carton with all the empty strips in the bathroom because she alerted my mum, who then called Colin. In a panic, Mum told Jacqueline to make saltwater and she forced me to drink it. I vomited immediately.

Colin Derby arrived along with the ambulance. I was rushed to Alder Hey Children's Hospital on Eaton Road in Liverpool, and all the way in the ambulance Colin was calling me a 'stupid fool' and a 'stupid little boy'. He seemed to be mumbling a load of stuff, but I was slipping in and out of consciousness and only caught the odd word. At A & E, they asked me what I'd taken and were given the packaging from the Bolvidon tablets by Colin. They pumped my stomach with a ghastly brown liquid, which launched me into a violent fit of projectile vomiting, probably just in time to save my life. Colin was talking as if I was just attention-seeking and believed I 'probably hadn't taken anything'. Then I filled a cardboard kidney dish with bile and mucous and there within it were frothy white remnants of the pills. At that point he shut up. I looked at him with a scowl and asked: 'Are you happy now?' I'd end up saying that again to him soon afterwards but for very different reasons. This was all part of my hellish experience, the scars of which never started to heal until that fateful backstage meeting with the wise and kind-hearted Gil Scott-Heron. Some of that damage, however, will never be fully undone.

CHAPTER 4

CRIME OR MUSIC

To say that I was overcome with excitement at the idea of going on tour with Gil when I took that coach down from Liverpool to London would be an understatement.

This was an incredible adventure. I mean, I'd never even been to London before, so can you imagine what all this meant to someone in my hopeless situation? I was living in a hostel for the homeless in Liverpool. I had no qualifications to speak of, and my job prospects were zilch. If I made an application for a job, they'd ask, 'Where did you go to school?' The response was always something like a long list of institutions. I had no prospects at all.

When I look back on that time, I remember thinking I had a choice: I was facing either a life of crime – this was where most of my peers were headed – or I could try going into this music business. A few years later, when I'd learned to read and write fluently, I wrote a song called 'Crime or Music' which spoke about this dilemma.

When I got to the Norfolk Plaza Hotel in Paddington, I went to the reception and asked for Gil. To my surprise, the woman at the front desk was expecting me. 'Are you Mark?' 'Yes,' I replied. 'Gil left this for you.' She handed me a room key and told me that the band had already left to play the show but Gil had told her that I was coming and had left me the key. He told her to tell me to 'go freshen up', and he would see me after the show.

I had no idea what to expect, but when I entered the room, I realised that it must be Gil's. There were brown envelopes strewn all over the bed, stuffed with cash, all £50 notes. I estimated there must have been about £50,000 which, even now, is a hell of a lot money, so imagine how much it was worth in 1984. He'd also left some jewellery, positioned quite deliberately on the bedside cabinet in a box which was flipped open. It contained a solid gold ram, encrusted with diamonds and rubies.

I'm not going to lie, the thought of taking the lot and disappearing did cross my mind briefly. The thought left my mind as quick as it'd come. I said to myself, 'Don't even think about it, this is Gil Scott-Heron, he's a good man and he's trusting you.' Gil had set me a test.

I took a shower, freshened up and then went downstairs to the bar and waited for the band to return. When I saw them come through the doors, buzzing from the energy of the show, I walked over to greet them. Gil cracked a smile and said, 'So you made it then?' 'Yeah, the bus was delayed, sorry I missed the show.' 'Yeah, we waited as long as we could, but we had to get to the gig. Did you go to the room and freshen up?' 'Yeah, I did thanks, here's the key.'

Gil threw his head back and started to laugh; then with a smile on his face he called out to the Count. 'Count! Get brother Mark a room.' And the Count did just that. I hung with Gil and the band in the bar for a while, then we went back to Gil's room. Gil produced another bulging brown envelope from his jacket pocket and threw it on the bed. Another bunch of £50 notes fanned out. One by one, the band members came to the room, each one laughing and joking with Gil, staying for a brief chat, then Gil would pay them before they left. Gil's hotel room was like a dysfunctional office but this was how business was done on the road, as I later found out.

Gil told me, 'Look, life is busy on the road, we've got shows every day, so this is the only time we get to talk. You wanna talk about anything with me, we gotta use this time. Tomorrow we start early; breakfast is at 7 a.m., we leave at 8, it's a long ride. Call the reception and order a wake-up call, 'cause these guys will leave you behind.' He never mentioned the money and I didn't ask. Perhaps even then, he knew the potential significance of our meeting. It seemed he had bigger plans for me, and he needed to know if he could trust me.

Gil's band at that time were called Amere Facade. They were a collection of world-class musicians. I knew who most of them were because they were on the latest album and my brother Reynold would talk about them. He talked about the bass player Robbie Gordon a lot because Reynold was learning to be a bass player and he would copy all of Robbie's basslines. This tour was the best education an eighteen-year-old wanting to get out of the ghetto could get.

Most of the band were from in and around Washington DC, as that was where Gil had been living at the time. The drummer was a guy called Steve Walker, who had played with the legendary soul singer Dionne Warwick. Since then, he had got into the go-go scene. Go-go was a style of music that had developed predominantly in DC at clubs and parties.

People would go to the go-go in DC like we'd go to a West Indian 'blues' party in the UK, in that they both went on all night and were often unlicensed. But the go-go sound was not based on reggae, like the blues was. It was based on drumbeats, changing up the rhythm, and rhyming, singing or rapping over the top. The beat didn't stop. It was constant, all night. The timing, the rhythms and the musicians playing or singing on top might change but the go-go beat was steady. There were some famous go-go artists, such as Chuck Brown & the Soul Searchers, Trouble Funk and Salt-N-Pepa's backing band EU (Experience Unlimited); but while people in the UK might have heard of these guys, they wouldn't necessarily associate them with go-go. Most people outside of DC didn't know what go-go was.

It was rumoured that Steve had been shot at a go-go, leaving him with impaired coordination and hearing. His days playing with Dionne Warwick were over, but Gil continued to support him, and he was still a very, very good drummer.

On tenor sax was Ron Holloway, a veteran of the jazz scene, from Takoma Park, Maryland (on the border with DC). Holloway went on to play with Dizzy Gillespie, with whom he toured until the great jazz trumpeter passed away. The guitarist on Gil's tour was Lyn Oakey, an English guy brought in by the Manchester-based promoter Alan Wise. On percussion, we had Larry McDonald. Larry was from Jamaica and had started out playing with the famous trombonist and bandleader Carlos Malcolm. He went on to play with all the big ska and reggae acts – the Wailers, the Skatalites, Stranger Cole, Toots and the Maytals, Lee 'Scratch' Perry; more recently, he had been playing with the blues star Taj Mahal.

But the guy I got closest to was Robbie Gordon. The other guys were older, and many had been college-educated. Robbie was younger and came from the south-east side of DC – which was then the murder capital of the USA and a really tough place to grow up – so, like me, he had had a ghetto education. Going on tour with Gil was Robbie's ticket out of south-east DC. We connected, and he understood me instantly.

At first, when I joined the tour, the guys were asking, 'Who's he? What's he doing here?' but Robbie just gravitated towards me – he made me feel part of it. Robbie was also an amazing musician. He was completely self-taught – he had an incredible style of playing, completely unique, and had already built a reputation as a top bass player.

The stage manager on the tour was an English guy called Pete Hooker – he was the guy Gil always called for when he was touring the UK. After a show we'd load all the equipment into the tour bus; there would be a second bus and Pete would drive that one with the 'backline' (all the amplifiers, drums and so on) and I would sometimes ride with him. He was very close to everyone and the whole band loved him.

On that first tour, I tried to make myself as useful as possible. I'd carry equipment, I would help the road crew strip down the stage after the shows, I would assist the band by running errands. If someone needed batteries for a tuner, or strings for a guitar, or an adapter for a US appliance, whatever it was, I'd find a way to sort it out. Sometimes the band would arrive in town and I'd have laundered their clothes, ready for the show. I'd hold doors open for people, I'd run errands, I'd go and get pizzas, you know, whatever was needed. I'd also supervise the dressing room during performances and make sure nobody got in there. Ironically, part of my job would be to stop people getting backstage, providing a little bit of personal security – literally whatever was needed to make the show happen or to make the tour run smoothly I'd do it. My mantra was 'If it's no one's job – it's my job!'

I learned to read a map, so I could help to navigate for the driver when we were touring Europe. Over the years, I ended up acting as a roadie; then later on, as a road manager and even tour manager for Gil, both in Europe and in the States.

On tour, we'd wake up around 7 a.m. in the hotel and would usually meet up for breakfast. Most of us would make it for that because it was included in the room fee. It was usually a buffet, with lots of choices of juice, drinks, cereals and hot food, which was great because you could eat as much of whatever you wanted. Also, when you're on tour, your options for food later in the day are usually limited.

Sometimes we'd drive for hours and, if in Europe, it could be whole days before we'd stop somewhere we could properly sit down to eat. Most meals were just pit stops at motorway cafes. They weren't like they are today; back then, all you could get was fuel and snacks, so the hotel breakfast in the morning was the best meal you'd get all day.

Gil would rarely come to breakfast, preferring to eat in his room, so I'd make it my business to make sure that someone in reception was told to send his breakfast up.

At the hotel, I'd usually stay with Rob, as often – in the early days – I wouldn't have a room. If Gil noticed, he'd say to the promoter, 'Get him a room.' If Gil didn't notice, the promoter generally wouldn't and I wouldn't ask, so Rob would say, 'Hey brother, I got a twin, you can share with me.'

Rob was really kind to me, and I'll never forget his kindness. The promoters, on the other hand, would be like, 'Who's this guy?' and 'What does he want?' Not all of them, but some. The worst was promoter Alan Wise. He was always trying to cut me out of the tour, trying to separate me from the band and making snide comments like, 'So you're going home after the next show, yeah?' Stuff like that. He was always snarling at me when Gil wasn't looking. Wise promoted the northern shows at places like Liverpool, Manchester, Sheffield and Leeds. Sometimes promoters would double up as road managers if there were a lot of shows on the tour, and that meant they also rode with the band. I usually did too but when Alan was around, he always wanted me to ride with the crew.

The band was in a Mercedes-Benz 'Splitter', which was a luxury tour bus at the front with a segregated rear compartment to carry bags and equipment. You could put a few flight cases in there – guitars and stuff that didn't need setting up before a show, and some bags – but there wasn't space for all the backline as well, so that would go in a crew van.

When it was arranged this way, the crew van could leave earlier and set up the band's equipment at the venue while the musicians would travel a bit later, allowing them some time to rest. The crew van was OK to travel in as it was usually driven by Pete Hooker, who was a cool guy. We got on well. He'd teach me things and I appreciated that. Hooker was always glad of a spare pair of hands too, so it worked out well for both of us.

Once the stage was set up at the venue, usually around midday or early afternoon, the band would arrive for the soundcheck. If it was a festival gig, we didn't do soundchecks, as there wasn't time, you'd just run a quick line check and then go straight into your performance, but at venues it was a lot more organised. As soon as the stage was set up and Pete was happy, I'd head for the dressing room to see if the rider was in place.

The rider was an addendum to the performance contract, which stipulated all the hospitality that was to be provided by the venue, or the promoter, to the artist and the band. Some artists have crazy riders, there were rumours that Elton John demanded loads of fresh flowers – expensive ones – in his dressing room.

Gil's rider at that time included a bottle of brandy, beers and soft drinks, a cheese platter, nibbles, a hot meal, and usually fresh fruit including lemons and honey. A lot of vocalists have honey and lemon because singing every night can put a massive strain on your vocal cords. Honey soothes the throat, while lemon will allow you to sing a couple of songs after your voice has already given out: it kind of elongates what you can do after the damage is done and at that point, it's about getting through the show, resting your voice and delivering again the next night. Often the venues wouldn't have the rider requests in the dressing room, so I'd make sure it was all there and ready by the time the band arrived for soundcheck.

Being at soundcheck was an incredible privilege. You would get to see this amazing group perform when there's no audience except for yourself and a few crew members. It's about as intimate as a show can get and you find yourself noticing every aspect of the music, because it's being performed instrument by instrument, in isolation.

Gil had some of the most amazing musicians in the business in his band and watching them play was awe-inspiring. Witnessing the behind-the-scenes performances and then watching it all come together on stage, with a full house, was the most incredible experience for a man of eighteen, just starting out and on this remarkable road trip. It was like living a dream. It was the most exciting and delightful time of my entire life. At that time, I felt as if I would have been happy just doing this forever, without a second thought.

The highlight of the soundcheck was when Gil arrived. The band would do their thing individually and then, as they were getting ready to do it collectively, I'd ask someone from the venue to get me to the hotel to rouse Gil and get him to soundcheck. Once he sat at his iconic Fender Rhodes piano, the whole vibe came together. It was magic.

The level of musicianship was 'off the chain' as the band would say, and the way the band was in perfect sync would always bring a wry grin to Gil's face. He'd put his head back, look to the ceiling, crack a smile and then hit the keys with some strange, diminished chord to get his signature sound and as its dissonance filled the room with vibes, they'd launch into a slew of musical masterpieces.

We often travelled with our own sound man. He did what is called 'front of house' sound, meaning he was the guy mixing the sounds coming off the stage and piping them through the PA system to the crowd. The house engineer would differ from venue to venue. Sometimes you'd get a really good one who was attentive to detail, and occasionally you'd get one who'd set his levels and then read the paper while the band were on stage. This was frustrating and had a big impact on the show. I'd see the band on stage motioning to the sound man, and I'd see him ignoring them. So, what I started to do was stand by the sound man during shows. I'd watch intensely and if I saw the guy slacking I'd point to the band and say something like, 'look, the sax can't hear himself' or 'the bass needs more in the monitor'. I came to understand the signs and what they meant, and I made sure the sound man was paying attention.

This was most important when the solos started. Gil's band did the most incredible solos, and nothing pissed me off more than when one member of the band launched into a solo and the sound man ignored it or caught it halfway through. If there's a guitar solo, all the attention should go to the soloist: lights, prominence of the volume level of the guitar and so on. So I started to tell the sound man who was going to solo and when it was coming in. That way, they could prepare their levels and give the soloist due prominence straight away. I knew every aspect of the music, all the parts and all the nuances of the performance. Sometimes the band would change it up a bit but mostly it followed a format linked to the set list and I knew it inside out, every solo, every word of every song, every bit of audience participation. So I was an asset to the sound man, who didn't know the band, and who had never heard the music and had no idea who was doing what, apart from when they were at soundcheck for an hour or so.

The band started to recognise my worth and would often tell me to make sure the sound man did this or that, while Pete

Hooker would stay on the side of the stage in a posture like a sprinter ready to start a race. If even the slightest thing went wrong on stage, he'd shoot out like a bolt of lightning and sort it and then be gone as soon as he'd arrived. We made a good team. So much so that whenever Gil arrived in the UK, the first thing he'd say was: 'I need Hooker and I need Mark.' We'd get the call and by that night we'd be there – ready to go wherever he wanted us to go – for however long he needed us. It was never a question – we were just there and that's how it went, for years.

When he was available, Gil brought his own sound man from the States. His name was Dave McClean. Dave was an old head in the business and had toured with many of the greats. Dave taught me a lot. He'd send me into the crowd during shows and ask me to listen out for specific things in different parts of the venue. He was stationed at the sound-mixing desk when the show was on, so he couldn't move, and sometimes he'd want to know if a certain thing could be heard from a certain vantage point. That's when I started to understand the complexities of acoustics and how certain rooms sounded, depending on different factors, like whether it was full or empty. This means what sounds great at soundcheck might not be so great when there are a thousand people in the room. This was all experience that would help me later on, when I got into music production and started performing myself.

In the early to mid 1980s, Gil would play at a lot of the festivals – Glastonbury, WOMAD, Phoenix and so on. In those days, Glastonbury was nothing like the corporate event it is today, and tickets were a lot less expensive. Back then, it was a fundraising event for the anti-nuclear movement CND. Having said that, it was beginning to attract bigger-name acts, and by the mid-1980s a lot of major bands would play there.

In 1986 when Gil first played that three-day festival, the Psychedelic Furs, the Cure, the Wailers, Black Uhuru, Amazulu, the Pogues, and Lloyd Cole and the Commotions were among the bands at the top of the bill on days one and two. I have distinct memories of it, particularly on day three, because we were next door to the Portakabins for Madness and Level 42. My brother was a massive Level 42 fan, and since he himself was a bass player, their bassist Mark King was one of his heroes; like Phil Lynott of Thin Lizzy, Mark King led the band. I was, however, disappointed that day when Level 42 came out of their Portakabin and King was flanked by a security detail on either side, just getting from his Portakabin to the stage some thirty metres away. There was no crowd, just a few other crew members from our band, and Madness. There were no fans or audience in the backstage area. It was overkill, and this sense of narcissism made me feel uneasy about King's ego. I stopped listening to Level 42 after that. It kind of burst my bubble.

Another memorable night on the 1986 tour was a show at the Irish Centre in Leeds. During the gig, I met a local guy who told me of a blues later that night in the ghetto and he invited me to go after the show. He took me and Robbie Gordon as well. The blues was in Chapeltown – the black area of Leeds, up in the north-east of the city, at the Chapeltown Road Boys' Club – and it was a purely West Indian crowd. The air was thick with ganja smoke and the music provided by a local 'sound system' was heavy dub. Afterwards, the local brother (whose name escapes me now) took us back to our hotel and asked if he could meet Gil. We took him to Gil's room, and we all sat up smoking joints for a few hours and talking. I recall the brother saying to me: 'He's a prophet.' That stopped me in my tracks.

A few days later, we were in another hotel and the boxing phenomenon that was 'Iron Mike' Tyson was fighting, and Gil and I watched it on TV. Gil was providing an incredibly funny running commentary, but it shocked me too, as everything he was saying seemed to be repeated by the commentator just afterwards. It freaked me out a bit 'cause the fight was live. I recalled what the guy in Leeds had said to me, and I asked Gil, 'Are you a prophet?' 'No,' he replied with a chuckle, 'if you know all the elements, it's possible to predict the outcome, that's all. I ain't no prophet.'

On that 1986 tour, Gil also played at the legendary Manchester club the Haçienda. I saw a girl dancing and I remember saying to Robbie Gordon, in my cocky, cheeky-chappie Scouse accent, 'I want her.' She was beautiful. She had jet-black hair and looked like a model.

Manchester was different from Liverpool. In Liverpool girls danced in pairs around their handbags and you couldn't just cut in on one, you had to ask her up, off the floor, and then if she agreed you and she could dance. If she was already dancing with her friend, you'd have to wait. In Manchester, girls danced alone, and in the Haçienda, there were no rules at all. It was a wild place, where anything went.

I remember walking over to this girl and just cutting in and dancing with her. I told her I was with the band, and she asked if she could come backstage and meet them. She was a singer and had a band of her own. She'd released some tracks on a

Manchester label called Bop Cassettes. I took her backstage and she met Gil and the band. She ended up back at the hotel with me and we spent the night together. The following day, when the band and crew left to go on to the next show, we exchanged numbers. She reached out to me as I was about to get on the tour bus and asked me to be her manager. I have to admit, as a twenty-year-old, I was a bit bemused by that.

At the end of the '86 tour, I moved to London. Gil had encouraged me to 'get out of Liverpool'. He could see that there were no real prospects for me there and he wanted me to broaden my horizons and was introducing me to people who might be able to help. By 1987 Robbie Gordon was also living in London. Rob had taken me to meet Leslie Palmer while we were on tour. Les was a Trinidadian, and he was one of the founders of the infamous Notting Hill Carnival. We met at his amazing community arts space on Willesden High Road, in north-west London, called the Brent Black Music Co-Op (BBMC). It had a restaurant, rehearsal rooms, a small performance space and a full recording studio. The recording engineer was a bit of a legend in the music industry – a Jamaican guy called Sid Bucknor; and another charismatic Jamaican called TJ was the manager. It was an important hub in the black music scene at the time. British reggae band Aswad had just recorded their album at BBMC, and Sid had a reputation back in Jamaica that was second to none due to his incredible discography from his time at Harry J Studio in Kingston. It read like a who's who of reggae music.

Rob had arranged a session at BBMC where he was recording a tribute to Bob Marley, called 'The Marley Scratch'. He'd asked me to drop a few bars on the track, so I came up with a little ragga riff and dropped it in; it was my first ever recording. You hear many hip-hop and R & B records these days with a ragga verse in them, but in 1987 it was something new. Barbadian guitarist Jimmy 'Senyah' Haynes was producing the track. He had just won a Grammy Award for his production of Steel Pulse's album *Babylon the Bandit*, only the third-ever reggae album to achieve that honour at that time.

Robbie needed a female vocal on the chorus. I told him I knew this singer in Manchester who wanted me to manage her. I was only twenty and had no idea how to manage anyone, but I guess when you tour with a famous artist, everyone thinks you know everything about the music business. Robbie told me to ask her to come to the studio in London. I called her and she was thrilled. I hadn't seen her since that night in Manchester the year before, so when she arrived, there was some anticipation.

We got her in the vocal booth, gave her the lyrics and the melody, and she killed it. She was great. But it soon became apparent that she was more interested in Gil's band than me, as she kept avoiding me. I thought this was a bit weird, since I'd brought her in. It honestly never occurred to me that I was simply a stepping stone. Later Rob told me, 'Forget her man.' I was like, 'Yeah, but you don't understand ...' He then produced several pictures of her posing in a bikini. He said: 'Look, she gave these to me, so I'm telling you, she's not about what you think, just keep it professional and forget her. That's how it is on the road, man. Everyone wants a piece of you because you're with Gil. Get used to it and don't get caught up in your feelings. This is the music business.' It was one of many, many lessons I learned in those early touring days.

CHAPTER 5

BEYOND PARENTAL CONTROL

If you'd said to me when I was a schoolboy at the start of the Eighties that in a few years I'd be a confidant of a major American recording artist and a trusted member of his touring crew, I'd have laughed in your face. Back then, life was tough and there was no sign of things getting much better.

After I was expelled from Gateacre Comprehensive for that fight with Floyd, and my failed suicide attempt, the social worker, Colin Derby, made good on his threat. Once I was discharged from Alder Hey Children's Hospital, he took me straight to Dyson Hall in Fazakerley (the unit that replaced Menlove). Dyson Hall was a new-build institution and – like Menlove – it was pretty secure.

Three of the staff from Greystone Heath – all former teachers of mine – were now at Dyson Hall. This was going to prove disastrous for me. They wanted me punished and I was sent from Dyson to Mobberley Hall within two months. Colin Derby, who was in many ways naive and easy to manipulate, helped them get their way.

Mobberley had been set up as an 'approved school for boys' in the 1930s but had become a 'community home with education' in the early 1970s, and now also accepted girls. An approved school was an institution where young people could be either sent by a court for committing an offence, or for simply being considered 'beyond parental control'.

Mobberley was to gain notoriety in the late 1990s as one of the institutions investigated by Greater Manchester Police as part of Operation Cleopatra. Officers investigated 350 complaints of abuse in that investigation and six men were prosecuted; £2.2 million was paid in compensation to victims.

The headmaster at the time was a short Welshman called Mr Llewellin John.

I was in a unit there called Curtis House and our housemaster was a boxing enthusiast, a cruel man called Mr Fane. The warden was Mr Southcott. Fane had tried to establish a regime in his unit that was based around sports and physical exercise, but it was really a cover for his violence towards the kids.

He took to making me put on boxing gloves and punching me from one corner of the unit to the other. Although I was a pretty big lad, I was still only thirteen. What I didn't know was that the frequent beatings and bullying I received from Fane were scare tactics used to keep the smaller and younger children in check. If he could take down the big black kid, what would happen to them if they resisted? Within a few months at Mobberley, I'd already been stabbed in the leg. A few weeks after that, I got savagely beaten by a gang and had a front tooth knocked out.

This second incident sparked an 'emergency case conference' that had me taken out of the institution for my own safety. I was released after only five months, which was unprecedented in the institution's history.

When I sued the council years later, I got access to my social services files. There was no mention of the beating, or of the 'emergency case conference'. I often wondered if Colin had fabricated the report: there was no other way to explain how apparently, in five minutes flat, I'd gone from this 'degenerate', 'rebellious' 'delinquent', to a 'model pupil' who deserved 'immediate and early release'. When I saw this, I realised how corrupt the social services were and it made me sick.

I remember when Colin visited me at Mobberley and I smiled sarcastically, with my front tooth knocked out and a stab wound still fresh in my thigh, saying to him: 'Is this what you wanted? Are you happy now? Did you teach me the lesson I deserved?'

Colin dipped his gaze, put his head in his hands and said: 'I'm going to get you out! I'm never going to put a boy in here again.' I remembered being back in the hospital bed, when the pills came out of my stomach, thinking what did I have to do to make this guy believe that I was the victim here?

By the time I left Mobberley, I had just turned fourteen and at this point my life was absolute hell. This scenario was a typical manifestation of the degree of corruption that was prevalent among the social workers, police and the local councils back in the 1970s, all of which would be publicised years later in various investigations, trials and prosecutions. They suppressed all manner of abuse to maintain their salaries and jobs, and to protect their colleagues or themselves. They abjectly failed in their responsibilities to protect the children placed in their care. It would take twenty years for the truth to come out.

There was only one occasion when I ever bumped into a former inmate from Mobberley Hall. Ironically, it was at that Glastonbury show with Gil. I recall sitting backstage, outside our Portakabin, when a man came up to me whom I recognised immediately. His name was Martin Donaldson, but we called him Dougie. On the day I'd been set upon at Mobberley by the gang from Moss Side in Manchester, Dougie was the only kid who didn't jump in on me. Despite being so far away from my time in care, it was a reminder that sometimes your old life can creep up and surprise you. Dougie was touring with one of the other bands on the bill and it was the weirdest of coincidences that we should both end up doing that on the same festival, with two different bands. We reminisced a little and he was quite apologetic about how I was treated in Manchester, but Dougie and I were always good, so it was nice to see him. Somewhat serendipitous that the one guy I liked at Mobberley was the only one I ever bumped into again.

My next destination was Sydney House, a boys' hostel in a grand-looking double-fronted Victorian villa in Aigburth in Liverpool. A man called Richard Aspinall and his wife had set up the hostel, originally housing refugees from the Hungarian revolution, but later, taking in teenage boys from troubled backgrounds. The boys there would go to normal state schools and often do jobs in the evenings, as back then, putting fourteen-year-olds into work was not uncommon. The hope was that the boys could get jobs in the local community and become useful members of society. After the Mobberley episode, this was the softest landing Colin could find for me. It ended up being my easiest time served in the care system.

Bill Crabb had recommended me for a job at the nearby three-star Alicia Hotel, working as a kitchen porter, and they had accepted me. On weekdays during term time, I'd get home from school at 4 p.m., drink a pint of milk and eat a packet of crisps – supplied by Marie, Sydney House's cook – then climb over the back-garden wall and go to work in the hotel's kitchens, washing dishes. I stayed there 'til 10 p.m. every weeknight. Working at the hotel was among the best of my childhood memories because the staff there treated me like an adult, and I had a degree of freedom and financial independence. I was after all earning £1.10 an hour, and was able to buy my own clothes and records.

I had devised a dishwashing system and it worked really well. This success helped in other quarters. Even though my social worker received dismal school reports – I was still struggling enormously with my lessons – those from Sydney House were glowing. The hotel told Colin that I was a hard worker, which meant I got to live in the hostel in relative peace.

We had all sorts of characters at Sydney House, but a particular sixteen-year-old boy called Stephen stood out. He was rumoured to have been a rent boy. One night, someone plucked up the courage to ask him directly and he confessed. He even went as far as giving us details about how he'd 'scope out businessmen' at the train stations and what he did with them in the restrooms. We were horrified.

One day, Sydney House organised a camping trip to the Lake District. We travelled there in a minibus with three staff members, one of whom was the charismatic Bill Crabb. Since Bill had agreed to take me into Sydney House and had saved me from more grievous harm in Mobberley, I always felt beholden to him. Anything he asked, I did without question.

At the campsite in Keswick, two staff members led us on a hike up a hill. We'd gone halfway up the road, before I realised that I'd forgotten my cigarettes in the tent. I'd started smoking at the age of nine and many of the care homes allowed the children to smoke. In Mobberley we'd been allowed to buy cigarettes and tobacco; it was the same in Dyson Hall. I decided to dash back for them. When I got to my group's tent and threw back the flap, there were Bill and Stephen. They were both in their underpants, sixteen-year-old Stephen was giving Bill an oil massage. Everyone present froze like deer caught in headlights. I uttered an 'excuse me', grabbed my cigarettes and ran out and caught up with the others.

I didn't know what to think. I was fifteen years old at this point, and this man was my saviour; he'd got me out of a deadly situation at Mobberley. I guess I just put it out of my mind and never spoke of it.

Still, I'd made a friend whilst at Sydney House. He and I knew that sixteen-year-olds could live independently so long as they had parental consent, so we'd resolved to split the rent on a small apartment in Liverpool when I hit sixteen. Freedom seemed like it was close, but it never happened.

Though I'd put the incident between Bill and Stephen out of my mind, Bill hadn't. He became hostile towards me. Where previously he'd been kind, he became harsh and began to complain about me to Colin, who as you might expect took his side; and Bill eventually used his influence to get me out of Sydney House and back to Greystone Heath.

I was back to square one and enraged.

Greystone Heath could only keep me until I was sixteen and had sat my examinations. Given my past difficulties, I had no consistent education to prepare me for O-levels, so I ended up put in for the less-respected Certificate of Secondary Education (CSE) exams.

I was taken by a staff member to Penketh High School in Warrington to sit the exams. I can recall seeing a huge Nazi sign on the school gate, with National Front initials. I was the only black kid in this terrifying space. I had little to no understanding of most of the subject matter in the exams I took. I had been out of formal schooling for so long and was so traumatised by experiences in care homes, I couldn't focus. My reading was not at all fluent, my spelling atrocious, and I ended up scoring a paltry mean grade of 4 in woodwork, art and English. My literacy levels were rudimentary at best, and in maths I did an exam even lower than a CSE called an RSA (Royal Society of Arts). This was a qualification for people who couldn't make the grade for even a CSE and the elementary level RSA was the lowest one they did.

Later, when I eventually came back to Sydney House, I never breathed a word of what I'd witnessed on that cold afternoon in the Lake District. Indeed, I'd blocked it from my mind. I didn't connect the dots until much later. Bill had shown me that he had the power to remove from me the most precious thing I had, my hard-won freedom. He'd shown me that he was, in fact, very much in control.

Upon my return, I came to learn that he'd thrown my friend onto the streets. When I tracked my friend down, he told me about Bill's lewd advances to him. He was living rough, so I took him to Ujamaa House hostel in Toxteth, where my brother Reynold was then staying, and they took him in.

After my second stint at Sydney House, I was released back home to my mum, but I only stayed there a year or so. My sense of family had been shattered. It seemed like my siblings now regarded me more as a visitor than a brother. I'd been externally toughened but internally dismembered by the care system. I couldn't talk to my mum. We were strangers living under the same roof.

I guess she felt guilty about not being able to get me out, or even stopping the social services from taking me in the first place, but perhaps she just didn't know how to talk about it.

By 1982, my eldest sister Jacqueline had moved out. She'd narrowly escaped the care system after being expelled from Netherley Comp for fighting with a boy who'd racially abused her. They used to chew paper with spit, roll it into balls and throw it in her afro, then they'd all laugh at her. But Jackie didn't take any shit and she would never shy away from a fight, even with the hardest of them. She was placed in the Garston Guidance Unit, a sort of community centre for kids who'd been excluded from school. They played snooker and table tennis and did virtually no schooling. If you went to the unit, you didn't sit any exams, so Jacqueline left with no qualifications. As a black family in 1970s Liverpool, it seemed like we were doomed. The whole system was against us. We were expected to achieve nothing and the system, it seemed, did everything in its power to ensure that was the case.

I connected most with my younger sister Michelle but was totally detached from Reynold, who was also taken into care at age twelve, but who appeared to have had a far less traumatic experience whilst there. He'd gone in when he was much older than me and was in places with more lenient security.

The bottom line, though, was that we didn't know each other anymore. I didn't feel like it was my home – and my siblings, perhaps unwittingly, made me feel unwelcome. I had not at that time considered that they might have resented the fact that I was getting three square meals a day, while they often went hungry. I found out later that my mum would try to do something extra on the weekend 'when Mark comes home', like have meat or something, and that my siblings felt the sting of this. They, of course, had zero idea of what I was actually going through. I would have gladly traded hunger for beatings and solitary confinement, but trauma is trauma and in truth, we had all suffered a lot, in one way or another.

Low on cash, I started hustling and running the streets. Within a year I was bringing trouble to my mother's doorstep. Being a black child in a white ghetto was one thing, but being a black man there was a whole other issue. I knew I'd never be safe on my mum's estate, so I left to return to Toxteth in Liverpool's 'South End' where my brother had a flat and where my sister Jackie had one too.

While at Sydney House I'd been using my wages to buy and store up furniture in anticipation of getting my own flat. Reynold got a flat first but was destitute so I'd given him all the furniture that I had, on the understanding that he'd replace it when he could and then give it back. When I showed up homeless myself in 1983, Ujamaa didn't have a free bed. I'd been couch-surfing from house to house with very little to eat. I'd asked Reynold if I could stay with him but he refused. I ended up sleeping next door at the flat of his neighbour, a guy called Peter Akinyemi.

Peter couldn't understand how my brother had a flat exactly the same size next door and wouldn't take me in when I was homeless. I lived with Peter for a few weeks, until it became a strain for him. I had no money and couldn't contribute.

I slept rough a few times when I couldn't find a couch to sleep on. I'd hit the lowest point of my young existence. Even in those brutal care homes, we had a bed to sleep in and food to eat and we were at least kept warm and shielded from the elements. I lost a lot of weight, became unhealthy and was totally destitute. I was seventeen years old.

Colin Derby had long since left me to my own devices. I certainly wasn't reaching out to him and neither was he reaching out to me. Eventually he passed my case to a guy called Eric Long. He was OK, not intimidating as Colin had been. Eric Long was charged with formalising the end of the care order, which would expire on my eighteenth birthday.

CHAPTER 6

RIOT AND REVOLUTION

I had spent a lot of time in Toxteth when the riots broke out in the summer of 1981, so I had a first-hand account of the action to share with Gil. They were incendiary days and nights, when that part of Liverpool became front-page news across the world.

Most of the looting took place on Lodge Lane, by Ujamaa House where Reynold was living at that time, but there were burnt-out buildings on Parliament Street and Kingsley Road too, and the burning and looting went on throughout that week in July, with only a day's pause for the protest march. On the first day of the riots, the police had tried to arrest a guy called Leroy Cooper on Selborne Street, close to the city centre. Leroy was about sixteen and from a very influential family in Toxteth, and word spread fast. But in fact this was just one of hundreds of incidents involving the police and the black community. Back then, the police were in the habit of arresting black people for no reason, using what was called the 'sus law', which allowed them to stop and search those they suspected of potentially committing a crime. This almost 160-year-old arcane law was intended to criminalise 'vagabonds' in Georgian times.

The police would grab you off the street and throw you in what we called the 'meaty' or 'meat wagon'. They'd beat you up inside the meaty and then dump you up the road. The police always prevail, however, 'cause they're the good guys. Anyone who still thought that after the Toxteth riots, and the beating of Rodney King in LA, needed their head examining. That's before we get anywhere near the recent murder of George Floyd and so many other black victims at the hands of racist police.

People witnessed the arrest of Leroy Cooper and ran to Granby Street with the news. A crowd soon gathered, a mob surrounded the police van and tried to pull Leroy out of it; things just erupted from there. Within hours, a battle was raging across a big swathe of Toxteth.

On July 3rd, 1981 – the night it all blew up – I was fifteen years old. It was a Friday night, I'd just got paid by the Alicia Hotel and me and the waiter from the Alicia were going out with his posse from Berkley Street. We were all dressed up to the nines. We weren't involved in the rioting – but we were trying to get across the police lines.

We saw lots of police getting bloodied and ambulances coming to take away injured officers but, weird as it might sound, we were oblivious to it. Back then, we were just interested in girls and wanted to get to the club. It was all a bit surreal.

I had a problem with the authorities given my experience in care, but this issue with the local police was alien to me. I'd been in homes for years and off the streets, so I had no idea what went on, but it soon became apparent that this was the prevailing experience of the black community in Toxteth. As the riots progressed and I found out the reasons why, I decided to attend a march that was being organised to oust Ken Oxford – then Chief Constable of Merseyside Police.

The police, who were losing control and had no idea what'd hit them, had called in reinforcements from all over the country, including armoured Land Rovers from the war in Northern Ireland. They started driving them into the crowds at speed, targeting rioters: a tactic only ever used before in Belfast. A local man called David Moore was killed by a police Land Rover. He was disabled and couldn't get out of the way in time. People said he wasn't involved in the riots, he was just trying to get home, and was an innocent victim of police brutality.

The rioters responded by stealing milk floats, setting them alight and jamming sticks on the accelerators so they rammed them into the police lines. At one point, a JCB mechanical digger was used. It was surreal. The whole place became a war zone. Hundreds of police were injured, and hundreds of people were arrested and beaten by the police.

The riots took a day off when David Moore got killed, and I decided to join the 'Anti Ken Oxford march' against the Chief Constable who'd been in charge of policing the riots.

As we congregated at the obelisk, just across from Sefton Park gate on the morning of the protest march, I saw that someone had made a mock coffin with the words 'RIP David Moore' scrawled on it. Someone had brought a real pig's head from the butcher's and placed it on top of the coffin. A police helmet – which had no doubt been taken by a rioter – was subsequently placed upon the pig's head and the coffin led the procession all the way to town, with the Liverpool Black Sisters organisation leading the march and singing the famous disco song 'Ain't No Stoppin' Us Now!' – 'We're on the move!' I marched behind them in the second row between the 'Oxford Out' banners.

At that time my perspectives on racism and police brutality had not yet merged. I had dealt with the possibly more acute and overt racism of an all-white care system and all-white neighbourhoods and had become – to a large extent – impervious to it. In some ways, even apologetic.

People would say 'nigger!' to me and I would reply, 'sorry!' My father had always been the complete opposite, a fan of Malcolm X and Muhammad Ali. I was also relatively naive at that time with regards to what was happening on the streets of Toxteth in the run-up to the riots, having left the area in 1969 at the age of three.

During the riots, there was a lot of destruction of property but the most significant upshot to come out of it all was that the

L8 Defence Committee – Anti-Ken Oxford march during the Toxteth riots.
© Mike Abrahams

police got their arses kicked by the black community and others. This was something the police had clearly never even imagined. They were bussing reinforcements into Toxteth from all over the country and sometimes even those buses were being attacked. Many police officers were literally carried off the buses and straight into ambulances.

Amid fears that the riots would spread into the city centre, business leaders eventually got together and asked the black community organisers to engage in dialogue. The community leaders who came together formed the Black Caucus in response. They told business leaders: 'The reason that the kids are rising up is primarily because of police brutality but it's also the fact that you, as the white business elite, exclude black people from any prospect of social mobility in this city. We cannot become upwardly mobile, we cannot become economically active, because you won't give us jobs. So you need to embrace positive action and give opportunities to black people, so we can be economically included.'

The riots had become leverage for that change; and because the industrialists figured that if they didn't do something for the black community it would have a disastrous effect on Liverpool's businesses, they responded and some jobs were created – not enough, but it was a start.

When Gil arrived in Liverpool in 1984, I had already moved to Ujamaa House, and three years after the riots, we had our own little uprising.

There were seven kids there, but it was a dump. While Sydney House was primarily for white kids and run directly by social services, Ujamaa was mostly for homeless black youths.

There were four staff members on rotation. There was no decoration, barely any furniture and never any food in the pantry. The day-to-day running of the place was managed by a local black guy who was the warden. He had recently served time in prison. The way it worked, then, was that we all applied for the dole and as we lived in sheltered housing we got about £40 a week instead of the usual £8. Of the £40 we were required to hand over £32 to the warden for food and rent, but we never saw any food. If we were hungry, he might give one of us a few quid to get some fish and chips for everyone.

'We should run this place ourselves,' I said to one of the other guys – a kid called Alan 'Marty' Martins – a small but strong lad a couple of months younger than me. He agreed with me, so we had a meeting with the seven of us and I said to everyone: 'Let's kick the staff out and run the place ourselves.' At first, some of them were unsure about this but Marty helped me persuade them.

We barricaded the doors so the warden couldn't get in. Needless to say, he was furious. Then the other staff tried to get in, but we told them we were not letting them in either until we saw the whole management committee and our demands were met. Then Simon Starkey – the vicar, who was on the management committee – came round and was furious too, shouting: 'I am not in the habit of having kids telling me what to do!'

So we didn't let him in either, and told him, 'No one is getting in until we put our demands to the whole management committee.' We wanted decent furniture, proper food and the place to not look like a dump.

From then on, Marty and I told the others, 'We're running the place ourselves.' Marty told everyone to give each of their £32 contributions to me and I would then pay the rent, buy the food and keep some petty cash. I told them we were going to have a menu for each day of the week, and we'd buy the food needed to keep to that menu. We would have three meals every day. No more fish and chips when the warden could be bothered feeding us and no more empty food cupboards.

That first pay day, we all went down to Kwik Save and spent £100 on food. That was two trolley loads – some of the lads had never been shopping like this before and had never had that much food. When we got back, we had enough to fill the empty pantry.

Three of the seven of us knew how to cook. I'd learned at Greystone Heath, where they taught you stuff like that as it was like being in the army – and a little bit at the Alicia Hotel and some restaurants where I'd also worked at locally on Lark Lane, while I'd been at Sydney House. But we decided that everyone had to learn so we could maintain a proper rota. I assigned to those who couldn't cook someone who could – as a mentor – when it was their turn on the rota, and it worked well. We had good, cooked meals every day, for the first time since any of us had entered Ujamaa.

We also had a cleaning rota. We went out and bought mops and detergents. Some were not keen to help out, but Marty enforced that edict – and we soon had the place looking spotless, whereas before it used to stink. This rota system went on for two weeks and subsequently the management committee all came around and finally agreed to our demands. They were shocked at how organised we were.

Another thing that was a big surprise to them was how efficient we had been at paying the rent. The housing association said the rent we had paid in the last fortnight was the first they had been paid for years (when I later left in 1985, I got a bill for £3,000 rent arrears, we all did). It turned out that the warden hadn't being paying our rent to them. He'd threaten us with eviction if we didn't pay him but instead of paying the landlord and buying the food, he'd been pocketing it – so he was sacked. The housing association also claimed they had not carried out any repairs because they hadn't been receiving any rent – so that's why the place was such a dump. When the warden got sacked, the other staff were put on notice.

After the revolution at Ujamaa House, the management committee offered to move us into a better house. It was newly refurbished, subdivided into six flats, two kids per flat, with one flat for the staff. It was agreed that the staff would come back but with our new system in place.

It was here that the new and last social worker I had, Eric Long – who'd assumed my case after Colin Derby abandoned me to the streets and my own fate – found me. He gave me £100 and got me to sign a document declaring that I 'wouldn't ask for any more money from social services', then he left. That was the end of my time under the yoke of social services. I was officially out of care, detached from my family, abandoned by the state and left to fend for myself.

The experience at Ujamaa House had shown me that I always had the mental tenacity to survive and even perform well. But after nine years of having my life deliberately mismanaged by those who'd forcefully put me in their care, freedom had come with a flimsy document and a paltry pittance. £100 for nine years of my childhood. I vowed to myself that this was not the end and that one day they'd have to pay for what they did to me.

I'd always had a radical free spirit; my father's Guyanese friends had called me 'Spartacus' (after the Thracian captive who'd led a slave revolt against the Romans) since I was able to walk, a name that the Guyanese in Liverpool still call me to this day. But my so-called 'care' experience, looking back on it, and my struggles within it, were manifestations of that spirit and the very foundations of what would later develop into my lifelong revolutionary mindset, which so endeared me to other activists.

By the time I first met Gil Scott-Heron, boy was I ready for revolution. Later when I became more literate, I summed up my feelings in a poem I wrote and posted in a letter to Gil for his appraisal, called 'Freedom Is a Funny Thing'.

Freedom is a funny thing!
We all believe that it can be.
But dreams of youths in poverty,
when shattered by reality,
make me question our democracy,
I ask, 'Are we truly free?'
If so, then freedom is a funny thing.
Freedom is a funny thing!
'Ha ha!' You think.
'Not so!' I say,
'To freedom we must find a way.'
'You're free!' They say,
'Why can't you see,

long gone are chains of slavery.
This is a free democracy!
We're both as equals you and me.'
'If so,' I say, 'we're neither free.'
You talk about democracy
and equal rights for blacks and whites.
But in your eyes, I see the truth,
your drunken mouth provides the proof.
There're chips on shoulders – I agree,
but fry your own before you fry me.
'Cause I'm aware of your contempt
for everyone except yourself,
I'm just another category
not welcome in your bigotry,
for all your views and flattery,
I clearly see your hate for me.
If the skin you wear, was black, not fair;
you'd suffer in-equality.
You'd hate so-called 'democracy'.
You'd writhe in pains of poverty.
If bigots said, 'Why can't you see?'
And told you that, 'You're truly free!'
You'd stare them right between the eyes
and from your soul I'd hear the cries;
'God help this damn democracy!'
Why can't there be equality?
Won't anyone just listen to me?
Lord! When can we be truly free?'
When from your race, you've been outcast.

You're scared and hungry and on your ass.
A song of freedom I would sing.
Now isn't freedom a funny thing?

CHAPTER 7

'MAHOGANY SUNSHINE AND TEARS'

After I sent a letter to Gil, I'd wait until the next tour to see him. I'd turn up at whatever locale I'd heard the band was performing at, or sometimes I'd get a call from the promoter, but either way, whenever I arrived at the show, I'd join the tour from that point onwards.

On those early tours in the 1980s, Gil took it upon himself to spend whatever time he could spare mentoring me, giving me encouragement and trying to foster in me a sense of self-worth. From the age of nine, I had been indoctrinated by the care system to believe that I was 'beyond parental control', 'maladjusted', 'a menace to society' or 'a product of my environment'; and to an extent British society – in general – reinforced those notions. Gil refused to accept these popular misconceptions. Despite my ingrained tendency towards self-deprecation – something Gil loathed and would literally stop in its tracks, if he got the slightest whiff of – Gil recognised potential in me that I did not see in myself at that time.

As soon as we'd get on the tour bus, Gil would pull out my letters. He'd always reach for the poems attached to them and then start his critique of my work. It was like watching your teacher as they marked your paper, but much more fun, because even when Gil criticised something, he did it in a way that made you feel special. It was never disparaging but always honest. I'd take his points on board and use them to improve my work. This process went on for years and a whole body of poetic works evolved – as did I. As a young man, with a positive role model, I was becoming more and more conscious and self-assured.

My most touching memory of those days was when he used to introduce me to people as his son, despite the fact that he had his own children. I'd lost my father at the age of fourteen and when I met Gil at eighteen, he'd adopted that role and had taken it on seriously, backing it up with money from his own pocket, paying for my flights, hotels and food.

Back then, I had so many problems; my mind was like Birmingham's 'Spaghetti Junction'. There were so many narratives going on in my head and I couldn't unravel them alone. Gil would listen to them all. At the end, he'd invariably say one or two sentences that would sum up what had taken me so long to say, and then he'd direct me to what I should do about each one. And invariably, his analysis was spot on.

He taught me about poetry and the music business, especially contracts and entertainment law. He politicised me and encouraged me to become productive in society. He also warned me of the dangers of drugs. A lot has been said and written about Gil's problems with drugs but back in the 1980s pretty much everyone was doing them.

Whenever we were on tour, drugs were readily available – but back then drugs were prevalent in a lot of walks of life. This was the era of the yuppie; stockbrokers, lawyers, fashion designers, bankers, journalists and politicians – anyone who had the money was partaking in the pleasures of illicit substances. There was always a notion that drugs were the scourge of the working classes – and they were – but they were just as widespread in the upper classes, only the perception was different.

In the music world, whenever you walked into a dressing room, people were chopping up lines of coke, rolling spliffs and drinking heavily; it was very hedonistic. I don't remember Gil being so different to most others where drugs were concerned back then, but he used to warn me of their dangers and always advised me not to make the same mistakes that he'd made.

I often wondered why Gil wanted to play this role in my life. In the ghetto, everyone had an angle, no one did anything for nothing, so one day I flat out asked him: 'Man, what do you want from me?' He threw his head back and laughed as he was apt to do, and he said, 'I want you to be successful!' From that moment on, I felt like I had a duty to succeed, that Gil had placed this responsibility upon my shoulders, that if I somehow failed to live up to his expectations of me, I was wholly unworthy of all the time, energy and money that he had invested. It was perhaps the best motivation that I could have had. Here was the person whom I cared most about in the world (besides my mum), even more so than myself, and his only ask was for me to succeed; it seemed like the least I could do.

People who knew Gil would always say two things about him: how clever he was and what a good heart he had. They'd say things like 'when you spoke with him, he always made you feel a little cleverer', or 'conversations with Gil always stayed with you forever'.

I loved to sit and watch him being interviewed by journalists. I'd often be the only one there besides the reporter, and Gil would always say 'take his details' and I would. Later I'd follow up and collate the press articles, to see how they'd turned out. One always stuck in my mind. It was a review of one of Gil's albums by New York journalist Neil Tesser, where he described Gil's voice as a blend of 'mahogany, sunshine and tears'.

Woodwork was one of the things I'd developed skills in whilst in care, and I'd worked with mahogany. It has an unusual lustre when it's polished, with layers of texture that only become visible when turned towards the sunlight; a bit like a hologram or the semi-precious stone they call tiger's eye. When you listen to Gil's voice, you can also hear a variety of textures which become more apparent the more you tune into what he's singing and to the intonation in his voice as he sings. For me, that reporter described Gil's voice perfectly. His vocal textures would ignite your senses, while the often melancholy messages, inherent within his lyrics, would move your heart and could bring tears to your eyes

During those early years on tour, I'd manage the backstage area and make sure that anyone who'd come round before or after the show was either on the guest list or there at the request of Gil or the band. We had to do this as there were valuables around – people's bags and so on, and sometimes there was money in the dressing room – so it was my job to protect them whether or not the venue security was present.

As such, I encountered many of the people whom Gil had arranged to meet with and some – like me, that fateful night at

Liverpool's Royal Court – whom he hadn't. But one such guy, who'd been invited to the show, came backstage in London one night in the early 1990s. He was a very cool-looking white guy, with ringleted light-brown hair and a somewhat calming demeanour. He had two books in his hand. He asked to see Gil and I enquired as to who he was. He said, 'My name's Jamie Byng and I'm interested in publishing Gil, he's expecting me.'

He passed me the two books as if they were his calling card, and I was perplexed to see *Lonely Crusade* by Chester Himes and *Pimp* by Iceberg Slim. They both bore the publisher's name – Payback Press. I was intrigued – these were iconic black authors – the messenger didn't appear to fit the message, but his literary tastes were right up my street.

I'd read Iceberg Slim and I was aware of Chester Himes. Though I hadn't read Himes's works, I knew he was one of the authors of the infamous Harlem Renaissance, along with Langston Hughes and Zora Neale Hurston, whom I had read.

Gil had recently published his volume of poetry *So Far, So Good* with Haki Madhubuti from Third World Press in the States. I knew this, 'cause I used to sell copies at the shows. But Gil had bigger ideas for his books and when I informed him that this white guy called Jamie was backstage, with Iceberg Slim and Chester Himes in his hands, he smiled and said, 'Yeh, man, he wants to republish my novels, he's cool man, let him in.' So I did, and like many other encounters on tour with Gil, it was to become the beginning of what would be a lifelong friendship, not only between Gil and Jamie Byng, but also between me and Jamie.

Gil's kindness was indicative of something within his conflicted and complex spirit. He was in many ways a tormented soul, but he had a need to help others in a practical way, not just uplifting them by writing and singing songs. Like many others in the civil rights struggle, Gil made sacrifices within his own personal life to be the revolutionary troubadour we all expected him to be. As such, he was constantly on the road and that must have put a tremendous strain on his relationships, not least of which would have been with his own children. Gil also had the kind of persona that made him want to be a father figure to others, and I think much of that was to do with the fact that he didn't meet his own father until he was twenty-six, when Gil Heron Snr returned to the US from Scotland, where he had played football for Glasgow Celtic and was known as the 'Black Arrow'. It's therefore ironic, that for many years, he was either wholly or at least partially estranged from his own kids, whilst being so paternalistic to people like me. I guess it was that we were on the road together so much, or perhaps it was his attempt to compensate – if that were somehow possible – for his shortcomings as a father himself, as contrasted to his own father's failure to raise him. It's a dilemma that I was never able to get to the bottom of, as I never met his kids throughout all the years I toured with him.

He wrote a poem about his own childhood, which he recited to me while he was writing it in 1988. It is called 'On Coming from a Broken Home'. When Gil was sent to live with his grandmother in Jackson, Tennessee, activists within the civil rights movement were fighting hard for political and social change, against the racism that was still rife in the Deep South. But in reality, racism was festering throughout American society in the 1960s, and as recent political events since the election of Donald Trump have shown us, it still festers to this very day.

Gil was one of three black children chosen to 'integrate' at a segregated elementary school previously reserved for white children only, and he received daily abuse from racist parents and pupils who refused to accept the change. This was after the landmark Supreme Court case 'Brown v. Board of Education' which forced the desegregation of US schools.

Gil knew first-hand how backward the racism in the South was, in particular, and it came through in his music. Songs like '95 South (All of the Places We've Been)', 'The Klan' and 'Cane' – a song very dear to my own heart, as a descendant of slaves on a Demerara sugar plantation myself. He'd also learned the blues while he was down South, listening to all the old-school tunes that he talked about, like 'Mississippi Goddam' by Nina Simone and Billie Holiday's rendition of 'Strange Fruit'. Gil was also a big fan of John Lee Hooker, B. B. King and Muddy Waters, not to mention Bessie Smith, and Robert Johnson – whose version of 'Me and the Devil Blues' Gil would later cover.

He went on to describe himself as a 'bluesologist', claiming that 'if you ever want to make something sound scientific, just add an -ology to the end of it.' He was incredibly skilled at crafting words, particularly new words, that sounded like they should already be a part of our lexicon. Many would later find their way into the urban dictionary, like his famous idiom – 'The Revolution Will Not Be Televised'. Other terms he coined, like the 'vibosphere' (a combination of vibrations in the atmosphere), will no doubt eventually find their way into our everyday language.

His musical prowess started early in his life. His grandmother bought him an old piano for six dollars, from a funeral parlour next door to her house, so that he could learn to play hymns. He started listening to Blues Radio from nearby Memphis in Tennessee, but his grandmother didn't approve, so as a kid he used to mix up the blues with the hymns when she was around and play the straight blues when she wasn't. When you listen to Gil's voice, you can hear the soulfulness that comes from blending that cacophony of diverse and often contradictory music, which collectively represents the quintessential sounds of the southern states.

Though Gil's music emanates primarily from a blues and jazz heritage, he is often referred to as 'the black Bob Dylan' because of the astonishing power of his lyrics. This crafting of words went back to his days as a teenager. He once told me that when he was in college, he worked at a dry cleaners and he'd think up jingles to promote the business on local radio. He even sang some of them to me and we laughed incessantly. I just couldn't imagine him working at a dry cleaners. I never liked that Bob Dylan comparison though, as I always felt that Gil's substance surpassed Dylan's and was far more significant, despite Dylan getting better exposure and therefore more fame. The exposure was always greater for the white artists as they were considered 'mainstream', while black artists were treated as 'niche'. Anyone who'd heard Big Mama Thornton's 'Hound Dog' would be hard-pressed to say Elvis Presley's later version was 'better'. But the truth is, everyone's heard Elvis's version, while hardly anyone ever heard Big Mama Thornton's; and when people used to say to me about Gil being 'the black Bob Dylan', I'd say that 'Bob Dylan was the white Gil Scott-Heron – just not as good'.

When his grandma died, Gil went back to New York to live with his mother in the Bronx. That was when he began to experience urban life, which was perhaps the biggest influence on his music and lyrics beyond the blues and jazz.

But whilst in New York, Gil was also exposed to the black writers and artists of the Harlem Renaissance; people like Langston Hughes, whose regular column in the *New York Post* had a satirical character whom Gil loved, called 'Jesse B. Semple' (or Jesse B. Simple). Jesse exemplified the small-town southern black man who comes north and has a simple way of looking at the complexities of northern life. Hughes used his column to deal with the issues of the day, such as war or political upheaval, through the simplistic and somewhat naive eyes of this southern caricature.

Gil also had a serious side to his nature and was similarly influenced by the more militant works of LeRoi Jones, later known as Amiri Baraka, the mentor of front-line in-your-face New York activists such as the Last Poets. LeRoi Jones had been a publisher of the Beat poets, who were seen as somewhat apolitical, but after the assassination of Malcolm X, he took a more radical stance like many of his contemporaries. He founded the 'Black Arts Movement', denounced his former apolitical stance with the Beat poets, and became a mentor to the Last Poets and other radical writers emerging from the Harlem Writers Workshop.

Gil and his mother had moved from the Bronx to a Puerto Rican area called Chelsea in Manhattan, New York. There were only a handful of black people in this neighbourhood – and this perhaps gave Gil an alternative perspective on what was going on around him, within other marginalised and stigmatised ethnic groups. He learned Spanish. At that time, the works of former Last Poet Felipe Luciano were inspiring young Latinos towards direct action, through the political movement called the 'Young Lords'. Born out of a gang in Chicago, they were the Puerto Ricans' answer to the Black Panthers and Felipe co-founded their New York chapter when he left the Last Poets in the late 1960s.

This was the political climate within a post-civil rights era America from which Gil emerged as an author and a poet. In Chelsea, again, he was exposed to a set of socio-economic and geopolitical issues that would appear within the lyrics of his later repertoire, with songs about Latino immigrants, such as 'Alien (Hold On to Your Dreams)' and those seminal Spanish intros such as 'Ah, uno, dos. Uno, dos, tres, cuatro' on Gil's biggest hit record 'The Bottle'. But that's what Gil did, he absorbed knowledge from everything around him. He was a perpetual student, never satisfied that he knew enough, always questioning everything and seeking to know more. I learned a lot from this approach and recall him once telling me: 'Don't believe what you read in the newspapers, if you want to really know the truth, go and ask people yourself.' This is something I have continued to do ever since. I guess that's why he attached himself to me, when he came to Liverpool. The city had hit the global headlines and made a big noise with the Toxteth riots of 1981, and when Gil arrived in 1984 he already had questions. I guess it was serendipity that brought us together.

Black people talked in rhythms and rhymes; in the pool halls, playing dice on the streets, in the clubs and the gambling dens. 'Talking jive' and 'spieling' were common tools in the vernacular of black people of urban America. Taking words and twisting them to convey different meanings in a rhythmical way was a part of everyday life, and commonplace on the streets in most black neighbourhoods, spawning what we today call 'rap'.

Wherever you found black people in New York, you'd hear rhythm and rhyme in everyday folks' dialogue. Questions like 'How're you doin', brother?' might get a response like 'It's all good in the hood.' Or 'What's going on?' someone would say. You'd reply 'Ain't nothing cookin' but the peas in the pod, an' they wouldn't cook, if the water wasn't hot.' Gil typified this sort of street dialogue in his poem 'The Ghetto Code' – a play on 'Morse code' but the jive talking version.

It was also a way of communicating whereby the authorities couldn't understand you; a method that had evolved from the time of slavery, when enslaved Africans were forced to speak English or French and developed patois and creole so they could speak in code. It is ironic, however, that Morse code itself was derived from Africans' communication across distances with drumbeats. When the colonisers came to understand what was being done and how African tribes were alerting one another by drum and decoding messages, the colonisers developed it into the system of Morse code that we know today.

Gil went to Lincoln University as an undergraduate and it was there that he first met the Last Poets, who were touring on the college circuit on the back of their first hit 'Niggers Are Scared of Revolution'. Gil dropped out in his second year – 1968 – to write his first novel *The Vulture*. It was a murder mystery, but its main theme was the devastation drugs were wreaking on black lives in American cities. He'd actually written the novel before he emerged as a serious recording artist, though it was published the same year as his first album – 1970 – when he was just twenty-one years old.

Gil later went on to attend Johns Hopkins University, where he achieved a master's degree in creative writing, despite having failed to graduate with his bachelor's degree. No doubt his admission was a recognition of his incredible intellect, as well as the commercial success that he was enjoying from the combined impact of being a published author and a signed artist, achieving national and international critical acclaim.

But I think Gil knew that music had a more prominent role to play than literature, in the black American tradition. One day, when I was merchandising his books at the show, I'd asked Gil a question about how we could increase book sales. 'Black people don't read,' was his response. I was a bit taken aback and must have looked perplexed. He elucidated: 'People buy them as a souvenir, an' put 'em on the shelf, just to have them. Ask 'em if they read it? – No! They don't read – most of them that is.' That's when I started to understand why he'd taken the musical rather than literary route to activism. People will listen to a song and hear the words, but they will be unlikely to pick up a book and read the words. For Gil, it was about the effective communication of the message, and it was futile if it was being done in a medium that people didn't engage with; even if sales showed that they had bought something, it didn't mean that they'd read and understood it. This was when I came to understand from him that the oral tradition was an effective means of transmission of knowledge, from one generation to another, unhindered by people's literacy or lack of it.

Gil saw that combining music and the spoken word retained the African oral tradition by using modern means. We are not sitting under a baobab tree and telling stories, like our ancestral griots; we are using modern forms of communication, technology and more explicit terms to explain the realities of what's happening politically in the world, through entertainment that is educational. Gil was therefore a modern urban griot.

Some people would call it 'edutainment'. I guess Gil's place in that oral tradition is evident from his influence on hip-hop today. He used to shy away from the moniker 'The Godfather of Hip-Hop' – that accolade he later ascribed to the Last Poets, but it's difficult to deny that his work was a vital component in hip-hop history.

If you look at the number of artists who have sampled his music in their own, you'll get a sense of the gravity of his contribution to the genre – Kanye West's 'Who Will Survive in America' (which uses Gil's 'Comment #1') and his and Common's 'My Way Home' (on which you can hear Gil's early hit 'Home Is Where the Hatred Is'), the Game's 'Angel' (using Gil's 'Angel Dust') and Rihanna and Drake's 'Take Care' are just a few of scores of examples to date.

Gil was a master at 'edutainment', he was able to teach people and make them dance at the same time. They would learn the lyrics and replay them in their own minds. The songs would tell stories and provide a source of information on a given topic, for instance the Vietnam war, the re-election of Ronald Reagan, the Watergate scandal, apartheid in South Africa, the scourge of the Ku Klux Klan, or the city life experience of black people in the urban ghettos of America. It was like an alternative news source, with in-depth analysis, tongue-in-cheek humour and a killer backing track all at once. It wasn't just an enjoyable, self-indulgent experience; his audience would learn something too. It was a process of trying to raise consciousness against things that were clearly wrong in society and the wider world in general, providing a way of escaping the propaganda of the white-dominated news channels and telling our people the truth.

Gil used to say to me: 'One of the few ways to get an accurate picture of black history is through our music and songwriting.' Having taken this lesson on board, it was imperative to me, when I was writing poetry, that I was explicit about what I meant so that there could be no ambiguity for future generations about what I was saying. Don't get me wrong, some poems are deliberately ambiguous, but my use of double or triple entendres is designed to make you think about each possibility, to determine which one I meant to say. If the truth be told, I meant to say all of them, so it doesn't matter which one you see, they're all correct. For example, my performance poetry band is called Malik & the O.G's. People understand an 'O.G' to be an 'original gangster' meaning either a real gangster or someone who fearlessly deals with a given situation. As such, both Gil Scott-Heron and Jalal Nuriddin of the Last Poets are classed – in the world of hip-hop – as 'O.G's', Jalal having been a gang member (of the Fort Greene Chaplains) and therefore both a street gangster and an O.G of the rap world, along with Gil. My debut album *Rhythms of the Diaspora, Vol. 1 & 2* by Malik & the O.G's, features both Gil Scott-Heron and Jalal Nuriddin, along with myself (hence Malik & the O.G's). Beyond that, my debut collection of published poems, from which the album is derived, is called *Ordinary Guy* (O.G) and my paternal ancestral lineage goes back to Guyana (making me also a 'Guy'). So the layers of meaning are all there, they are all deliberate and they are all correct, whichever one you choose to understand. In years to come, people will be able to read back these poems, listen to these songs and know what I meant. This will hopefully ensure that I could not be misinterpreted, or just omitted from history altogether.

In 1988, Gil gave me my first real road management job whilst touring the east coast of America, which was a baptism of fire for me. It was a low-budget tour for 'Black History Month', so the band didn't have big venues or an entourage to support them. That's when Gil started teaching me the contractual side of things. Making sure we got the contract rate and ensuring the promoters paid up. Normally, when you book a show, you get half the money up-front – upon signing the contract – and the other half when you turn up at the venue. However, some of the more, shall we say, 'shady' promoters will put clauses in the contract to stipulate that you get paid 'when the band goes on stage'. So if you're on stage, how can you get your money? The danger is, you come offstage, the promoter is gone, the show's over and you don't get your money.

The gigs with the shiesty promoters are usually the low-budget ones, in what they call the 'Chitlin' Circuit'. During the period of segregation in America, under what were the 'Jim Crow laws', black artists couldn't perform in white venues. In fact, black people couldn't go into white venues at all. This wasn't just limited to schools, but theatres, diners, hotels, public lavatories and so on. So an alternative network of venues emerged, which were safe for black performers, but these were usually low-class joints in the seedy parts of town, or in the backwaters down South. They were 'dangerous' but 'happening' at the same time. They were named after 'chitterlings', a food that slaves ate, a kind of sausage made from pigs' intestines and filled with the offal that slave masters didn't want. They stank, but were a staple food of the enslaved, particularly in the Deep South. As they represented the waste of the animal and the lowest-quality part of the meat, the term became synonymous with the network of black venues throughout America, which catered to black entertainers and black audiences on the fringes of urban and rural ghettos.

I recall one such show in Massachusetts, where Gil showed me the contract rate and instructed me to get the money when he went on stage. As soon as he got up to perform, I went straight to the box office where the promoter was counting the money from ticket sales. I introduced myself, presented the contract and asked for the fee. 'Sit down,' the promoter said as he reached for the drawer; he pulled out a pistol and placed it on the desk. He then made small talk and tried to change the subject. I had one intention only – and that was to get paid, in full. I won't lie, I was shocked, but I wasn't going to be intimidated by the presence of a gun. I held my nerve, as one of the first lessons I'd learned as a teen from the gangsters in Toxteth was the mantra: 'Never show fear in the ghetto!' I continued as if the gun wasn't there, and unflinchingly demanded the full fee. When the guy saw that I wasn't intimidated, he grudgingly started counting the money.

The band was playing by now and the first song was in full swing. In my mind I figured, you have two choices, either shoot me, in which case you don't have a show – which I knew wasn't an option, or pay me now, because if you don't, I have instructions to go out and tell Gil and he's gonna walk off the stage and out of the venue and leave you to explain it to your angry audience. I called his bluff and he counted out the money. As desperate as I was to get out of that office and out of range of that pistol, I meticulously counted the cash. Lo and behold, he was $350 short. 'It's short!' I declared. 'I need another $350.' The promoter said, 'Didn't Gil tell you? I gave him that as expenses when he came backstage, he said he needed to pay someone.' I was stuck; there was no way I could stop the show to ask Gil, and he knew it. I also couldn't get into it with this guy, as I would in any other circumstances, 'cause he had a loaded revolver next to his hand on the desk. It was a stalemate, so I let it slide – for the moment. After the show, I went to Gil and he said, 'Did he pay up?' I said, 'Yeh but he was shy $350, said he'd advanced you before the show, is that true?' 'Hell no, I didn't get a cent from him, go tell him to pay up.'

As expected, when I got there the office was locked, the box office was closed and there were only bar staff, cleaners and a stagehand – none of whom had any authority. We'd been had. I was worried that Gil might think I'd taken it, but he didn't for one moment suggest that. I guess he knew what to expect from these kinds of shows, which was why Gil insisted that I collect when I did. I'm sure if the show had gone on and I wasn't there, the band would have come offstage to nothing. But Gil had a solution in mind. The next morning, it was time to check out of the hotel. I was holding all the cash, so it was my job to settle up the bill. There were six of us, and the bill was about $500. I'd had breakfast and told Gil that I was gonna check out and settle up. Gil said: 'Wait, get all the band out into the taxis, and when everyone's outside, give him all the keys at once and tell him the promoter's paying for the rooms. He did the booking, so they have all his details.' So that's what I did; we left him with a bill slightly bigger than what he'd shorted us on, in much the same manner, but this time there was no gun involved. We'd just outsmarted him, in a fashion that he thoroughly deserved. I must admit, it did feel good; I'd agonised over the loss of that $350 all night, even telling Gil to take it out of my pay – which he refused to do – but in the end, poetic justice (pun very much intended) was served.

When Arista Records got bought out by RCA in 1983, things started to go downhill for Gil. Gil had been going through a highly productive period, recording and releasing nine studio albums and a live one with Arista in just seven years, between 1975 and 1982 – but it was all about to change. He'd been the first artist signed to Arista when it was founded by Clive Davis, but Davis's successors had no interest in honouring that relationship. The new management didn't see eye to eye with Gil. A stand-off unfolded between Gil and Arista, resulting in Gil not only being constrained from recording any new music, but also in Arista holding on to his master recordings, preventing him from releasing any music at all.

By the late 1980s, Gil filed a lawsuit against Arista for the return of his recordings and publishing rights. The bitter dispute dragged on for years. He couldn't sign with another label because Arista wouldn't release him from his contract, but they also weren't releasing any new product, so Gil was left to do tours to make a living. That's why he was touring constantly during that period, with no new album to promote.

It was as a result of this dispute that I began to learn the contractual side of the music business from Gil. When he sued Arista, I became the one who carried that huge beige suitcase full of contracts, through airports and on and off tour buses and in and out of hotels. It weighed a ton. Gil didn't at all accept Arista's interpretation of these deals. We would sit up all night reading them. I had never seen recording contracts before, but now Gil was passing me complex paperwork. He'd pass me a recording contract. I'd read it and then we'd discuss it, the split between the artist and the label, the tour support and promotion, the obligations for both parties to record and release and so on. I'd ask a question and he'd say, 'Ah, that's because of this ...' and pass me a distribution deal, or a publishing deal, or a licensing deal.

We'd sit up for hours reading contract after contract, until I was exhausted. Then I'd go to my room, sleep for a couple of hours before breakfast, and then we'd be back on the road, heading to the next town for the next show. In hindsight, the whole tour was one big training course. I was constantly learning, and Gil was constantly teaching. Gil taught me about all the different facets of the music business: merchandising, production, promotion, tour management, licensing, territorial distribution, release forms. He exposed me to all its nuances and complexities. It was a thorough industry education – particularly to its legal side – and it gave me a foundation that would put me in good stead later on, when I was running my own record company.

Gil would always find a way round a problem. The record company wouldn't give him CDs to sell at the shows, so Gil moved back to his original form of artistic expression: literature. Arista also had no control over this aspect of his work, so books became a key component of the merchandise he sold during tours.

In 1990, when the American Afrocentric poet Haki Madhubuti published Gil's collection of poems *So Far, So Good*, we finally had merchandise. When Gil came over to the UK in 1992, he gave me a couple of hundred copies to sell at the shows. I remember asking Gil, 'Have you got any more books?' 'Yes, in the back of the bus,' he replied. 'No. They've all gone,' I countered, pulling out a wad of cash and putting it on the table. 'There's your books!'

There wasn't a secret to what I was doing. I was simply passionate about Gil's work and the causes he stood for. I worked the crowd and canvassed everyone I could. Later I'd learn that sales are all about hitting your target audience, and any fool could see that every crowd at a Gil Scott-Heron concert was a direct target market. Plenty of people at the shows were activists – Gil was very aligned with Artists United Against Apartheid and the anti-nuclear lobby group Musicians United for Safe Energy – and knowing his audience, his repertoire and him personally certainly helped me close deals and determine very quickly who might buy his books. The merchandise soon became an integral part of the tour and a substantial supplemental income stream. Finally, I was paying my own way, more than covering my own costs and turning a healthy profit for Gil.

I think Gil saw something of his younger self in me, and wanted to give me the opportunity to shine in different ways. He once told me that when he was growing up, he felt he didn't have much choice but to sing, like when he was working at that dry cleaners as a young guy, coming up with radio jingles as a way to make some extra cash. Gil said this was how he managed to find a way to express himself musically, whilst doing a job he didn't really want to do.

When he first told me this, I recognised something in his words. I realised I needed to find where my own creativity lay so I could continue to be on the road and do whatever errands were required to be done; but being around all these creative people, I needed to find my own sense of artistic expression. For me, that was where the writing and the poetry element came into play. By getting involved in selling Gil's books, I was working in the area where I knew I wanted to hone my creativity and I hoped that one day I'd be selling a book of my own.

With Gil in 1988.

Once Gil realised that I was a good salesman, he started ordering more books. This felt like a real endorsement. Previously, no matter how hard I worked, it never seemed enough for some people. There had always been questions about what I was doing on the tours. Gil would be like, 'Leave him alone. I'll be the judge of that. Just let him be.' But it didn't shut everyone up. Promoters, in particular, would often question my role; and some band members too wondered if Gil didn't have to pay the expenses of this young kid, perhaps they could be paid more. But when they saw the volume of cash I could generate by selling merchandise, it soon quietened this sort of talk down. Some nights, I was doubling the take on the show, which more than covered my costs and contributed greatly to theirs. That was the point at which I really felt like I was making a valid contribution.

When Gil finally signed a publishing contract with Jamie Byng and Payback Press, the merchandise came back hard and fast. Jamie was from an aristocratic background but was a very down-to-earth guy and a huge fan of Gil, having already published an impressive list of black American writers and musicians. Now, seeing Gil's previously out-of-print first and second novels, *The Vulture* and *The Nigger Factory*, back in print and available for sale, I felt a renewed vigour when merchandising at the shows, and the cash came in even faster. Gil and Jamie became great friends, and so, when those two books came out with Payback Press, their relationship was cemented and remained solid – right up to the end of Gil's life.

The biggest hits were behind him when I met Gil, but I don't think anyone measures Gil's music through its commercial success, and he certainly wasn't bothered by this. His career is defined by one set of statistics – he made thirteen albums between 1970 and 1982, and after that he made just two more, and one of those he made in 2010, the year before he died. And yet as anyone who knew him or worked with him will tell you, he never stopped writing songs and creating things, it was just disputes with record companies that stopped him recording or releasing material. To make a living, he needed to go on tour – and that meant I would go on tour too. With Gil's mentoring and the experience I was getting on the road, I grew in confidence, expanding my knowledge and developing a political and creative focus in my life. In a nutshell, I was changing fast from the teenager who had turned up the stage door of the concert at Liverpool's Royal Court Theatre in 1984 – into the man that I could be and would be.

CHAPTER 8

DEEP SEA

After seeing life on the road, I had new aspirations. They weren't just pipe dreams anymore; I had contacts now, so my dreams had the possibility of being realised and that gave me a whole new perspective on things. I wanted to get myself established back in Liverpool. Having left Ujamaa House in the summer of 1985, I knew that there was no going back and that I now needed to put down firm roots somewhere, so that whatever happened I'd always have a place to fall back on and call home. I never wanted to be homeless again.

I rented my own flat in Sefton Park and I was determined to get my driving licence, as I felt that driving would give me options that I currently didn't have, and I hoped that one day I could drive Gil on tour. I had developed a very rudimentary working life in Liverpool between tours, doing menial jobs that my friends – who were hustling at the time – would mock me for. But I needed money to pay for driving lessons and that kind of work didn't pay so good. So instead of just getting a job, I got three of them.

The first was making sandwiches for the staff canteen at the retail and betting company called Littlewoods in the heart of the commercial district, in Liverpool's city centre. I was the only man and the only black person on the line in the kitchen. I worked with fifteen middle-aged white women, who were intriguing to observe and, if I'm honest, a little intimidating. I decided on day one to keep my head down, keep my mouth shut, do my job well and get paid. This was a means to an end for me. Initially, the women were very cagey about a man being on the production line, so for the first few days they hardly spoke to me. That didn't last long. Once these women felt comfortable enough, they let loose with all kinds of stuff. It was a sight to behold. They were hilariously funny, raunchy and sometimes borderline disgusting, but I got the sense they'd dialled it back a bit for my benefit, as I was barely a man – at just twenty years old – and some of these women had kids who were older than me.

The catering manager at Littlewoods was a light-skinned mixed-race guy from down south. We all wore aprons, but he wore a suit and was hardly in the kitchen at all. This was the Thatcher era and the retail sector was under pressure to phase out full-time workers and bring in part-timers, like me. We'd all get taken off the line, one by one, to discuss whatever changes the company was proposing to our work patterns, shifts and contracted hours. I decided to act ignorant, stay out of the politics and keep my head down. But my work started to get noticed. I'd soon devised more efficient ways of prepping the food and was turning out sandwiches faster than anyone else.

117

As soon as lunchtime hit, hundreds of people descended on the canteen and the food would fly out faster than you could replenish it in the cabinets. At first, the women didn't mind my work rate, because it meant they could slack, and we still made our quota.

But before long, some of them, mostly the full-timers, became suspicious of me – wondering if I was a spy for the company. And as my work rate was so high, it was starting to make the women on the line look bad. It was getting a bit uncomfortable for me, but I soldiered on. Having the manager constantly notice my work and him coming on the line, telling me I was 'management material' and saying things like 'What are you doing down here with this lot, get up here with us' didn't help endear me to my co-workers.

My hours at Littlewoods were from 8 a.m. 'til noon. Two or three times a week, I'd book a driving lesson from the city centre, which would drop me off at my second job, waiting tables at the popular and trendy – if somewhat bohemian – Keith's Wine Bar on Lark Lane. Keith was an unusual and rather awkward character, who was reputed to have been quite wealthy but – like so many middle and upper-class yuppies at that time – liked to come to Liverpool to 'slum it'. Keith's only served vegetarian cuisine and had a rustic period feel in the decor. If you wanted a steak and kidney pie and a pint, there were a few pubs on Lark Lane for that. It's only now, upon reflection, that I'm realising how stratified Liverpool society was back then, along social class lines; people really didn't cross the divides that much at all. And everybody seemed to know their place. Not only did they accept it, but they appeared to be quite content with the status quo.

After I'd finished my shift at Keith's from 1 to 5 p.m., I'd walk up to the top of Lark Lane to start my evening job as a commis chef, at an upmarket French restaurant called L'Alouette.

Leaving Toxteth and moving to Aigburth was like casting off old clothes and putting on a three-piece suit. Toxteth never shook off its negative image from the 1981 riots, as a 'crime-ridden ghetto' full of 'angry black youths – fighting and looting'. Having an L8 postcode at that time made it difficult to do even the simplest of things, like get a job, or open a bank account, such was the stigma attached to it. Hence, ironically, the rationale for all the hostility and the justifiable social unrest that ensued in response to decades of social deprivation, structural racism and police brutality.

The lack of opportunity led many in Toxteth to resort to crime and live out a dangerous, yet alluring, street life. Hustlers targeted vulnerable black youths, recruiting them into street gangs, as drug dealers, or into a variety of other criminal pursuits, arguing that the system didn't care about them, that the white man hated them, and the only ones who cared enough to put money in their pockets were the gangsters. That was the narrative and it sold in the ghetto, because – as ludicrous as it sounds – it was true.

Having decided that it wasn't a life for me, my choice to find a way out working three jobs on low pay was laughable to my former friends, many of whom had taken the other path and some of whom were emerging with all the trappings of wealth, cars and jewellery – and on the streets, they had what everyone craved: respect! In their eyes, there was nothing worthy of respect in washing dishes in a hotel, making sandwiches in a department store, waiting tables in a wine bar, or preparing starters in a restaurant. But to me, there was dignity in it, and I took great pride in every aspect of my work. I wasn't content to just be a dishwasher, I developed a system to make myself the best and most efficient dishwasher that the hotel had ever hired. I applied that same attitude to every task in every job, no matter how menial, and it developed a work ethic in me that has survived to this very day.

One day, as I was leaving Littlewoods and walking along Church Street – a boulevard in the city centre's retail district – I bumped into an old acquaintance who we called 'Frisco'. I knew Frisco from the summer of 1984. We'd met when I had worked on an Isle of Man Steam Packet ferry called the SS *Ben-my-Chree*. Frisco had been a cook on the rival Sealink ship, the *Manx Viking*, and as we were among only a handful of blacks on the island, we'd become friends. It was great to see Frisco, as he was one of the more positive brothers in the black community. He had a job as a chief cook, and he didn't get embroiled in all the petty ghetto politics, but he was a martial artist and could handle himself so no one messed with him. Everybody liked Frisco, he had a magnetic personality. Rumour had it that his father was a San Franciscan from the US airbase at Burtonwood – just outside Liverpool – and that's why people called him 'Frisco'. I never did ask him if that was true or not.

As we were catching up, I asked him where he was off to, and he replied: 'I'm going back to the Isle of Man, to get a job on a BP oil tanker. Why don't you come with me, they're hiring?' A light went on in my head and I decided I wanted in. So we went straight to Liverpool Airport, and bought two 'fare cracker' discount tickets for £25 each. We caught a flight and went to see Wollems – the shipping agents that were crewing up.

My previous experience as a pantry boy on the Isle of Man ferries could earn me a position as a steward, but I didn't have the necessary documents. However, the agent assured me that should I return with the right papers, I would get the job.

I headed for the pool, in Mann Island at the Pier Head in Liverpool, where they issued seamans' discharge books and seamans' cards. The man at the counter wasn't forthcoming initially.

'We're not really issuing them anymore, so whoever's got them's got them, who hasn't, tough.'

I pleaded with him, telling him of my father's thirty-five years at sea and my own experience on the ferries, but he was adamant that he'd only issue me a seaman's card and discharge book if I had a confirmed seafaring job. I gave him the number of the man at Wollems but when he called they couldn't agree on which would come first, the job or the papers.

In the end, I made a joke of it. 'C'mon, mate, he's saying I can't have the job without the discharge book and you're saying I can't have the discharge book without the job. You give me the discharge book and he'll give me the job.'

The guy burst out laughing. 'You're a cheeky little bastard, aren't ya?' He said, 'But I like you, so I'm gonna give you the documents. Come back here tomorrow with your birth certificate and passport photos and you'll have your discharge book and seaman's card – but you'll have to join the union and pay your subscription – £35.'

I literally danced out of that office. How did these things happen? One minute I was making sandwiches with a bunch of raunchy middle-aged women in a department store, the next I was about to embark upon the adventure of lifetime by going away to sea, all within twenty-four hours – it felt surreal.

The next day, Frisco and I returned to the pool in Mann Island and my documents were issued on the spot.

'You're a lucky bastard you are, I don't do this often these days, but I sense something about you. Don't make me regret my decision.'

I couldn't believe it; I had a seaman's discharge book and a seaman's card. I was now officially in the Merchant Navy. Back then, you could travel overseas on your seaman's card without a passport, but I decided to get one of those too, as I wanted to be prepared for anything. Finally, I felt like I had an identity – as a seaman – but the reality was, I hadn't been to sea school and I had no idea what I was letting myself in for.

I called Wollems and gave them the details from my papers, and they put me on the list for the next available post as a steward on one of their BP oil tankers. Frisco got shipped off immediately. About four weeks later, I got a call from the agent. 'We've got a ship for you, it's on its way to Houston, Texas, in the US. We need to fly you out there to join, when the ship docks.' I was as ready as I was ever going to be. I was also about to take my second-ever aeroplane ride, but this time it was transatlantic.

I made arrangements for my little sister Michelle to move into my flat and look after it while I was gone. She was the last of the kids still at home with my mum. My mum was a bit apprehensive about Michelle going out into the world on her own. She was only nineteen years old then, but I assured her I was going to send money home and make sure that everything was paid for. It was more like house-sitting than anything, as I intended to come home after the trip to sea, which was scheduled to last about six months. My mum reluctantly agreed, Michelle moved in and I left for my first deep-sea adventure. People who went 'deep sea' didn't rate people who worked 'on the ferries'. They treated ferrymen like they were not real seamen. I knew this from the old seamen I'd worked with on the ferries; they'd become ferrymen but their hearts were still 'deep sea'.

When I touched down in Houston and was leaving the customs area, I saw a chauffeur with a board with my name on it. It seemed like overkill for a steward, but who was I to question BP?

He drove me in a black limousine for about an hour, and then checked me into a hotel. He said, 'I'll give the agent your room number, they'll be in touch when the ship docks and someone will come to collect you and take you to the ship. It may be a couple of days. If you need anything – food, drink, whatever – charge it to the hotel room and the company will pay the bill.' Two days later I got the call, and the agent came to pick me up and took me to board a 109,000-tonne British Petroleum oil tanker called the MV *British Skill*. It was bound for the Caribbean, then West Africa.

I soon discovered that most of the guys on the ship had just had their BP contracts terminated. This affected their pensions, redundancy packages and other retirement benefits, and the union would no longer be recognised. This was another of Thatcher's policies to break the power of the unions. Ships were now re-registering in offshore territories, flying 'foreign flags', and were no longer subject to British maritime law. The guys who worked onboard were serious 'company men'. They lived and breathed BP. The company had taken them on as schoolboys, put them through sea school and then straight on to BP tankers. They'd fed, clothed and trained them, then taken them all over the world. BP were like their parents. Now these guys faced two options – to leave BP or sign new contracts with Wollems. They felt betrayed.

I was the first of a group of foreign flag seamen arriving on what these guys considered as their ships – in what was, in their eyes, a contravention of union and company regulations, as well as the conventions long-established in the seaman's cardinal rule book, UK maritime law. The fact that I was black further complicated things. It turned out that some of the Wollems men didn't want a black guy on the ship either, so my first deep-sea trip was doomed before we even lifted anchor.

The other steward on the ship named Ian – a burly 6'4" fellow from Penzance – felt sorry for me and decided to train me. He realised immediately that I didn't know the job; it was very different from the ferry, where I just worked in the pantry. Here, I had many more responsibilities, and we carried highly volatile dangerous cargo, not passengers. No voyage lasted four hours like the Isle of Man boat journeys, some of these voyages were weeks or months at sea between ports. It was a totally different job. Over the next four months, I'd learned the ropes, but the damage was already done, and my card was marked from day one.

It was when we arrived in West Africa that I figured out exactly why the voyage was destined to fail. We dropped anchor off the coast of Angola in a place called Cabinda. A local African crew came onboard to work cargo. They'd floated a pipeline out on a pontoon, to where we were anchored about half a mile off the coastline. The local crew came out on small launches. As they approached, I saw that there was one white guy with them. He wore clean white shorts, a designer shirt and an expensive pair of shoes. He had a solid-gold Rolex watch on his wrist, and he was clearly the boss. This was in sharp contrast to his African crew. They were all black, mostly barefoot and in dirty shabby overalls that didn't fit. Those with boots didn't fare any better, as they were splitting at the soles.

These guys were working in a dangerous environment, with virtually no protective gear or even basic workwear. Besides that, everyone was referring to them as the 'coons'. They were fed a fraction of what the rest of the crew were given. I was horrified when I saw how they were treated. As it turned out, the crew didn't see me too differently. One night, one of the crewmen got drunk and came up to me in the bar and said, 'You know everyone calls you "the coon", don't you?' From then on, I started spending the evenings alone in my cabin, preferring not to keep company with anyone onboard – except when I had to.

I was essentially ostracised. In their eyes, I was the black man who got what they considered to be a white man's job, or the foreign flag crewman who took a BP man's job. As far as they were concerned, I should have been 'down aft' – a dirty, dingy spot at the back of the ship, where everyone used to hang their overalls – with 'the chogs', the derogatory term that the white crew used to describe Filipino or Thai crew, who would occasionally come onboard and ride with us from one port to the next as what was called 'a riding gang'.

I actually elected to spend a lot of time down aft. The Thais in particular were lovely people. They'd come onboard and do the donkey work, such as chipping the rust off the decks and painting and repairing them – work that the white crew thought was beneath them. They were paid a pittance in comparison to everyone else, and were treated like slaves, but they got on with it and never complained.

The Thais taught me how to cook Thai food, and I learned some basic words in their language from their head man, Tospon. They made my stay onboard bearable. The space and time away from the hostile white crew was also a relief. With Gil's words in my ears, encouraging me to be creative, I was able to experiment with my writing, alone in my cabin at night, while the white crew members were getting drunk in the crew bar.

At that stage of my life, my literacy was relatively poor, and I still could not read well although my writing was improving. I found it a bit easier to learn to write than to read, as what I was writing was from my own imagination, while what I was reading was from someone else's.

I was twenty years old, and the gaps in my education had taken a terrible toll. Not only had my schooling been completely disrupted after the age of nine but I had been doing manual labour for so long that what little I did learn, in the limited classroom experiences I'd had, seemed a far-distant memory. What I also didn't know then – because it wasn't diagnosed until much later – was that I suffered from both dyslexia and dyspraxia.

I soon realised that poetry could be a great introduction to literacy. It served two functions; firstly, it taught me how to use words in creative ways, giving me a higher understanding of the use of language. Secondly, I was not learning by rote, having devised my own system to learn words by myself. This meant I was not constrained by conventions, nor was I doing it because someone had told me to, so I became totally absorbed in the learning and I loved it. My thirst for knowledge continued to grow, as my capacity for it expanded with each day. At sea you have nothing but time, interrupted only by your required daily chores. I was a social leper on the ship for the most part, as there was always some reason to ostracise me – being a black man, a non-BP man, or a foreign flag man – all these factors conspired to afford me plenty of alone time on the ship, and I made full use of it.

I started looking into the etymology of words, I wanted to know what their origins were. By understanding the roots of words and where they came from, whether Latin, Ancient Greek, Arabic, Germanic, I could get a deeper understanding of their meanings. Poetry gave me the ability to really stretch language to its limits and refine my writing, which would help me in other areas, later in life. I would spend six hours a night in my cabin, learning new words, experimenting with language and ploughing through books. That was how I came to write my first raft of poetry. One of the things I'd always dreamed of doing was going back to the ancestral origins of all black people, and this had finally been my chance to visit Africa. One of the first things I wrote was about this experience, and this mighty and mysterious continent. It didn't quite happen for me in the way I'd hoped on that first trip, but I came close. When we dropped anchor off the coast of Angola, in Cabinda, at last I could see it, I could smell Africa. There was a mist on the horizon, from which the mountainous coastline protruded. In the crisp morning air, as I waited to glimpse a light through the mist, the inspiration came over me to write what I saw and felt in that moment. It manifested itself into a song, which I simply entitled 'Africa'.

Africa!
With your misty morning.
Hear my heart!
It's beggin' I'm calling.
Africa! Won't you shine a light for me?

Though I travel as an English man.
I've been searchin' for my fatherland.
At last, I'm so close I can see,
my Africa in front of me.

Oh, Africa!
With your misty morning.
Hear my heart!
It's beggin' I'm calling.
Africa! Won't you shine a light for me?

Deprivation is in our land.
But starvation I just don't understand.
When there's enough food for everyone.
All we have to do is spread it around.

In Africa!
With your misty morning.
Hear my heart!
It's beggin' I'm calling.
Africa! Won't you shine a light for me?

I know you're a troubled place.
You're carrying the burdens of every race.
I hope that one day you'll be free,
so I can go home through my family tree.

To my Africa!
With your misty morning.
Hear my heart!
It's beggin' I'm calling.
Africa! Won't you shine a light for me?

Onboard, the animosity from the white BP crew grew more intense towards me as the days went by. I spent long hours attempting to write poetry so as to avoid worrying about it. We'd set sail for America to discharge the oil from Angola. By the time we docked at Wilmington, Delaware, on the east coast of the USA, I had a stack of poetic works.

When the ship's agent came onboard in Delaware, I asked him to deliver my mail, which included a letter to Gil, enclosed with four or five of my first poems. I'd hoped Gil might appreciate them and perhaps offer his opinion. Gil was living in Washington DC at the time; he never wrote back but I later learned that he did read the poems.

Meanwhile, the crew had become so hostile towards me that the captain decided it was too disruptive to have me onboard. He told me that the best thing to do was to fire me, so that I could go home and claim my benefits. If I resigned, I wouldn't be entitled to anything. I had only been at sea for four months and I didn't want to lose my job, but the skipper insisted it would be in the best interests of the ship. One thing I couldn't argue with was the fact that I hadn't been to sea school. Some of the crew contended that this would jeopardise their safety, because I wouldn't know what to do in the event of an emergency. But I'm sure I wasn't the first person to go to sea without sea survival training, and I wouldn't be the last.

The worst aspect of the situation was that even though I had been fired, we had a few more weeks at sea before I could disembark, so I had to carry on working among the scumbags that had stitched me up. If I was in a room, they'd all walk out. If they were talking in a space and I came by, they'd all go quiet. It was a form of mental torture, which was designed to make me so unwelcome as to make me leave and never come back. Seamen were pretty ruthless, and I could see that this job was not for the faint-hearted. Nonetheless, I'd been to America, Africa and the Caribbean; I'd started reading and writing and I was on the way to greater and better things, so even though my time as a seaman was disastrous, it served a purpose. I also had my seaman's papers, which they couldn't take away from me once they'd been granted – so it wasn't all bad.

The way I looked at it, in twenty years' time, these guys would still be seamen, but I would be on a new kind of journey: educating myself, and dreaming bigger dreams.

Not long after, when I finally paid off – that is, when I left – that ship in August 1986, I went on tour with Gil again. To my surprise, he had the letter I'd sent him from Delaware. One morning on the tour bus, he started reading the poems out loud. He asked why I'd used this word and not that, what I meant here … things like that. He became very intrigued by my work and started to compliment me. That was the first sign that I was on to something, that maybe my writing was coherent, after all. Maybe I had actually broken through a learning barrier. For the first time in my life, it felt like I had a real teacher and it just made me want to write more. This process went on for years. I'd write poetry and post it in letters to Gil; we'd meet on tour, he'd appraise the poems and I'd write some more, refining the ones he'd assessed.

After my experience on the MV *British Skill*, I began to doubt if going sea was the right thing for me. I discussed it with Gil. He had never understood why I wanted to go to sea in the first place anyhow, but it made sense to me – I was following in my father's footsteps, trying to understand why he set down roots here, why he fought wars for a country that didn't want him or his kids.

While we were on tour, Gil introduced me to a Kenyan Indian woman called Ramona Da Gama. Ramona was an advertising executive – middle-class, well-spoken and very sophisticated. She was living with her partner Corrie, who had studied at Harrow and went on to be a successful accountant with a big City firm. They owned a smart townhouse in west London, whose basement was transformed into an office area.

Ramona had first met Gil when she'd gone to one of his shows at Ronnie Scott's Jazz Club, in London's Soho. Ramona had tried to buy one of Gil's records after the show and when she went to the merchandising desk, the guy there had for some reason asked her to cover the desk for ten minutes. As Ramona was a top saleswoman, she sold lots of merch in those ten minutes and was introduced to Gil. When they were talking one time on this tour, Gil had asked Ramona if she could take care of me – to help me out if I was in trouble. It hadn't occurred to me that there was a reason I was suddenly meeting influential people like Ramona.

After the tour I moved into a squat in Harlesden in north-west London and went to see Ramona. She was running a small advertising agency out of her house in Shepherd's Bush. She had been running the recruitment advertising at the *Times* newspaper and then the *Mail on Sunday* but had realised there were lots of small magazines needing advertising specialists, and so had set up her own company.

When I went to see her, I asked for a job, but I don't think she thought that was what Gil meant when he'd asked her to take care of me. She was used to hiring university-educated people and had a reputation to protect – she was clearly worried about the image of the firm and how I'd be with her high-profile clients.

She had eight people in the team and was also concerned about how I'd fit in. Three of them worked in her basement office. She explained to me that I was a big risk to gamble on. But I think she liked my spirit and energy. I guess she also knew that though I may not have had a traditional education, I was streetwise. Another one of her employees was the daughter of a politician. She wasn't getting results selling ads, but Ramona didn't know how to let her go because of who her father was. In short, this girl wasn't hungry, but I was.

I said to her, 'Ramona, I understand what you're thinking but give me a chance? Don't pay me for a month and if I'm crap, get rid of me. But if you do that, I'll be going back to a ship to peel potatoes. If you show me what you do and I can do it, then pay me whatever you think I'm worth, just give me a chance.'

At that point the penny dropped. She gave me some training in the morning, then after lunch she put me on the phone with the first clients. She gave me a tough job, selling space for a new American football magazine called *Touchdown*. American football was just arriving in the UK and had a very small niche audience here. As such, people weren't exactly falling over each other to advertise. There was also a competitor magazine called *Gridiron*, which specialised in British American football, so the niche market was further split.

The first client I spoke to on the phone was the owner of a sportswear supplier called Ealing Sports. He'd always advertised with the competitor, Gridiron. I sold £3,000 of ad space on the first day to him. Ramona was astonished.

She said: 'That's great but do you really think I'm going to give you a job?'

We laughed and had a drink. I was in. The next day, I sold Ealing Sports a double-page spread on every six issues of the mag, so I think Ramona knew this was no fluke.

Although I was still struggling with my literacy then, I found it wasn't a problem with this job. It was all telesales so I didn't really need to read stuff, just reel of some demographics and circulation figures, the rest was all blag.

In my first year – 1987 – I pulled in £120,000 worth of ad revenue for Ramona; and I earned £10,000, which was more than any job I'd had to date, even exceeding the salary on the ship. I started bringing in business from the top London advertising agencies, which handled all the major clients – Saatchi & Saatchi, J. Walter Thompson (who had Pepsi-Cola), YellowHammer, BBDO, Boase Massimi Pollitt (who had the Labour Party campaign). I was selling ad space for several magazines. For me, it was all just a hustle. Once I understood how it worked, it was straightforward.

I was also finally beginning to make enough money to live in a bit of comfort. I moved from the squat in Harlesden to a studio in Leytonstone. It was nice but there was an hour's commute on the Central Line packed in to the Tube train like a sardine. I relented on the luxury and took a dingy room in Cricklewood, which was nearer to work. Finally I landed a flat share in a two-bedroom apartment in Neasden, north London, with an American guy called Victor, who was a backing singer with the 1980s pop star Hazel O'Connor. Victor and I had met through work.

My advertising days also gave me a big break – but this came about more by accident than by design. I'd convinced Ramona to take on a very small music and lifestyle publication called *The Buzz*.

The guys running this mag were all hippy kids on All Saints Road, in Notting Hill, west London, with big ideas and even bigger ideals. Lovely though it was, those projects are never financially viable. They saw me as a guy who did business with the devil. I wore a suit to work and a Burberry trenchcoat and looked pretty slick to the outside world.

The guy selling the classified ads at *The Buzz* was called Anton Brooks. Anton would later go on to do PR for the US grunge band Nirvana, after discovering and supporting Kurt Cobain when nobody thought they were anything special; but back then, he was working on this small mag. I think Anton really saw me as the big corporate advertising man, but we got on. We had a bond with each other which we couldn't really explain – just a natural empathy – and as I was to be bringing in the advertising the magazine so desperately needed for its survival, and Anton was doing the grass-roots classifieds, which brought the street cred that the readers loved, we needed to work together.

Many years later we came across each other again on Facebook, and then he read an article about my life with Gil Scott-Heron in the *Guardian* newspaper. I guess I never spoke about Gil at *The Buzz*, so he didn't know anything about that side of my life until he read the article. They just thought I was the corporate guy with the posh boss. It turned out that Anton, who was from Barnsley in Yorkshire, was adopted; he also had dyslexia, and could barely read or write back then either. I guess sometimes in life, you form bonds without consciously knowing why – but we had more in common than we knew back then.

I approached Carlsberg to sell ad space in *The Buzz*. I didn't bother with the media planners at the agency – the people who normally assigned which publications they were going to aim campaigns at – but went straight to a brand manager at Carlsberg itself.

Just as a bit of small talk, I asked the guy if Carlsberg was still selling a beer called Carlsberg 68. It was a boutique lager, sold in bottles – it was rare in the UK, and one of the only places you could get it in Liverpool was in a club called Kirkland's, one of only two clubs back in the early 1980s that would let black people in. It had made Carlsberg 68 a very popular drink among Liverpool's black population.

By a strange coincidence, Carlsberg 68 was this brand manager's product. He had been marketing it – clearly without too much success – in the UK. I had struck gold. He was personally invested in the brand and had found a disciple. He took out a double-spread in *The Buzz* at rate card (a document that generally shows the maximum price you would pay for an advertisement) – and that opened the floodgates to all the big advertising campaigns. When one corporate sees another in a magazine, they figure they're tapping into a new market and they should too. It's all smoke and mirrors but it's how the advertising world works. Clarks desert boots, Gold Label barley wine, Virgin Games, Yamaha DX7 – they all wanted space. *The Buzz* went from a small quarterly black-and-white A5 fanzine to a full-colour, A4-size bimonthly magazine, financed by the corporate ad revenue I generated. My strategy had worked.

The Carlsberg effect didn't stop there, *The Buzz* were putting on a big promotional music and fashion event at a club called Heaven in London's West End. The concept was that of 'a living magazine'. They wanted to bring all the sections of the magazine to life: music, style and fashion. Carlsberg put up £3,000 to support the event and gave us 1,000 free bottles of Carlsberg 68 for the night. There were several bands on the music bill, and I had asked Gil's bassist Robbie Gordon and his band to play. *The Buzz* had also booked a band called Soho (who went on to have a top 10 hit called 'Hippy Chick' later in 1991). Soho were going to be top of the bill and play last.

Robbie was living in London at that time, as he had an English girlfriend. He had just fired his drummer – a Jamaican guy, who used to drink so much Wray & Nephew Jamaican white rum in rehearsals, he kept missing his cues and losing time. So I got my brother Reynold to come down from Liverpool to play. He was a big fan of Robbie's, and knew all the songs – and as well as playing bass, my brother was also a drummer.

When we got to soundcheck for the show at Heaven, and Soho heard Robbie's band, they said it was too hot an act to follow and refused to play last. Robbie's band were now top of the bill.

This change of running order messed up the schedule for the sound engineer, and when Robbie's band came on stage and started playing, the electronic drums were not set up on the sound man's desk. Robbie called me on to the stage to explain to the audience there was a technical issue. Unfortunately, the technical issue took a bit of time to sort out. The crowd was getting impatient, so Robbie shouted to me: 'Do some poetry!' I put aside any apprehensions and recited a poem I'd written and sent to Gil called 'Power'; I followed with another called 'Freedom Is a Funny Thing'. It was inadvertent and not by design, but it turned out to be my first ever poetry performance in front of an audience – and they loved it. It went down great and bought us the time needed to sort out the tech.

Advertising also gave me an opportunity to mix in other musical circles. Through marketing contacts, I was given backstage passes to loads of shows, including Tina Turner, B. B. King, Hugh Masekela, Chick Corea and Miles Davis. Despite my literacy problems, I was even given the chance to interview Miles Davis's band – I took them sightseeing in London, too – and the recorded interview was transcribed and turned into a magazine feature in the next edition of *The Buzz*, using the revolutionary pseudonym which my father's Guyanese friends had given me in childhood, 'Spartacus'.

But by 1988, I wanted out of the advertising world. I had certainly made a success of it but there were aspects of the scene that I didn't like.

There was one incident involving a media planner at the big US ad firm McCann Erickson that made my mind up. I'd gone to see this woman to make a pitch, but she shut me down before I even began. She wasn't interested in advertising but insisted on engaging in conversation. I was puzzled.

A few days later I got a call from a rival magazine's advertising manager, offering me a job. I had been headhunted. I asked them how they found out about me and the woman mentioned the name of the media planner at McCann Erickson. Apparently, she'd sung my praises as a salesman, though she hadn't even heard me pitch. The woman at McCann Erickson later called me, asking if I'd got the job? I told her I was still considering it. She asked me to visit her office once I'd 'accepted the new gig'.

That's when the penny dropped. She'd taken a fancy to me and had told the advertising manager to offer me a job if they wanted her business. She then called me to ensure that I knew it was her who had got me the job.

I neither took the job nor called the woman back. The magazine came back with an offer to double my salary. But I didn't relent. I closed the door on that, because my integrity was more important to me than the things they were offering me. There was a similar incident involving a fashion show – Afro Hair & Beauty – at the Hackney Empire, when one of the organisers invited me to her office, exposed most of her breast and asked me if I'd like to win their competition for a modelling contract. Once again, I turned the offer down and came in third place. All these episodes did was to persuade me that this wasn't the world for me. I needed something real and meaningful, I was done with the superficial.

It was now January of 1988. At that time Gil was preparing to go on a tour for Black History Month, which is February in the US. Gil wanted me in the States. Ramona wanted me in London. There was no room for a compromise. I was at a crossroads in my life, but I knew what I had to do.

CHAPTER 9

BLACK HISTORY MONTH

Though I had toured with Gil a few times prior to 1988, I'd never been on the road with him in the US before. Now, arriving in DC for this Black History Month tour, I was about to have my eyes opened to the respect Americans held for Gil. His peers in the music industry especially held the guy in high esteem.

Kim Jordan, Gil's keyboard player, remembers once playing at the Blue Note Jazz Club in New York, when a barman came up to her piano and told her that someone sitting in the corner wanted to buy her a cognac. She told the barman she didn't like cognac. The barman said to her, 'You better take this one.' It turned out that the man offering the drink was Prince, who was a big fan of Gil's.

In 1988, Gil shared a booking agent with an artist called Richie Havens. He was the singer and guitarist who'd shot to international acclaim for being the opening act at the iconic and world-famous Woodstock festival in 1969. He had a kind of folky, soul sound and a manic guitar-playing style that was unique to him.

Until we got out on this tour, I had no idea who Richie Havens was. But I was to learn all about him years later. Because it was Black History Month, their mutual booking agent decided to combine Gil and Richie's tour dates and put them on the same bill for each show.

I had flown into Washington Dulles Airport from London – and Gil, the band, and I drove up to Huntington, Long Island, for the first show. The band was doing their soundcheck, and Gil and I were chilling backstage, when this far-out-looking guy appeared in the corridor. Richie, who had Native American and West Indian heritage, had a long beard and was dressed head to toe in African clothes; he wore a dashiki top and a cool kufi skull cap. He looked like he'd just fallen out of the 1960s.

When Richie saw Gil had arrived, they made eye contact in a manner which seemed to connect their very souls. I was stood between them in anticipation, aware of the good vibes but with the beholden sense of a subordinate who hadn't yet earned the right to speak. I had no idea who he was but he looked cool.

I later discovered that Richie had started out in New York as a performance poet in Greenwich Village, before becoming a big name on the folk scene. He was a very tall guy, as was Gil. Gil looked at Richie and just said, 'What it is?' Richie replied: 'What it is?'

That, I came to understand, was a sort of 'What's up' in their Sixties New York vernacular. These guys obviously went back many years and were being drawn together again. In fact, there were very, very few words said between them then, or for that matter throughout the tour. There was just a mutual understanding and respect.

They were both activists and wrote protest songs and they had a camaraderie. In place of conversation was a kind of vibes-based communication, almost like telepathy – or as Gil called it, 'the vibosphere'. Each seemed to know what the other meant and they didn't really need to use words to convey this.

Standing between them, in anticipation of some more substantial conversation, was a bit awkward. Gil broke the ice, he just looked to Richie and said, 'Yeah, man, this is brother Mark! From England.' Richie didn't speak, he just nodded his head, and then Gil said, 'Yeah, man, I met this brother on the road. Brother-man was looking for the truth.' Richie just said: 'Way it should be, man. Way it should be.' And that was it. The end of the conversation. But Richie and I were cool from then on in and he got used to me being around backstage at the shows.

People often say that Gil looked at me like a son, and this made other people look at me in a different way. I guess it meant I was accepted. And now here I was being inducted into a company of spoken word titans, with Woodstock legend Richie Havens, though I still hadn't grasped the gravity of his status at the time.

On that night, it was Gil's show, so Richie went on first as the support act. In the dressing room after Richie went on stage Gil declared, 'Man, fuck it! Ritchie ain't no goddamn support!' That's when I realised that Richie was a significant artist. Because he was before my time I'd never heard of him till then – in fact, it wasn't until years later that I discovered he'd been the opening act at Woodstock.

Perhaps Richie was thinking he was back at Woodstock again, because he played and played and played – song after song after song after song. After a while Gil said to me: 'Go speak to the promoter and find out what time curfew is?' In other words, he wanted to know what time the venue was closing. There was an hour to curfew. By this point, Richie had been on the stage for an hour and a half.

So Gil said to me, 'Look, you need to tell him, get a message to Richie and let him know he's gotta come off stage, otherwise we're not gonna get a show.'

I wrote a note to Richie that simply read, 'Richie, it's time to get offstage for Gil's set.' Richie was sitting playing his guitar and singing in front of Gil's Fender Rhodes piano, so I put the note on the piano, right in front of him. He looked at the note, nodded his head and carried on playing.

By the time he finally finished – after two hours – Gil got just forty-five minutes for his headline set at his own show. How Gil reacted to this shows you the kind of person he was. Instead of complaining, Gil just kept saying: 'Man, Richie ain't no support.'

One of the other venues on this tour was Blues Alley in Washington DC, a small, intimate spot. Gil played several nights running at Blues Alley. Richie wasn't playing this batch of shows because they weren't strictly part of the tour.

On the first night we played at Blues Alley, there was a lady working on the door who was a fan of Gil's. We got to talking and got on really well.

Her name was Katea. It turned out she was related to 'jazz royalty', and was the daughter of the late, great Sonny Stitt, a saxophonist who had played with Thelonious Monk, Art Blakey and Dizzy Gillespie. She was a politically conscious black woman. At that time, I was still discovering my blackness, having been brought up in a very white environment. I'd lived in a predominantly white country, on a white council estate, I'd been to all-white schools, was taken into white care institutions. I was made to feel that it was almost a crime to be black.

I had grown up being taught that *Ten Little Nigger Boys* and *The Story of Little Black Sambo* were normal books, and not something I should be offended by. I was nonetheless offended, but somehow resigned to the reality that white people were never going to stop being racist – I believed I just had to find a way to stop letting their prejudice offend me.

It was a shock to me to come across a black woman who was so proud of her blackness, who was so self-assured in terms of who she was, who was so content in her own skin. Many of the black people I knew in the UK were also apologetic for being black. The first notion of black pride had come with the Toxteth riots of 1981; but by 1988, they were a distant memory and the black community that I'd come to know there had largely been forgotten again by white society. The influx of drugs into the community had all but annihilated the riot-era sense of black unity and pride. Now, it was everyone for themselves. Thatcher – it seemed – had prevailed in the end – and black people were back at square one, trying to fit in where they were not welcome, like gate crashers at a party.

I fell for Katea. It was a revelation to be in a relationship with someone who was also introducing me to a new set of values and a new way of looking at myself, as a black man. Her warm, welcoming persona took me by surprise, too. Most of the black women that I knew in the UK tended to be quite hard – probably because they had been through very traumatic life experiences, like my own. Most of the black women in my neighbourhood in Liverpool were as streetwise as the guys, if not more so. In Liverpool, we didn't really have a black middle class, we were all in the same class – the black class, which was considered the lowest class.

In America, there was a black middle class – folks who made good money, enjoyed comfortable lifestyles, some had even had a private education. They didn't have the kind of hang-ups that black British people had. But then again, they were ahead of us in development, and they had the numbers. We were only about two per cent of the population of the UK, whereas black people made up over twenty per cent of the population in America. DC was called 'Chocolate City'. The band used to joke that the only white people in DC were in the White House.

That's not to say that I wasn't fully aware that most black people's lives in the US were not much better than ours in the UK. The ghetto experience in the US was far more extreme in terms of poverty and violence than anything even I'd encountered in the UK. But Katea belonged very much in the black middle class. Her father's success as a musician had presumably enabled him to give his kids greater opportunities. She was educated, cultured and genteel. Everyone respected her and you could see why. This sister was for real.

In the same month I met Katea, Gil made a discovery about me whilst we were sitting in a hotel foyer in Virginia. He had already started to think that perhaps I had difficulty with reading, and having seen my poetry, he was also aware of my limitations in writing. I hadn't previously shared this information with him or Katea, as I was still ashamed of my literacy at that time.

One day, Gil put me on the spot. He passed me a book that he was reading. (Gil always had a book with him – no matter whether he was on a train or on a plane, he was always reading a book.) He asked me to read a page to him. I froze! I fumbled with the words for what seemed like an eternity but in reality was just a few terrifying moments.

At some point, he realised that I wasn't going to read the whole page, so he asked me quite bluntly: 'What's the problem? Aren't you fluent in reading?' I had never considered that a person could be fluent in reading; I always considered fluency to be associated with speaking. Gil said that I needed to do something about it and that literacy was the key to everything. He reiterated that it was 'nothing to be ashamed about, but something to be addressed'.

To help me improve, he told me to break words down into syllables. He said to read each part of the words out loud – phonetically – to capture the image of each part in my head and memorise the image, so I could recognise it next time.

I didn't know then that I was also dyslexic. If you are not dyslexic, you don't even need to think about words in this way – you just see them and immediately put their meaning to them, but for dyslexic people like me, you have to go through exactly the process that Gil outlined. While Gil encouraged and helped me to start to reading fluently, Katea really gave me the incentive to improve. She made me believe that I could be a proud black man, and I wanted to show her that I could be a black man whom she could be proud of.

At the end of Black History Month, she presented me with two books. One was Cheikh Anta Diop's *The African Origin of Civilization: Myth or Reality*. And the other was W. E. B. Du Bois's *The Souls of Black Folk*. The first was an anthropological work and is about how all civilisation began in Africa. The other is a socio-logical study, written by a mixed-race man, who graduated from both Harvard and Fisk Universities not long after the abolition of slavery, and who challenged perceived notions about black people's rights in post-slavery America. Both are seminal works, and both had a huge impact on me and were great places to start my self-education into black consciousness and pride. Diop's work showed me how Africans have a lot to be proud of. We were not what we were portrayed as being by European eugenicists, but were in fact cultured human beings, civilised, but dehumanised by white supremacist colonial propaganda, which had permeated every level of Western thinking since the days of slavery.

I admired Du Bois for challenging white people's long-held beliefs on where black people were in the years after slavery was abolished. That they were 'completely uneducated' when, in fact, there were several positive role models in the black community in this era, albeit few and far between where literacy was concerned due to the ban on enslaved people reading and writing.

I started reading Maya Angelou, beginning with *I Know Why the Caged Bird Sings*, which I devoured passionately. Angelou's writing helped me understand black history from the point of view of a black American woman, and I was fascinated by all the perspec-tives I could find on race relations in America. I then resolved to read every book that Maya Angelou wrote, all her novels and her poetry. They were a revelation.

To me, there seemed to be no black middle class in the UK, and there was almost an acceptance that black people were lower-class citizens. This was not being challenged on a mass level – there might have been individuals challenging white supremacy, but there were certainly no mass civil rights movements as there'd been in America. There were pockets of resistance here and there, usually on the back of a riot, and there were individuals who were trying to do things, change things. But there were few if any marches on Parliament, in the way people from the civil rights movement had marched on Washington. And we didn't have a Malcolm X or a Martin Luther King or a Black Panther movement in the UK black community.

After reading Maya Angelou and other contemporaries of hers, like Bell Hooks and Alice Walker, I moved on to the Harlem renaissance. Langston Hughes, Rosa Guy, Zora Neale Hurston and others. It was like a voyage of discovery – these were books that were relevant to me.

When I was in school and they were telling me we were going to read *Little Black Sambo*, how was I supposed to be interested? Maybe this was a factor in why I hadn't developed reading skills. Who'd want to read that bullshit?

CHAPTER 10

GIL FIRED ME

At the end of the 1988 tour with Richie Havens, Gil fired me. That sounds dramatic – and in some ways it was – but Gil fired people all the time. He was a super easy-going guy, but sometimes, if he needed to assert his authority, he would sack people. I often used to get asked by the crew: 'Have you been fired yet?'

I guess in my case, Gil was questioning my loyalty to him and suspected I was now more dedicated to Ramona in London. It was a complicated situation, as I had left London and my job with her to join the tour – against her wishes – but in the end, it was his decision to make so I respected that, as difficult as it was.

When I got back to London, Ramona fired me, too, for going out to the States and staying longer than the two weeks' holiday I was due. She had contracts to fulfil and couldn't have someone disappear off to the States for a month, like I had just done. I understood Ramona's point of view, too; she couldn't leave things open-ended like that.

Katea was still writing to me and wanted to make a go of a long-distance relationship. She said she'd even 'come to London' to be with me, but I couldn't offer her any accommodation. I had no job and was couch-surfing at friends' places again. I felt torn. My family and the people I'd come to love were all estranged from me. My mother, my sisters and brother, now Ramona and Gil and even my girlfriend, Katea. If there was ever a time I felt truly alone since leaving the care system, this was it. History was repeating itself; I'd been sacked from BP at the end of October in 1986, before I'd left for London that Christmas, and now I'd been sacked again in March of 1988.

Since the earlier BP sacking, my sister Michelle had been living in my flat in Aigburth, which ironically was across the road from Sydney House. I couldn't ask her to leave. I started working at a company called IDC Communications on the Strand in London. They sold telephone equipment, fax and telex machines, and photocopiers. They provided comprehensive product and sales training, and, after my induction period, I decided that there was the least competition and the most earnings potential in the sales of telephone key systems. I sold them door-to-door, to companies in London.

I was going around cold-calling at offices in places like Oxford Street and Hanover Square, drumming up good business, but the problem was – you didn't get your commission until the installation of the telephone systems, and that could take months. There was no basic salary, it was commission only. I was staying with a friend, Steve Carney, who was being extremely generous but he needed rent after a while. I was also eating his food and though he was cool about it, I didn't want to overstay my welcome.

I got a transfer to an IDC office in Liverpool. The problem there was that the guy who ran it was a crook – and it wasn't just a case of waiting to get paid, he didn't pay you at all.

I needed a drastic solution to the financial situation. As well as having no money, I had managed to rack up a £3,000 credit card debt during my time in London, before I went to the States. This debt was starting to cost me a lot of money at about thirty-five per cent interest per month, plus charges. I considered the possibility of going back to sea. I had a discharge book from my time on the ships two years before, which meant I could now legitimately get a job on any ship.

Gil and others often questioned what it was that fuelled my desire to go to sea. More so after the racism I had faced during my earlier experience with BP. I guess they never understood that it was important to me to follow in my dad's footsteps. Dad was at sea for thirty-five years – and bearing in mind his traumatic life in England – I was determined to see what he'd seen, to understand what had made him want to come to a place like the UK, where he was made so unwelcome.

I'd developed a whole new set of aspirations. Ramona had mentored and trained me to a high standard; I had developed a refined phone voice, through all the telesales training. I'd been in boardrooms and had done deals with big corporates and their agents, so going back to manual labour would be a massive anticlimax. I was determined not to claim state benefits when I came back to Liverpool – being back on the dole represented failure, and I couldn't bear that thought.

So I sank further into debt, and soon the stark realisation dawned on me that without Gil or Ramona's patronage, I was back at square one: homeless and broke in Liverpool. In May 1988, needing to stem the haemorrhaging cashflow deficit, I reluctantly took a job for the summer season, working as a steward. I would be back on a passenger ferry, but I was really hoping to work deep sea again.

I had all the right documentation – a seaman's card, a discharge book – and by this time most of the big shipping companies had relocated their operations to the Isle of Man. I was perfectly situated to scour the island and talk to all the manning agents in my search to join a foreign-flag ship. I was fortunate to get an offer from an agent called Britship, who were crewing up for the Danish oil company Maersk, so I jumped at the chance. And in December 1988, I flew to Rhode Island, in the US, to join the oil tanker, the MV *Maersk Nautilus*, which was bound for the Caribbean.

I'd started to keep a diary, in the hope that one day I'd write a book and tell my story. The first entry was from when I got the call from Britship saying they'd got a ship for me. As the entries progressed, day by day, years later they would prove a useful aide-memoire of what life at sea was truly like.

MONDAY 19TH DECEMBER

Started work, very easy-going atmosphere, catering department consists of myself (steward) and the cook-steward (Len). Talk of the ship being bound for Colombia. Still offloading cargo. Destination not yet confirmed. Went ashore. Visited two local bars in the marina. Quiet night, turned in (half-cut).

TUESDAY 20TH DECEMBER

Orders confirmed. Due to set sail at 6:00 p.m. for Colombia.
ETA – early morning, 26th December (Boxing Day). Weather
pretty poor, 8:00 p.m. set sail. False alarm missed our tide, so
the ropes went back out and we tied up again. Due to sail a.m.
(Wed now).

THURSDAY 22ND DECEMBER

5:30 a.m., weather overcast. 10:45 a.m., weather now picked
up. Quite sunny. Just received news of a Pan Am air tragedy.
No survivors. Flight 103, London to JFK New York, same one
that I'd flown on less than a week ago (747) over a place called
Lockerbie. Thank God I'm alive!

It never hit me until much later, the gravity of what had happened
on that Pan Am flight, as once we were away from the coastline,
we were out of range of radio and TV, and apart from telex
communication, we were all but incommunicado until we got
close to land again. This kind of lifestyle was going to have its
dangers, but it was hard to appreciate how real they would be
when I was just starting out. Back then, I put it out of my mind
and got on with the job.

There were sixteen of us onboard, with eight officers – including the captain, engineers, radio officer – and eight crewmen.
Usually on a ship like this, there would be a chief cook, a second
cook, a chief steward and two stewards to look after the catering.
But on the MV *Maersk Nautilus* there was no second cook, no

chief steward and no other steward. It was just me and the cook – that was the whole catering department.

I ended up doing my job as a steward, which was from 8 a.m. until 6 p.m., and the second cook's job as well. I did that role for no extra money, for both that trip and the next ship also – about a year in total – with the idea that in the long run I was training myself up to one day be a chief cook, a post that earned double what I was getting as a steward.

Taking on this extra role meant I was working even longer days. I would start work now at 5.30 a.m. to bake bread for the crew for the day, before they rose for breakfast. That was part of the extra second cook's role. This meant that when the rest of the crew would wake up and start 'turning to' (that's how they described getting ready for work at sea), there would be fresh bread and pastries for them. At 6.30 a.m., after I'd served breakfast, I did the 'strap-up', which meant cleaning everywhere in the galley and the crew mess. Then at 8.30 a.m. I was on to my stewarding duties. This meant cleaning all of the officers' cabins, throughout the morning. Then I would clean the pantry and restaurant before preparing for the lunch service.

I'd prep all the cold meats, salads and condiments, set the tables in the crew and the officers' mess and then serve the crew lunch from the pantry. After lunch I'd clean the officers' mess, lay the tables for the evening dinner service and then 'knock off'. I had two hours free and I would rest or read and write poetry in that time. Then at 3 p.m., I would start cleaning the ship's passageways and landings, scrubbing decks and 'stripping and polishing'. On oil tankers, men are walking around the ship in oily boots and it's always dirty, so the passageways and decks would have a glaze applied to them. My job was to strip the lacquer off the decks, apply a new layer of glaze and polish it. I would use a buffing machine, but you needed to get down on your hands and knees to get in the corners. It was a tough job and took up most of the afternoons.

After that, I would prepare for the dinner service, which was between 5 p.m. and 6 p.m. I'd strap-up again before cleaning the crew and officers' mess. My final job of the day was to throw the rubbish overboard. This was my favourite time of the day, because, if the weather was fine, I would then sit on the deck and watch the sunset. I'd usually take a moment to update my diary.

FRIDAY 23RD DECEMBER

Weather good, Captain's birthday so we had a party in the officers' bar. Sailing through the 'Bermuda Triangle'!

MONDAY 26TH DECEMBER – my sister Jackie's birthday (it's actually the 27th but I'd always got it mixed up).

'Happy birthday Jackie.' Arrived at Cartagena, Colombia. Loading just offshore at loading bay. Shore leave available, but no one wants to go ashore, too risky. Beautiful city within sight. Lots of tropical rainforest and jungle. Weird flying insects and mosquitos everywhere. Dug-out canoes surrounding the ship and men in them selling baby crocodiles and ganja.

TUESDAY 27TH DECEMBER

3:00 a.m. Pirates boarded the ship while we were loading. They grabbed Davy – the watchman – and put a cutlass to his throat and made him sit there while they robbed the ship. Second mate on the bridge raised the fire alarm and startled them, Davy got away. Pirates scattered over the side. They took a few fire extinguishers and some tackle. I was fast asleep.

WEDNESDAY 28TH DECEMBER

Left Cartagena at 8:30 p.m., bound for New York and possibly on to Boston from there?

SATURDAY 31ST DECEMBER – New Year's Eve

Weather good, 80° or so in Caribbean. Captain has put up another bar tab. All drinks free, what a party 7:00 p.m. local time – midnight GMT. Celebrated again.

TUESDAY 3RD JANUARY

Arrived 6:30 a.m. in New York. Got half day. Went ashore. Broadway, 42nd St. Times Square. Bought a tape – Gil Scott-Heron rerelease 'The Revolution Will Not Be Televised' digitally remastered. Sounds excellent, good to see him on the rebound. Uphill – all the way.

SATURDAY 7TH JANUARY

Postcards to Mum and Dianne. Wrote to bank. Ordered payments: Calvin – £125/Bank Loan £140/IMB Loan £600. – Subs £135. Tot: £1,000.00 from Dec/Jan wage. Wrote Reynold with letter for insurance company (have copy).

MONDAY 9TH JANUARY

Finished poem 'Urbane Guerrilla' – posted to G.S.H. [Gil Scott-Heron].

Although I lived by this working routine, my days and weeks could be very unpredictable in some ways. Tankers are basically vehicles for hire. Anyone can charter a tanker and a crew, send them to pick up and deliver a cargo from anywhere in the world. A ship like the *Nautilus* had a different charter almost every cargo.

Once they had filled up the ship's hold with the cargo, you could be going anywhere – they would wait until the oil was sold and then head there, to pump the oil ashore. There were often no fixed arrangements, so the company would just buy oil where it was cheap, fill up the tanker and tell us to sail into international waters, drop the anchor and await orders. As soon as they'd sold the cargo, we'd get orders and head off to wherever the buyer was, to discharge the cargo. Sometimes we could be floating aimlessly for weeks until we got a buyer. It all depended on the oil price. If it dropped after we'd loaded the cargo, we'd have to wait until the price went up again before the company would sell the cargo. It was always a waiting game.

The crew was pretty friendly to me at first. Although oil tankers are huge ships, there aren't many people onboard and you can be away from port for a long time, so it gets boring. You need people to talk to, as a way of relieving the monotony of the days.

I hadn't been onboard long before I encountered a problem. It was a much-reduced crew on the *Nautilus*, compared to what I was used to on the MV *British Skill*; and the chief cook, a man called Len Phillips, was also acting as chief steward, what this new system termed a 'cook-steward'. That meant he was in charge of the ship's laundry as well as the galley and I reported directly to him. There were washing machines onboard for the crew and officers to do their personal laundry but all the other stuff – tablecloths and tea towels from the canteen and the pantry, and bed sheets, towels, quilts and so on – would get thrown into huge linen sacks. When we arrived at a port and were waiting for a berth to dock in, the sacks would be loaded onto a launch using a 'derrick' – a crane on the ship – then laundered commercially and returned two days later. It was my responsibility to pack the stuff, get it to and from the deck, and back to the stores upon its return.

On one occasion, we had dropped anchor under the Verrazano-Narrows, a vast suspension bridge between New York's Staten Island and Brooklyn – and Len had arranged for the laundry sacks to be taken ashore and cleaned. After this had been done, he came to my cabin with a brown envelope. He passed it to me and said it was 'a gift from the laundryman in Staten Island'. I asked: 'Why would the laundryman give me a gift? I don't know him.' Len replied, 'Just take it and be happy.' I looked inside the envelope and could see it contained about $500 in $100 bills. I said to Len: 'Take it back! I don't want it.' Len looked me hard in the eyes and said, 'You shouldn't have done that.' This exchange was to radically change my relationship with the whole crew. What had clearly been going on was that someone onboard had been putting in invoices for the laundry – which Maersk was paying for – with a big inflation on the price. The proceeds of this scam were then being divided up among the crew and presumably the laundryman, because he'd settle the invoice with the company directly but was providing cash to the cook-steward as his cut.

I had decided, long before this, that I wanted to lead an honest life. I had seen how money had corrupted so many of my friends in Toxteth and Netherley; I was disgusted by what people would do to each other to get it, and I'd resolved that the only way to subvert that corruption was to be free from avarice. Part of that integrity which I wanted to establish and maintain involved never taking a bribe and not getting involved in scams. If you aren't greedy, then you can't be corrupted, I believed.

But I paid a price for refusing to accept that envelope, and that wasn't the only time. True to form, just like the BP crew before them, the men grew antagonistic towards me, and I was again ostracised on the ship. Word was, they thought I was a 'company spy'. If I walked into a bar, everyone would walk out. If I sat at a table in the canteen, everyone would get up and leave. Of course, if you didn't collaborate on a scam like that, the people involved always feared that you would grass them up. I'd lived long enough on the streets and in the institutions of the care system to know the cardinal rule – you never grass – but I also knew that I didn't want to be involved. I'd say, 'If you don't tell me, I won't know and what I don't know I can't tell. So don't involve me in anything and don't tell me anything. Just leave me to do my job.'

That wasn't enough though, the men were suspicious and couldn't understand what sort of person didn't want free money. Eventually they got together and hatched a plot. First, they asked me to run the bar on the ship. The way the bar worked was that everyone ran up a tab – and every month, your tab would be deducted from your wages. I was immediately suspicious when they asked me to run it and I refused. But that wasn't the end of it.

A few weeks later, we took on some new crew members at a port, and some of the hostile lot paid off. I was glad to see new faces onboard, and grateful not to be ignored by them, so I spent a rare evening in the bar having drinks. Mostly I avoided socialising with the others because of their hostility; I tended to stay in my cabin and read books or write poems and songs, preferring to spend my time studying the etymology of words and listening to music on my Walkman. But that night, I got a bit tipsy and forgot to mark off a few beers on my tally.

The next day the ship's boatswain called a meeting for the crew in the bar. He announced that there was 'a thief on the ship', that someone had been 'stealing from the bar'. Stealing on a ship is considered a heinous crime and everyone looked shocked. I realised I may have made a mistake the night before and not chalked off all my beers, which was not uncommon; people would often tally up the next day and the barman would simply reconcile the stock. I didn't want anyone else to be accused of stealing if they were talking about my few beers that I hadn't tallied up yet, so I told the boatswain this, in front of everyone. He leapt on my words as a confession. 'I knew it was you!' he said triumphantly. 'I was just waiting to see if you would confess to being the thief.'

I had walked into a trap. From that moment, almost the entire crew refused to talk to me again, including the new guys. Before, it was just the crewmen who had ostracised me, now the officers got wind of the boatswain's twisted story and refused to acknowledge me also.

In a way, this worked in my favour, as it meant that I spent all of my spare time from that point on writing new poetry and improving my reading. My long-term goal was to pay off my debts from London, go to college and get into university.

Writing became an exercise in catharsis for me. I'd resolved to write a book when I was ten years old, whilst I was at Greystone Heath, determined to expose all the injustices of the care system. Gil had encouraged me to acquire the necessary tools to hone my reading and writing, and the time I spent on the ship gave me the space to develop those skills. But it also gave me new context for the narrative I am writing now.

I captured my disdain for Len, who was at the root of this stitch-up, in a poem, so that people would know what he did to me. The poem was called simply 'The Ship's Cook'.

You piss me off most every day.
In your own sly-silly way.
You act like a child without a playmate.
You're about as exciting as a dirty steak-plate.

You pace the galley, all day long
And cringe each time I sing a song.
Which makes me sing a whole lot more.
If cringe you will, right out the door?

'cause when you had your boys aboard,
You schemed and lied and set up fraud.
And sent me off to Coventry
Because your thief, I would not be.

But now your boys have all gone home
And left you scheming all alone.
And I've returned from Coventry,
Except with you, which shows to me.

That you were at the heart of that,
Which turned a good trip into bad
And paved the way for more to come.
I hope one day you'll overcome ...

The rat that lives within your soul.
The hatred in your heart so cold.
The loneliness that you must feel
Resulting from your dirty deal.

Soon, almost the whole crew of the *Nautilus* paid off the ship – except me and Len. He lost all his power and influence after that. He was still my boss, but the fear factor was gone as I'd worked out his game and mentally got on top of it. Without his pack of cronies around him to bolster his ego, he suddenly became very small onboard and I barely acknowledged him.

The new guys who signed on the ship were as much of a threat as I was, because they didn't know about the laundry scam, and Len couldn't tell them without jeopardising himself. The balance of power had now shifted. He then tried to befriend me, but I ignored him. I'd walk round the ship singing and smiling and it had him totally perplexed. He was expecting me to be afraid and depressed, and I showed him the total opposite.

22ND FEBRUARY

South-westerly swell – 30ft waves – bit dodgy like. Force 9 gale. May get worse later. Received news of Panamanian flagged cargo, vessel *Cecil Angola* disappeared off the coast of Ireland. 17 people lost – believed drowned – (poor bastards).

28TH FEBRUARY

Last day of Black History Month. Although I couldn't be with my people this year, I had the good fortune of being accompanied through it by Maya Angelou's *Singin' and Swingin' and Gettin' Merry Like Christmas*, Gil Scott-Heron's 'The Revolution Will Not Be Televised'/*Best of Gil Scott-Heron/Live from Scotland 1987*. Stevie Wonder and Bob Marley put the finishing touches to it. You're never alone if you have music. God bless them all. Confirmed two-port discharge of cargo – both at Corpus Christi, Texas – Houston is out. Weather fine. Heard news of three ships sunk in – or around – the Bay of Biscay, no more than a week or two after we left. It looks like the bad weather we had got worse. God help them. No news of survivors. Wrote the poem 'If Only?'.

6TH MARCH

Passing Florida Keys – group of islands off the coast of
Florida, linked together by a series of bridges and also linked
to the mainland. Having problems with the chief cook, who
informs me I've been 'sent to Coventry' – (a bit)???

Said he gave me 'plenty of chances', but he 'got sick of it'.
He said it was my 'own fault', and that I'd marked my 'own card
a long time ago, trying to impress. But it didn't work – did it?'
This gives me the answer that I was looking for. The previous
beer set-up was all part and parcel of them getting something
on me, to get me off the ship. They had previously asked me
to run the bar in the hope (I presume) that I'd make a mistake
(or they could help me make a mistake) then they'd accuse
me of pilfering and get me off the ship. But I declined, so they
settled for this. I'm waiting to see how they intend to finish
the job. Sending me to Coventry – I believe – is supposed to
encourage me to leave. Weather a bit choppy, overcast.
Turned in early.

20TH MARCH

Hurray! Happy birthday to me. 23 today. 23 years on the
planet and I haven't learned a fucking thing that I didn't know
at 10 years of age. That must have been when I stopped
listening. Well, judging by recent years, I do need another
radical change in my life. This may be the last major one 'til
middle age. So I'd better get busy on it. Listen, look and 'see'.
Read and absorb it. Study, or rather learn to study, write as

much as I can and above all – shut the fuck up! That way, you may get to live 'til middle age. And, if so, who knows, you might just get to work too? Len gave me a half day. I've put a crate of beer on the bar. It's usually a couple of cases but I can't afford it this month, so it's better than nothing and I'm thankful that I'm here to drink it.

Every new place makes an impression on you when you're travelling the world. We had sailed past Turkey through the Dardanelles, a narrow strait about the width of the River Mersey, which connects the Aegean Sea into the Sea of Marmara – and then through the Bosporus into the Black Sea, where we docked at Constanța, in Romania, on 22nd May 1989. It was near to the end of the Soviet Bloc era, but several months before the Iron Curtain finally collapsed.

Shipping from the West was allowed in the Eastern-bloc ports but with constraints. In Romania, under the communist dictatorship of Nicolae Ceaușescu, ships were allowed to discharge and collect cargo. Seamen were allowed ashore but with the strict instruction that they must not carry any printed material such as newspapers or magazines into the Communist country. Romania was still effectively a vassal state of Mother Russia, and any information they might find that life in the West was much better was obviously not in the interests of the ruling party.

I was fascinated by Constanța. There was evidence of its grand past in the architecture but much of it was derelict – and anything modern was a grey, concrete-style monstrosity. Some of the Ottoman-style ancient mosques and older buildings still bore pockmarked walls – peppered with tank-shell and bullet holes from the Second World War, when the Russians had invaded and occupied the city in 1944, and had imposed Communism as the law of the land.

I went ashore in Constanţa and decided to have a proper look around, while most of the other seamen filed into bars at the quayside to drink the day away. I stopped by three girls on the street and asked where I could buy some American cigarettes. They all spoke English fluently. As they were giving me directions, an older woman approached me. She had a baby with her, and this infant was red-faced and looked ill with a temperature. She became agitated and started shouting at the three girls. The girls convinced her to leave and told me she was a professional beggar. Afterwards I saw lots of other women like her, all carrying sickly babies.

The girls – who turned out to be three sisters – said they would take me to a hotel shop, and I thanked them for their help. Then I said I was looking for things to do but there were no entertainment or tourist events happening. They said that was just the way it was – and invited me back to their house.

I remember clearly the house where they lived. It was in an area that had once been quite upmarket but had fallen into decline since the Communist invasion. It was a large townhouse, spread over several floors – and when we got there, we were greeted by a smiling old lady in a headscarf, who was their grandmother.

Inside, there were lots of antiques and old furnishings. There was a fabulous ornate piano – with original wooden keys and exquisitely crafted brass candelabras that pulled out on the sides. It was clearly the family's pride and joy.

As I was standing looking so impressed, the oldest sister, who must have been about twenty-six, started to play. She launched into a classical work – Tchaikovsky or something – and it was amazing, like a concert performance. I was astonished at her ability; she was clearly classically trained. Then the middle sister – who was about twenty-four – started playing. She was also good but not quite as proficient. Finally the youngest – who was about twenty – had a go, too. She could play but clumsily, and she was not as good as her sisters. Her name was Elena Dragomir. Her older sisters were correcting her, and then everyone started joking around. I felt very at home.

After a time, when we were all getting along, the grandmother reappeared with a plate bearing a slice of toast and a fried egg. The egg white seemed to be cooked but the yolk was raw and gelatinous. I didn't fancy eating it – but the way it was presented and the way they were all watching me, it soon dawned on me that the egg was a luxury item and they were offering it to me as their guest.

They watched me intently as I ate the egg, as if it was a prize that everyone wanted but only one of us could have. Afterwards, they asked me if I like Stevie Wonder. I was shocked. I was an avid Stevie Wonder fan, and I collected his albums. They produced a cassette tape of an album called *Characters* that I had never seen before. I thought, how did these people behind the Iron Curtain get to hear Stevie Wonder's new album before me?

Elena played it for me and when it came to the song 'Free', she said to me: 'I want to be free like a river – like Stevie Wonder says.' Her words melted my heart as it became clear that these people were prisoners of communism.

Soon after, there was a commotion at the front door. I could hear a man's voice and the grandmother shouting in response. The sisters disappeared to join the old woman. Later, they explained that a man had come to buy the piano. Things had been so tough in recent months that they'd put an advert in a newspaper for the piano. But the grandma, having heard her granddaughters play so beautifully to me, had changed her mind and told the man it was not for sale. He was angry because he'd driven all the way from Bucharest, but the old woman chased him off. The sisters said they hadn't played the piano in a long time before that day, and it had ignited in them a passion and nostalgia for the past.

I stayed with the family until late that evening and it soon became apparent that an attraction between me and the youngest daughter, Elena, was building up. The others had left us. We sat at the piano and exchanged kisses. We also exchanged addresses. But at about 10 p.m. they said I needed to get back to the ship since it was dangerous for me to be out in Constanţa at night because of the Securitate – the Romanian secret police. They would think I was a spy or something. The girls escorted me into the street, checking to see if the coast was clear. It was surreal. We were hiding in the shadows like criminals. They found a taxi to take me to the docks and bundled me in like I was a defector trying to sneak out of the country. We agreed to meet in the same place we had met that day, the following evening.

The following night was to be our last night in Constanţa. I walked to the square where we had met before, in a state of nervous anticipation, and caught sight of the three familiar faces.

The girls were all dressed up but as I approached them they avoided my eye.

'Shall we go?' I asked. I wanted to take them out for a meal, to repay them for the kindness they had shown me.

The eldest sister cast me a surly, hostile look. 'Go where?'

Then I noticed a man standing on their left. He was dressed in a black leather coat and looked displeased.

'You go!' he barked at me.

I was bemused. 'Who are you?' I asked, but the eldest sister urged me, quite desperately, to go.

In an accent I was unfamiliar with, he said, 'Passporte?' He gestured with his hand that this was a demand – not a request.

It was becoming increasingly obvious that this man was not a bystander. I asked again who he was, and he pulled out a badge of sorts.

'Securitate!' he said, and then reiterated his demand. 'Passporte?'

I relented and showed him my passport. Unnerved, I began insisting that these women had done nothing wrong but the sisters kept telling me to go. 'You don't understand,' they said in panic.

The Securitate officer slung my passport back to me. 'You go!' he said with fearsome formality. I was close to despair. What had I done? What had they done? I had no idea, but I knew I had to go, for their sakes, so I walked away. In my frustration, I boarded the ship, went straight to my cabin and wrote a song which I simply entitled 'Elena'.

Suspended in time in 1949.
Behind the iron curtain.
The 1980s she cannot not see,
Still she listened to a song of liberty.

When I asked her out with me
Our hearts and minds were one.
She played a Stevie Wonder song
And I was thinking while she sang along.

Oh why must you remain here – Elena?
To be free is your fantasy.
Free just like a river, in springtime,
Flowing down to the sea,
Is all you want to be.

But still she must remain here. Romania!
Her heart's in the west – her mind the east.
Thinking of a river.
I leave her.
Wishing that she were as free.
Through a blind man she can see.

Her golden hair, her skin so fair,
I'm locked in ecstasy.
Her fingers sing a song for me,
As they dance across her piano keys.

And when it's time to say goodnight.
In the shadows I must run.
The very next day our dream is gone,
When we're seen together
And the police come.

Oh! Why must you remain here – Elena?
Freedom's just a word within a song.
Freedom like a river, I give her,
All of my heart this day.
For her freedom I pray.

But still she must remain here – Romania!
Suspended in time and poverty.
Thinking of a river,
I leave her.
Wishing that we were as free.
Through a blind man we can see.
Only rivers in our worlds run free.

It would be months before I found out what actually happened that night in Constanța. On a subsequent trip to a place called Ascension Island in December 1989, one week after the Romanian revolution had started, I received a letter from Elena. It had been written that week, after the fall of the ruthless Communist dictator – Nicolae Ceaușescu – who was later executed on national TV. She explained that the man in the black leather coat that night was, in fact, Securitate – Romanian secret police – and that she and her two sisters had been arrested and accused of prostitution, but she hadn't been able to write to explain all this until after the revolution. She said that her grandmother had been forced to sell the antique piano to pay a bribe to release them from jail. I was heartbroken that their kindness to me had led to such sorrow for them, but it was good to hear that she and her family now had a new lease of freedom.

I paid off the *Maersk Nautilus* in Istanbul at the end of May in 1989, and flew home. Reynold still had his own flat, so I stayed at my place for a month looking for a new ship.

I was there for four weeks until June 1989, when I joined another ship in Sicily. The ship had a charter to deliver fuel to several British military installations in the Mediterranean and the North and South Atlantic Oceans. Most of the fuel came from Sicily, some from Italy. We'd load up and deliver it to places like RAF Akrotiri in Cyprus, as well as to Ascension Island and the Falklands in the South Atlantic, sailing via Gibraltar. As it was a military charter – the oil was for the British bases – everyone on board had to sign the Official Secrets Act.

Margaret Thatcher had declared war on Argentina for reinhabiting the 'Malvinas', as the Argentines referred to them, but to the British they were the Falkland Islands. Ascension was a vital refuelling and staging post, about halfway between the UK and the Falklands. If you're sailing southwards from Europe, there are no other islands after the Azores and the Canaries until Ascension, so you can see why the British have always wanted to keep hold of it strategically.

When we arrived on Ascension and went ashore on the first night, I met a couple from St Helena, which is about 1,300 miles south-east of Ascension. Brian and June Coleman were such open and friendly people. Like most of the locals, they were of mixed race, and whilst June had a lighter complexion than me, Brian was darker and had an afro like my brothers.

St Helenians – or 'Saints' – I was soon to discover, were a historically noble but downtrodden people, who were treated almost like slaves on Ascension. Where any other electrician might earn say £1,500 a month, a Saint doing the same job would be paid something closer to £200.

Furthermore, although they were black, they had almost no concept of black culture. Most Saints were descended from Africans who had been brought to the island as slaves by Portuguese settlers, or by British forces, who were preventing them from being transported to Brazil after 1807, when Britain supposedly officially abolished the so-called 'Africa trade'. In St Helena, these people were cut off from the rest of the world, and appeared to have been almost totally indoctrinated by white British culture.

From Ascension Island, the oil tanker sailed on. The South Atlantic, between Ascension and the Falklands, is one of the toughest environments on earth, and probably one of the most treacherous stretches of ocean. There was little or no life to see, save a lone Albatross that occasionally followed the ship. You don't see these huge birds anywhere in the northern hemisphere, but they start appearing once you cross the equator, pursuing ships like something straight out of Samuel Taylor Coleridge's poem *The Rime of the Ancient Mariner*. Sailors are very superstitious about these mighty birds – which seems a shame, since they're the only company you get in such desolate and remote places.

When we docked at Port Stanley in the Falklands under our RAF military charter, no one aboard was allowed ashore. However, I had been suffering from an abscess in my mouth for two weeks preceding, and had been using cloves soaked in brandy in an attempt to numb the gums and alleviate some of the pain. I needed the attention of a dentist urgently, so I alone was allowed ashore.

As far as I was concerned, the Falklands War was all about oil. The islands were needed by the British as a staging post to access oil reserves in the British Antarctic Territories, directly south of the Falklands. I wasn't particularly interested in the place, despite the rare privilege of being allowed to visit. But I do have a clear memory of my time there – and it had a strange conclusion.

Two squaddies escorted me to the military dentist on the RAF base. Like troops everywhere, they had a nickname for everything, and they called the native islanders 'Bennies' – because they all wore hats like the character Benny, from the 1970s TV soap opera *Crossroads*.

After I'd had my abscess drained and my tooth drilled and filled, I told these guys I needed to go to a shop, to get some supplies. On the base, they only have the NAAFI shop, which is a general store you find on any British military base. There, in one of the remotest places in the world – with not another black person in sight for a thousand miles – I found an audio cassette of Public Enemy's new release, *It Takes a Nation of Millions to Hold Us Back*. The album is now a hip-hop classic, notable for its angry, politically charged message. I played it non-stop on my Sony Walkman as I made the long ride back on the launch through the rocky South Sea outcrops. I swear, by the time I arrived onboard that racist ship, I was pumped up and ready to take on any racist fucker that came my way. The track that got to me was called 'Black Steel in the Hour of Chaos', and the lyrics went like this:

I got a letter from the government
The other day, I opened and read it
It said they were suckers
They wanted me for their army or whatever
Picture me givin' a damn, I said never

Here is a land that never gave a damn
About a brother like me and myself
Because they never did
I wasn't wit' it, but just that very minute
It occurred to me, the suckers had authority

Cold sweatin' as I dwell in my cell
How long has it been?
They got me sittin' in the state pen.

I gotta get out, but that thought was thought before.
I contemplated a plan on the cell floor.
I'm not a fugitive on the run
But a brother like me begun, to be another one

Public enemy servin' time, they drew the line y'all,
To criticize me for some crime.

Nevertheless
They could not understand
That I'm a Black man
And I could never be a veteran.

On the strength, the situation's unreal
I got a raw deal, so I'm goin' for the steel

I was thinking with a new political consciousness thanks to the influences of Gil and Katea, and I was now the kind of reader who devoured books at a rapid rate.

While before it had taken me up to six months to read one book, I was now tearing through Alice Walker's *The Color Purple* and Zora Neale Hurston's *Dust Tracks on a Road*. I read in quick succession a whole series of books by James Clavell – *King Rat*, *Tai Pan*, *Shōgun* and *Noble House* – each volume thicker than the next. After you read a book the length of *Noble House*, you realise that no book is beyond your reach, no matter how thick it is.

A few weeks later, after we had sailed back the way we came, we returned to Ascension. I spent my time ashore with Brian, June and the other St Helenians I was getting to know. They were wonderful people who seemed endlessly kind and hospitable. It made me all the more furious to learn how the white people of the island mistreated them.

I struggled to reconcile how black or indigenous culture seemed to be strikingly absent here, and the surest sign came when Brian took me to visit a local school. It was built for the children of Saints, and on the walls of the classroom I saw that all the black children's artworks were of white people. White faces – smiling, standing within family arrangements. I was stunned. One dark, imposing picture stood out – it was a depiction of a large black gorilla, over which was scrawled: 'Black! Black! Black!'

I was transported straight back to Netherley. What I was seeing here was the same racist indoctrination and brainwashing that I had experienced there. I remembered how, in that environment, I had started listening to white rock music and following white celebrities, contorting my interests and my behaviour to fit in with the very culture that oppressed me. My own former self-loathing held a frightening parallel with what I was seeing here – and I was struck by the thought of what might have become of me if I hadn't met Gil.

I had not quite escaped the pernicious experiences of my upbringing, being submerged in such a hostile culture for so many years, but I was meticulously unpicking those false narratives and reminding myself of the positive black narratives I'd absorbed in recent years. I was also opening my eyes to the truths I'd observed while travelling the world and witnessing the after-effects of the former British empire (which I deliberately spell with a small 'e' because, in my opinion, it doesn't deserve a capital letter).

I wanted to fight harder to reassert my own black cultural heritage and to further undo the white man's indoctrination of me. Reading had widened my horizons and shown me a side of history that my white teachers would never have taught, choosing every time instead to introduce their students to the likes of 'Little Black Sambo' in the jungle.

I had been travelling along this road for a while, but it was now registering with me, with new, total clarity, why Gil was so vociferous in his desire to educate black people about the game that was being inflicted on us. How we could escape the colonialist trap that was set by elevating ourselves through knowledge and culture – and why we needed platforms like music to disseminate those thoughts and ideas further. This was what the Last Poets later referred to as 'De-West-Toxification'.

Just as I had encountered corruption on the Nautilus, my time here wasn't to pass without an incident involving dishonesty and disaster. We had docked at Antwerp in Belgium for a pump over – the transfer of cargo between two ships – and we were to take on fuel oil. The man responsible for this operation was the second mate – a guy called David Humphreys. He was a religious man, and also a man who liked a drink.

That night, he and the watch keeper had made the usual calculations of how long it would take to transfer the volume of oil to be pumped – and while it was being transferred, they'd gone to the crew bar. But Mr Humphreys had made a big miscalculation on what time the pipes needed to be disconnected. After a while, oil started spilling on to the deck. At 80,000 to 90,000 tonnes, the ship's deck was a vast area. Thick, black oil covered it all and rose in inches until it spilled over the barriers and into the water below. Most of the crew were asleep, a few were still drinking in the bar. By the time someone finally noticed something was wrong, the ship was completely flooded with crude and it was spilling into the harbour fast. A major incident was declared and the authorities in Antwerp ordered the captain to get the owners to pay for a massive clean-up operation.

A costing was made for the clean-up, which was telexed to the ship's owners and forwarded to the ship's captain. It ran into hundreds of thousands of pounds. The owners told the port authorities in Antwerp that it would do its own clean-up, outside territorial waters, but would pay a fine to cover any damage in the port. The owners then ordered the captain to sail out into international waters. We expected some expert crew to arrive to start the process, but they never came. The next day a telex from the company came through and the captain ordered the crew to release 5,000 gallons of diesel onto the deck to break up the thick black crude oil. It was done, and the crew scooped the whole lot of it overboard into the North Sea, using apparatus that looked like snowploughs. It was an act of eco-vandalism, and it made me sick.

Soon after, it was announced that everyone on board – except Mr Humphreys, who was sacked and left the ship immediately in Antwerp – was to be paid a 'bonus'.

I was offered £300 from the company slush fund that the captain had been authorised to pay out but said I didn't feel comfortable with it, as I saw it as a bribe.

'I don't want it,' I told the captain. He looked at me with a sharp glare.

'If you don't take it, I will.'

Conversations had already started on the ship about people being 'lost at sea'. Rumours would spread about sailors getting thrown overboard and the captain and the crew telling the rest of the world 'the man had been depressed.'

I got the feeling that these comments were meant as a subtle warning and I knew that if I didn't take the money, I may never see the next port. I agreed to sign the list, and when I did, I saw that the Captain had been awarded £3,000. The hush money was paid by hierarchy, according to rank and as I was the lowest rank on the ship, I got the smallest amount. Everyone onboard took the money and though I was horrified by what I'd seen, I didn't speak out about the oil spill. But it caused me turmoil in my very soul.

I was near the end of my tether with life at sea by that point, my soul was in great turmoil – and the thing that clinched it was a hurricane. We were on the east coast of the US when we hit the bad weather. The hurricane was travelling on the same path as us, heading across the Atlantic to Europe. Following the old saying, our captain decided that the safest way through was in the eye of the storm – the thinking being that if you broke through the side of it, it could smash you into pieces.

This turned out to be the most horrific and frightening experience of my entire life. We were being tossed around like a rubber duck in the tub, and our vessel weighed upwards of 70,000 tonnes. At any given moment, it felt like the ship would snap, and we'd be sucked down to the bottom of the ocean. It was impossible to sleep. It wasn't just a couple of days either. This storm went on for two weeks, during which time to stop being thrown out of your bunk, you would have to place your mattress vertically in your cabin rather than in the normal horizontal setting – in this way if the ship lunged you would roll rather than be thrust out of your bunk. But it was still impossible to sleep, and we suffered day after day with nausea and fatigue. We were bruised and terrified, delirious and traumatised. The storm was so intense that you lost track of time.

One night, I lost it and started crying like a baby. I was calling out to God, Allah, Buddha whoever would listen, to 'get me out of here'. The fear was so relentless, the constant possibility of death so debilitating. I remember writing a letter saying, 'I love my family, if this is the end …' and sealing it in a plastic bag.

Then, the next morning, we sailed into the Bay of Biscay – and with the storm now arriving in Europe, we were told to find safe anchorage and wait until it finally subsided. It was too dangerous to try to put into port. While we were waiting at anchorage, we heard a Mayday message for a ship called the MV *Secil Japan*, which was breaking up on rocks at a place called Hell's Mouth off the coast of North Cornwall. Sea rescue had sent out a helicopter to winch the Asian crew off the ship, but the first guy to go up had fallen and perished on the rocks below.

It was at that moment, hearing of this tragedy, that I decided I wasn't willing to risk my life like this at sea anymore.

CHAPTER 11

THE LAST POETS

During my years at sea, I posted all the poems I'd written to Gil, along with letters detailing my experiences around the world. In the years after I got back to the UK, taking leave from whatever I was doing at the time, I'd join Gil and go on tour in the UK and in Europe. On the long journeys between venues, as always, Gil would read my poems and letters – making comments, correcting mistakes and laughing if something amused him.

I often used to find my letters in his dressing room, so I knew he had them to hand and took them seriously.

Our conversations roamed around every topic. What started off as me trying to understand the basics of Gil's geopolitical stance on things mentioned in his artistic repertoire – from apartheid in South Africa to the Iran-Iraq War to the Cuban Missile Crisis – developed into a dialogue. We were demystifying the issues, and I was coming to understand his material in real depth. We pushed each other to explain our thinking and, in some cases, diverged in ideological arguments which could often get heated.

My relationship with Gil had changed. Having taken the time to study his writing and the ideas he was espousing, I'd also formed my own views – some from books, but many from my own personal experiences travelling around the world. Gil was so clever and well-read that he would wipe the floor with most people in an argument.

I didn't dissent for the sake of it – I respected his opinions more than anyone's and always considered his view as a starting point on any issue. But we were coming to things from different perspectives. He might have views on Angola or a Soviet country, but he'd never been to these places. I had been to Angola and I'd been to communist Romania. Working on oil tankers, you were privy to some inside knowledge about the industry. I had grown used to reading the *Lloyd's List* magazine, which gave in-depth analysis of the shipping industry and issues in the oil business, so while Gil was forming his views from the *New York Times*, the *Washington Post* and the *Wall Street Journal*, I was involved first-hand, and often reading about the details that never made the wider press.

We had a blazing row once about the first Gulf War. I had formed a view about why Saddam Hussein had invaded Kuwait.

Gil's views on the war were formed by what he had read in the US mainstream media and he didn't agree with what I was saying. He would get angry if he didn't win an argument and he'd shout you down. But I wasn't going to be subdued – I knew what I was saying, and I argued my point vociferously. I think the band was quite shocked when we clashed over this on the tour bus, everyone else was silent. They would rarely argue with him, not like this – but then, they knew he had the power to sack them at any time. Gil later told me that he respected me for arguing back. He really didn't like sycophants. In fact, he was training me to hold my own and I was doing what I was supposed to do – challenging authority in search of the truth. Gil had made a career out of it.

My new-found intellectual confidence had certainly been helped by my time at sea. I now had far bigger ambitions than becoming a chief cook. I was starting to think I was not incapable of learning, and that I really wanted to do something new. I had often thought of going to university but it had seemed like a pipe dream as I knew I didn't have the requisite entry qualifications.

Despite the fact that I could now hold my own in a debate with someone like Gil Scott-Heron, getting a place at a college was no easy matter for someone with my lack of formal education. And you needed a college education to get into university. In the days when I was in the care system, people like me were effectively 'off the radar' as far as education was concerned. Nobody cared about us. Milestones and targets didn't matter, you were just contained – managed like a resource, then spat out onto the streets at the end. I guess there was some sort of afterthought that you might become useful if you were given some practical skills, like gardening or woodwork, but as far as academia was concerned, there was little to no consideration.

Even in care, though, I had been considered bright. With an IQ of 124, I had presented the authorities with a dilemma. Out of a hundred kids at Greystone Heath, they had wound up putting only three of us in for exams; and of the three of us, the other two, who were both white kids, attended what we referred to as 'outside schools'. I did not. Without preparation, with only the meagre scraps of education I was given, I was barely able to scrape an RSA certificate in maths at 'elementary level' which was lower than a CSE, which itself was lower than an O-level. I also got a few CSEs, but the grades were so low as to be irrelevant when it came to applying for jobs. I'd taken them with no preparation, a limited capacity in reading and writing, and for much of it I just ticked boxes and hoped for the best, which didn't work out all that well for me. Basically, I received the lowest level of the lowest qualifications you could take at that time.

The requisite qualifications needed to enter a college to do an A-level were four O-levels (equivalent to today's GCSEs in the UK) at grade C or above. I wasn't eligible even to gain entry to a college – let alone a university. Essentially, I was stuffed.

Gil's recognition of these hurdles – and his insistence that I was intelligent and had potential – was the initial driving force that opened me up to books. The difference between myself and people who'd enjoyed a formal education was that once this new world became accessible to me, I couldn't get enough of it. I likened it to an Aladdin's cave, full of treasures, each one so precious that you wouldn't be able to choose what to take first. Acquiring knowledge also gave me a sense of black pride and dignity – now that I had acquired a totally new perspective on history and, in particular, black history. There were some books that were particularly pivotal in changing my mindset about the relationship between white and black people.

One of these was *Roots* – Alex Haley's saga about an eighteenth-century African teenager, who was enslaved by white Europeans and taken to America, which also told the stories of his descendants. They made *Roots* into a television series in the late 1970s, but we weren't allowed to watch it at Greystone Heath. We were only allowed to watch cops and robbers programmes, like *The Sweeney* and *Starsky & Hutch* – which always had the same message: criminals never win. (And we were always made to feel like we were criminals, even if we'd committed no crimes.)

But in terms of getting into a university, thanks to my lack of requisite qualifications, the only option for me was to try to enter as a mature student. To do this, you had to demonstrate you had relevant life skills and work experience for a course, and some academic ability, even if it was acquired vocationally through your job rather than college or school.

Strangely, the Toxteth riots ended up inadvertently giving me the leverage I needed to get into college. That violent uprising in the summer of 1981 had scared the living daylights out of Liverpool's business leaders. They figured that if they didn't do something for the black community, riots would keep happening and adversely affect the local economy. There was also the vast cost of repairing the damage they wrought, which would need to be paid for from the public purse, which then took a toll on increased business rates and insurance premiums.

Among these businessmen was a guy called John Moores Jr. He was of the key figures in Liverpool's business elite who embraced the idea of social change, and was probably the most vocal about it. The Moores family owned Littlewoods, a massive catalogue retail business with a high street chain of department stores, where I had once worked in the staff canteen, and a football pools company. Littlewoods employed thousands of people in Liverpool. In 1981, it was through John Moores and his connection to the business community that a deal was brokered with the L8 Defence Committee to bring the riots to a halt – on the condition that opportunities would be opened up for the black community within their businesses.

John Moores led by example. After the riots, two of the Liverpool 8 Defence Committee members – an activist called Peter Bassey and an academic named Linda Loy – were brought into the Littlewoods organisation to help instigate an equal opportunities policy. They set up an equal ops department and then ran an annual 'positive action' scheme called 'Entry to Business' through which four black people from the community were employed by Littlewoods and put through a funded management training programme for fifteen months, in the hope that they would achieve an internal vacancy at the end of their time there. Just before going out for what would be my last trip I had got in touch with Linda Loy at Littlewoods and asked if a place on the entry to business programme was available. She'd told me to 'put in an application.' I got the job and was told I could start when I returned from sea.

So in August 1990, I paid off the *Maersk Ascension* for the last time, put away my seaman's card and discharge book and began working at Littlewoods again. It was a bit strange going back as a trainee manager, after having done the menial work of sandwich-making on the production line, at the Liverpool chain store, a couple of years earlier. Now, I was in a suit rather than an apron, and sat at the management table whenever I was in one of their stores. I guess I felt a tinge of imposter syndrome. Like I didn't belong there, as if someone like me didn't get to enjoy such privileges. My life was starting to change, and so were my

Malik fishing on the *Maersk Ascension*.

aspirations; but it would still take some time for dreams to turn to reality.

As part of the programme, after the initial three-month store management training, you'd be seconded to any part of the Littlewoods business that you wanted to work in for the subsequent twelve months. That department was obliged to take you in, train you and mentor you, but your salary didn't come out of their budget, it came from the equal opportunities department's funding. It was a win-win situation; they got free labour and you got exposure and training in an area that you'd probably have never got into if you'd gone through open recruitment, since traditionally black people were excluded from these processes. Apart from equal ops, there were a few people from ethnic minorities already working at the company. I met one South Asian woman – Aruna Arya – in marketing. She mentored me for a time and was perhaps the most diligent employee I have ever encountered. She always told me that we had to work twice as hard to get half as far as the white staff. I really respected her candour and strength. Aruna would set me tasks that had been piling up on her desk. I got a sense that people laid a lot of work at her door because she was so proficient and never complained. The result was that she never stopped working. We shared a common bond in that regard and when I left her department she gave me a sterling reference, saying I'd been an absolute asset to the team. Her approval meant a lot to me as she was the person I most respected there.

When Linda employed me, the first thing she asked was: 'What level of qualification do you have?' I had to reply: 'None to speak of.' So she said, 'OK, you're a mature student! We're going to get you to college and enrol you on a course. This is a BTEC (Business and Technology Education Council) course, so what we'd like you to do is study business and finance on day release, at our expense, and apply what you learn on the job throughout the rest of the week.'

I did a course at Millbank College in North Liverpool. I'd go there one day a week, and the other four days I spent at Littlewoods. After my three months' store management training in Southport, I decided I couldn't be a store manager. I felt far more at home with the workers than among management, and was scolded more than once for sitting at the lunch table with the workers. They'd say, 'You're management now, we don't fraternise with the workers.'

After the initial management training, I could book myself on any training course I wanted – internal or external – and they'd pay travel and accommodation if necessary. I booked myself on absolutely every course going, no matter how obscurely related. I found myself travelling regularly to Shaw Mill, the distribution centre in Oldham, and Spinney House in Liverpool – their training centre – directly next door to where I'd worked for them making sandwiches.

I had phenomenal support at Littlewoods through equal ops. If I had finance homework, for example, I'd get the top accountants there to help me. For computing, I'd do all the internal training but also have the trainers on tap if I had any IT questions. The company would send me away on weekend management courses, which they also paid for. One in particular stood out. It was a residential one-week summer school course on 'Responsibility at Work', and it was held at the College of Ripon and York St John (which is now called York St John University).

It was the first time I'd ever set foot on a university campus: it was a striking space with ornate flower beds, and there was a nineteenth-century quad, Gothic architecture and a bell tower. There were delegates there from all over the country. I recall being in a group exercise and asking a question, to which one of the other delegates looked at me and said sarcastically, 'Haven't you been to university?' It stopped me in my tracks. I quickly realised that I was among a group of management trainees who'd followed a conventional path to get here – and that involved graduating from university. I was deflated for an instant but then brushed it off and threw myself wholeheartedly into the training.

My group was awarded first place on that course and we were presented with an extra certificate in recognition. That was the moment I decided that these people were no better than me; if they could go to university, so could I.

The nurturing at Littlewoods was mirrored in my academic and training results. In the first year at college, when I got my notification of performance, I had achieved distinction in four out of five subjects towards my BTEC qualification in business and finance.

I had the option to work for one year in any department of my choice and initially picked group public relations. I spent a month or so shadowing the PR team, learning how they got editorial coverage for products, and how they'd report the effectiveness of a PR drive. This was somewhat familiar to me, as I'd done some PR with Ramona and *The Buzz* magazine in London – but this was a major corporation, so things were on another level altogether. I then went into the market information department. This was where they did all the number crunching. It was a lot of statistics and demographics, but I took to it like a duck to water. The buyers would come at me with a stack of Mintel market reports on various market sectors, and say things like: 'I'm going into a gold meeting tomorrow with a supplier, I know nothing about the gold market. Make me a summary?' I couldn't work on the floor, as it was all open-plan and it was hard to concentrate, so I found a stationery cupboard and I'd disappear into it, alone, for hours with a laptop; I'd emerge with a comprehensive summary of the market, which my colleagues would then use in their meetings to act informed in front of suppliers. I got so good at it, they all started coming to me: white goods, brown goods, sportswear, it could be anything – as long as I had the demographic and the market intel, I could churn out a comprehensive and valid report. But they still never offered me a permanent job – despite a sterling reference from Aruna.

I ended up working in an emerging brand within the group, as part of the Index marketing department, which consisted of a secretary, a marketing manager and the sales director, who'd been recently made the sales and marketing director. Index was an internal start-up, and was competing with Argos, another 'catalogue shop'. They had a hundred high street stores and were scheduled to open another twenty that year. Their marketing team were overwhelmed. The advantage, for me, was that I would have a clearly defined job – as 'National Sales and Marketing Coordinator', I got a budget of £300,000 for point-of-sale material, and I reported directly to the marketing manager and sat in on meetings with the director.

I worked all the hours – so much so that they gave me my own laptop, which I took home to work some more. There was one other guy there who was their main computer guru. This guy, Tony Bishton, was a genius. What he didn't know, didn't need knowing. He stayed late every night without fail, and so did I – usually the cleaners would throw us out. I was totally committed and became indispensable in the role – or so I thought.

Then, when my tenure on the 'Entry to Business' programme ended, they let me know, without a hint of ceremony, that there was 'no budget' to keep me on. I was dropped like I'd never been there.

It hurt, and Linda Loy was so livid she extended my salary from equal ops in the hope they'd find some budget – but that only prolonged the inevitable. John Moores's vision of equality was not shared by his board of directors and, rumour had it, he'd personally financed the scheme because the board of Littlewoods wouldn't.

The BTEC qualification – if you finished the two-year course – was the equivalent of two A-levels, enough to get you into university. The problem was that the course ran over a two-year period and my contract at Littlewoods on the 'Entry to Business' course was for only fifteen months. The assumption was that you'd be taken on in the end and then finish the BTEC in your new role.

You couldn't switch from the BTEC National Certificate (day release), which had work experience included, to the National Diploma (full-time), which was purely academic, to get the equivalent qualification – so if I didn't get kept on, I'd be unable to complete it. But I was, nonetheless, delighted to have my first-year notification of performance, which was awarded to me at the annual presentation of achievements at Littlewoods, in front of all the directors. I got an overall distinction and was presented with an award by John Moores himself. It was an incredible accolade for someone who had never achieved anything academically before. After the ceremony, Mr John – as we called him – made a beeline for me and we struck up a friendly but rather portentous conversation, which seemed mischievously contrived for the benefit of the audience. This got the attention of the directors, two of whom came over and tried to join in. As the owner of the company, Mr John had the power to completely ignore them, which he did, and then carried on talking to me. I guess he was making a point.

While Littlewoods was taking my life in one direction at this time – working nine to five, and then some – putting on a suit and tie every morning was a bit out of character for me. And seeing them charging a hundred per cent mark-up on products, plus interest – if sold on a payment plan – seemed excessive to me. I wondered if this kind of capitalist swindling wasn't for me. I persevered at Littlewoods, though I had lost my enthusiasm, seeing how they'd used me in Index marketing with a carrot and stick of sorts, holding out for the hope of being kept on, when there was never any intention of this happening. Going back to work afterwards was decidedly awkward for everyone. They would ordinarily have never had to see an employee again after their contract had been terminated. But now here I was back at my desk, with the full understanding that they had no intention of hiring me at all. My loyalty was done with, and so was I. At that point I was simply going through the motions and so was my manager. I was undergoing another far more fundamental trans-formation, and it had little to do with a salary or business: it was about my very soul.

Two years after I met Gil, I'd briefly met another black American poet and activist, Jalal Mansur Nuriddin. Jalal was a member of the New York group, the Last Poets – a spoken word outfit with a powerful political message, who had enjoyed success in the late 1960s and early 1970s with records like *This is Madness* and *At Last*, and their self-titled debut album *The Last Poets*. Discovered by Alan Douglas, producer of Jimi Hendrix, Jalal has been called the 'Grandfather of Rap' and, like Gil, his style anticipated the rise of hip-hop. In 1986, Jalal came to Liverpool to play at a festival called

Earthbeat, in Sefton Park. He was performing with another member of the Last Poets, Suliaman El Hadi. I was introduced to Jalal by a friend, a bass player called Lloyd Massett, in the backstage area. I mentioned to Jalal that I'd worked with Gil Scott-Heron and he said to me: 'Stay with the righteous and you will surely prosper.'

I bumped into Jalal and Suliaman again a couple of weeks later, outside the Methodist Church and Community Centre, on Princes Avenue in Toxteth. They were doing a residency at another community arts centre called the Blackie, and their 'artists in residency' programme was entitled 'Blessed Are Those Who Struggle' after the Last Poets album title. The Blackie (now called the Black-E) is an arts institution in Chinatown, where lots of local talent has passed through or been nurtured. From actors like Cathy Tyson (who won fame for her role in the 1986 film *Mona Lisa*) to Paul Barber (*The Full Monty*) and many others, it has spawned a lot of talented dancers, artists and musicians as well. The Last Poets had been flown over from the US by the Blackie to run a workshop for inner-city youth in Liverpool, and they also performed the concert at Sefton Park on this visit.

Jalal obviously enjoyed his time in Liverpool, because by 1991 he had moved to the city. I met him again that year at a Wailers concert, at the Town & Country venue in London. I reminded him how he'd said something profound to me in Sefton Park – 'Stay with the righteous and you will surely prosper.' He laughed and said, 'Yeh man. That sounds like something I'd say.' I asked him: 'But how will I know who the righteous are?' 'They won't be surrounded by the unrighteous!' he replied.

In the early 1990s, he was working at a recording studio called

Pink Studios on Lark Lane, in Liverpool. There was a big scene going on at Pink Studios at that time. A Greek guy called Hambi Haralambous, who'd had a moderately successful 'New Romantic' band – called Hambi & the Dance – had built the studio on the site of the old Lark Lane Motor Museum. Later, it would launch bands such as Atomic Kitten. Jalal would record there with Hambi's business partner, Andy McCluskey, of the Liverpool electro-pop band Orchestral Manoeuvres in the Dark (OMD).

There was another musical group being developed at Pink Studios called Bantu, whom Jalal was working with. They were sort of a British answer to the US hip-hop band Public Enemy. My brother Reynold had started working with Bantu, too, and had recorded some basslines on one or two of their tracks. Hambi was trying to manage Bantu, but they were a bit too street for him – and he needed someone to handle them. Knowing that I'd worked for Gil, Hambi offered me £8,000 if I'd work for him and handle Bantu. He'd signed them to a production deal at the studio and had pressed up some vinyl demo tracks and white labels to test the market, but he was a little scared of them. Hambi said to me, 'You can meet them, but I wouldn't take them to your house.' I entirely ignored Hambi's advice, and met the brothers Ibrahim Osi-Efa, Calvin Smeda and their DJ Kevin 'K-Delight' Philemon and brought them straight to my flat so we could talk informally. We clicked immediately and I told them what Hambi had offered me. After, I said, 'I'll represent you for free. If I can get you a deal, I'll take a manager's percentage; if not, you owe me nothing' – and that's what I did for a time. I thanked Hambi for his offer but turned him down. Bantu had already formed a strong relationship with Jalal, who I'd heard was living in the city. I asked the guys to take me to him and they did. That was to be the start of another profound period of spiritual transformation for me, and would lead to another lifelong bond, that only death could separate.

So there I was, doing the corporate stuff at Littlewoods in the daytime, while hanging out with an original member of the Last Poets at night. What I soon gleaned from Jalal was his deep understanding of the world – something that was very evident in his poetry. Jalal had become an orthodox Muslim in the early 1970s – and like Gil he was very spiritual. But I had a lot of religious questions that Jalal had comprehensive answers to, which Gil didn't. Gil had politicised me, but on metaphysical matters he was as confused as I was. Gil had made a record about these questions in 1994 called *Spirits* – but he didn't have the definitive answers I was seeking. His understanding was derived from his own concepts and prevailing Afrocentric ideology, which had taken root in America during the late 1960s and early 1970s and was not framed by any particular orthodox religious perspective. It was more akin to an American reinterpretation of West African tribal and cultural belief systems.

The questions I was asking Jalal were the culmination of a very strange introduction to Christianity during my childhood in care and my experiences of atheism at home. There was no talk of any God in our house, as a young child, but I was exposed to plenty of it during my years in the care homes. Attending church was part of the weekly routine at all the homes but at Greystone Heath, it had a particular significance as there was a chapel on the premises and we had a religious assembly every morning, presided over by the headmaster, Charlie Wells, who fancied himself an evangelical preacher. He had no religious training that we knew of, but he delivered a daily sermon and clearly enjoyed being in the spotlight and playing the piano accompaniment to the hymns that we were forced to sing. To us kids, rather than this being an introduction to the teachings of Christianity, it was just a performance by a cruel headmaster, who was doubling up as a pseudo-vicar.

On Sundays at Greystone, there was more of a ritual surrounding the whole God thing. We used to have to dress in our 'Sunday best' – black 'drainpipe' trousers, white shirt and tie, black blazer and these horrible two-tone mackintosh overcoats, which I can never recall being in fashion. The only one I'd ever seen, outside of Greystone, was worn by the dysfunctional old detective Columbo in the 1970s US TV series. Then we'd be split into groups of twenty or so, lined up in twos, to be frogmarched to our respective church – military style. What was surprising was that we went to different churches each week. It was either the Catholic church, in which case we were marched down Stocks Lane into Penketh, or the Methodist Wesleyan chapel, which meant walking down Liverpool Road by the train station at Great Sankey, or the Salvation Army, which involved taking the minibus into neighbouring Warrington.

It was the visits to the Catholic church that perhaps stick in my mind the most. After the humiliation of being marched in, we always had to sit at the back. None of the rest of the congregation wanted anything to do with us. Then, what really stood out, was the communion. The idea of drinking someone's blood and eating their flesh seemed almost pagan to me. The 'flesh' tasted like dried wafer and as for drinking blood – red wine – well, you can imagine what a nine-year-old thought of that.

So we were exposed to multiple versions of Christianity – and they seemed, really, like different religions – including the daily pseudo-ceremony at Greystone Heath's own in-house chapel. To my young mind, it all equated to people who were cruel to me, who wanted me to drink blood, eat flesh and sing happy songs, while treating kids like me no better than a leper. It all left a very bitter taste in my mouth.

But what these experiences did give me was a consciousness that there was a creator. This was something that my siblings didn't have at that time – because we had no religion at home and weren't otherwise exposed to it. I had big questions in my head: What if there is a hell? Why does the sun rise every morning? What happens when you die? How could drinking blood be holy? Why should I confess my sins to a priest if he's not God and can't forgive me?

I had articulated these questions to Gil, but he didn't have answers that satisfied me. He would say things like: 'The Bible says, "Thou shalt not have any other Gods before me!" Well, that means there must be other Gods!' That was both too simplistic and too ambiguous an answer, so in some sense I had never stopped searching for a better one.

I'd been hanging out with Bantu and had heard that Jalal was back in Liverpool and had been in the Pink Studios with the group, so I asked Ibrahim – the bandleader – to take me to see him. He appeared hesitant at first, but eventually agreed.

In Liverpool at that time, a lot of black folks drank the strongest of beers. For us, these were Carlsberg Special Brew, Tennent's

Super (Super-T) and Gold Label barley wine (I have no idea why it's called 'barley wine' 'cause it comes in a can and tastes like malt liquor). The day I'd turned up at Jalal's flat for our first sit-down encounter, I recall having a can of Super-T in my hands. Ibrahim had told me on the way there that 'Jalal don't like people drinking alcohol you know?' I'd replied rather arrogantly 'No one's gonna tell me I can't have my beer, man, that's his problem not mine.' Ibrahim ignored the comment and we proceeded anyway. I sat talking to Jalal with my beer in hand and he never mentioned it or expressed any displeasure, he was more interested in the depth of our discussion than what I was drinking. My questions came hard and fast, and the answers came equally rapidly. I told him at one point, 'Hold on, man, slow down! Let me absorb your answers?' He said, 'I'll slow down with the answers, when you slow down with the questions', and that's how my path to Islam started.

I posed the same religious questions to Jalal that I'd posed previously to Gil but he had a totally different take on things. We talked about the history of the time when Jesus was around. Particularly about the role of the Romans. Jalal would say things like, 'The Romans were Jesus's enemies, they wanted to silence him and kill him. Why should you then take Jesus's story from the people who wanted to kill him?' He also said, 'The New Testament was mostly written by Paul. Did you know that Paul never met Jesus?' This threw me, as I'd assumed that Paul was one of the disciples. In church they always referred to him as 'the apostle Paul'. Jalal explained that the Romans had a puppet king – Herod – on the throne and were forcing the Jews to reinterpret their scripture (the Torah) to accommodate Roman idolatry and decadence. That Jesus was not 'the son of God' but rather a prophet, sent to correct the Jews' misinterpretations since the Romans had started to corrupt their teachings.

He explained that these misinterpretations were propagated by corrupt rabbis, who'd altered the text of the Torah (the basis of the Old Testament) to confound the Jews, so they could align with the rich, pagan Romans, who worshipped families of Gods. Jalal explained that Paul was such a character, who took the Roman coin and was granted Roman citizenship; he was sent in by the Romans as an imposter, to misguide the Jews who believed in only one creator. It was in fact Paul who introduced the idea of Jesus being the 'Son of God'. That would make Mary the 'Mother of God' and God the 'Father'. This is how the Roman Catholic Church adopted the concept of a trinity. The trinity was already present in Greek, Roman and Egyptian belief systems – and the Romans were trying to craft these pagan myths onto the Hebrew monotheistic beliefs.

Jalal told me about the Essenes – Jews who were driven out of Judea by the Romans, for refusing to adopt these new, what they called 'Hellenistic', interpretations of the Hebrew scriptures – and how the Essenes preserved the original scriptures before the Romans had them edited. He told me about the 1969 discovery in the Qumran Caves of the 'Dead Sea Scrolls', which contained original pre-Romanic versions of the Torah and also other prophetic works, and which contradicted the version that found its way into the Old Testament. This started me on new lines of enquiry and ignited my interest in religious history. I wanted to understand the context in which these events occurred, because I had also noticed many discrepancies in the Bible that troubled me.

Jalal gave me a translated copy of the Gospel of Barnabas. I knew Barnabas was a disciple of Jesus but I wondered why – if he wrote a Gospel – it wasn't in the Bible?

Jalal explained that the Gospels of 'Matthew', 'Mark', 'Luke' and 'John' were all written by Paul and falsely attributed to the disciples – so as to appear credible. Paul himself was not a disciple of Jesus. He informed me that 'most of the New Testament was written by Paul' and that 'Paul had been instrumental in killing the followers of Jesus'. He told me that a story was cooked up of him having a vision on the road to Damascus, where he saw a blinding light, fell from his horse and repented his sins and believed. But even if this were so, it was after Jesus was gone – and although Paul is recorded as having travelled with the disciples, they described him as a having 'heretical beliefs' due to his assertion that Jesus was the 'Son of God'. This totally blew my mind but I wanted evidence. Jalal said: 'Read the Gospel of Jesus's disciple Barnabas. He explains it better than I could.'

I felt angry at this point, that if this was true all my life I'd been lied to by the clergy who had tried to misguide me. I took the Gospel of Barnabas and read it. It was like a key that unlocked all the discrepancies I'd found in the Bible, and explained why the Romans had co-opted Jesus's teachings and rebranded them in the image of Roman beliefs. I found out that Christianity was invented two hundred years after Jesus, in Rome, meaning that Jesus himself was never a Christian and that the beliefs he espoused were directly in contradiction to those of the Catholic Church. The Bible itself was compiled four hundred years after Jesus and the Romans decided which books went in and which didn't. They put in the books by Paul – whom Barnabas described as an imposter – which suited the Romans' purposes, of course, and they excluded all of the books by the twelve disciples of Jesus, including Barnabas's Gospel where he describes Paul as 'the liar' who is promoting the 'heretical belief' that 'Jesus is the son of God'. Barnabas goes on to say, 'I say to you that Jesus is the son of man.' It all became clear to me, that the Romans had done a major edit and shifted the holy lands from the Middle East to Rome – the centre of their imperial power base. But what to do with this new knowledge?

Through my conversations with Jalal, I started to understand Islam in a way I never had before, and found it gave me answers to all the questions I had spent years asking. At this point I had still not read the Quran – the holy scripture of the Muslim faith – but I was starting to understand that Prophet Muhammad was of the lineage of Prophet Abraham, and therefore had the same ancestral origins of all the Hebrew prophets. That the angel Gabriel revealed the Quran to Muhammad, as he had revealed the Gospels to Jesus and the Psalms to David. That there was a whole chapter in the Quran named after Mary, which described in detail the immaculate conception of Jesus but refuted entirely the story of the nativity. That the nativity story was identical to the story of the birth of the Babylonian god Baal. It was to be a momentous awakening. I started to realise why there was so much propaganda against Islam. It was a classic case of discredit the witness so they'll never listen to the evidence.

Jalal proved to be a great teacher. Within a few months, I was seriously contemplating becoming a Muslim but before embarking on this next step, I decided to take a break and get some perspective on where my life was going.

In December of 1991, I booked a holiday to go back to Ascension Island for Christmas. It was a place so unique and so full of natural beauty – a volcanic island that just popped up in the middle of the South Atlantic Ocean – and it was home to so much diverse and wondrous tropical wildlife: giant green sea turtles and every kind of shark, manta ray, porpoise and dolphin. It was a place where I could relax, think, and become one with nature, away from the hustle and bustle of the city.

As I was boarding the plane for my visit, they gave me a form that asked: 'In the event of death, who should be contacted?' I gave my mum's name. It then asked: 'What religion would you like to be buried as?' I wrote, 'Islam.' That was the first acknowledgement that Islam was going to be my religion.

I spent my month in the South Atlantic reading another of Alex Haley's books, *The Autobiography of Malcolm X*, about the black American civil rights activist who became an orthodox Muslim, before being assassinated by his black nationalist pseudo-religious former associates.

Malcolm X's introduction to Islam was through the so-called 'Nation of Islam'. This was – at the time – a relatively new religious cult founded in Detroit in the 1930s, which sought to co-opt Islam with a perversion of the faith in order to use it as a vehicle to recruit disgruntled black people to their black nationalist creed. I had been troubled by the Nation of Islam and had talked a lot with Jalal about this subject. Through Malcolm X's autobiography, I came to realise that whilst the Nation had some strong and valid perceptions of black history, it was in fact a cult, a skewed and pseudo version of true Islam. The book explains why Malcolm X left the Nation. Reading it, and understanding

Malcolm X's journey into and out of the Nation and finally on to Mecca and true Islam, helped me see the real faith – and from there everything clicked into place for me.

What the Nation was in relation to the actual religion of Islam, was no different to what the KKK is to Christianity. Alex Hayley's book was to settle any lingering doubts I had about becoming a Muslim. Malcolm X, like me, had grown up running the streets and had been incarcerated at a young age when he had a religious awakening – albeit a misguided one. So his life had lots of parallels with my own, to which I could definitely relate.

I also decided on Ascension Island that if I did convert, I needed to leave Littlewoods and move on. Despite my success there, all I was being offered at the end of the Entry to Business course was a trainee manager post, in a store out in Chester. I wanted to move forward in advertising and marketing, which was my chosen field. It was very demoralising to hit such roadblocks, after achieving so much – and I still believe there was an undercurrent of racism at the company that stopped me achieving more. Jalal was encouraging me to get back into the music business with him, based on what I had done with Gil, so I decided this was to be my new focus.

On my return to Liverpool, I headed straight for Jalal and told him I wanted to take the shahada – the declaration of faith – and become a Muslim. He asked me, 'Are you sure?' I said, 'Yes!' So I took the shahada that same day.

'*La ilaha il Allah Muhammad Ar Rasul Allah*. There is no Deity worthy to be worshipped except the Deity and Muhammad is the Messenger of the Deity.'

That night I performed my first prayer in congregation in

Liverpool. I recall shaking as we prostrated, feeling overwhelmingly that I was bowing down to the creator of all mankind and all creation. The following day, I went back into Index at Littlewoods. I took one look around and thought to myself, I've done so much for you guys and I've not been able to secure a decent job despite that. So I tell you what, I'm out of contract – the fifteen months have passed – so I don't need to give you notice. I'm leaving! I suddenly felt a great sense of clarity and did not hesitate in the slightest to walk out. They were shocked, as the marketing manager had just adjusted to the fact that she was going to get me for free for another few months, after Linda Loy's intervention – the marketing team had dangled the carrot to keep me keen but, really, they had shown no intention of keeping me on, and so I felt no loyalty towards them.

That day I left Littlewoods for good, and the next I boarded a plane for Nice in the South of France. It was the biggest date in the music business calendar – MIDEM, which is the Cannes Music Festival – and I was representing Bantu and Jalal.

I had to blag my way into the festival itself, but once I did I started networking hard in the hopes of securing a deal for either or both artists.

That night in MIDEM, I was offered a beer and tipped it back. It took a few sips to remember that I was a Muslim now, and that Muslims didn't drink. Those cold swigs of beer were the last taste of alcohol I ever had. I have never touched a drop since 1992.

My decision to become a Muslim was initially met with great hostility by my family. This was heartbreaking for me – I thought they would be happy, but the news came as a real shock. There had been no religion at home – no God – my mum was a socialist and my dad had been a black nationalist. I think if I had become a Christian, they would have been less taken aback, but Islam was a wholly foreign thing to them and they couldn't reconcile what it meant, or how it had happened. I remember my mum, when I told her, shouting in disbelief: 'But there is no God!'

The news wasn't well received by my siblings either, who also didn't understand much about Islam. Why should they? Reynold's perceptions were rooted in tropes such as 'Islam butchers women', a reference to female circumcision. I later found out that this was a pre-Islamic East African cultural practice, and that East African Christians, Muslims and animists all did it. It has no basis in Islam and the other ninety per cent of the world's Muslim populations abhorred the practice and outlawed it.

But there are common misconceptions and false perspectives that a lot of people have on matters like this, and in the absence of an alternative narrative, they remained unchallenged and wrongly construed as truth, when in fact they are not. I faced a lot of hostility initially, but as time went on most of my family became more accepting of my beliefs and were not so hostile to me, at least not visibly so. My new religion meant I also shed a good few friends, but I figured it was a release of dead weight.

It was the way that Islam allowed me to change for the better that helped the people in my life accept the change. First of all, I stopped drinking. I wasn't an alcoholic before, but I had always been a big drinker – and my lifestyle, one way or another, from London to the oil tankers, had been built around boozing. Suddenly I didn't drink at all. I stopped going to clubs, became celibate awaiting marriage, and in 1994 I even gave up smoking cigarettes.

I had always been the black sheep of the family, the one who got in trouble or brought drama to the door. I went from that, to being the one living a more wholesome life; it was a shift in the family dynamic. I had become a different person and they respected me for it. Years later, my mother even started giving my children presents for Eid, and my siblings would come for Eid parties.

CHAPTER 12

HUSTLERS CONVENTION LIVE

Earlier that same year, another drama was gestating and about to explode. It would not only reopen old wounds, which I was trying desperately to salve, but would also start a chain of events that would rip the mask off the whole pseudo-righteous network of institutions masquerading as the 'care system'.

I was sitting in my flat in Liverpool on a February evening in 1992, when the doorbell rang. I opened it to two plain-clothed police officers who identified themselves as being from Widnes CID. Widnes is the neighbouring town to Warrington and borders Great Sankey, where Greystone Heath was. After ascertaining who I was, the policemen asked me if I had ever been a resident at Greystone Heath. I told them I had been, on and off, between 1975 and 1982 – and asked why.

They wanted to know if I had come across 'someone called Alan Langshaw'? 'Yes,' I said. 'He worked on Poplars A unit.'

Langshaw was being investigated over allegations of sexual abuse against children at Greystone Heath. He had worked two periods of employment at the institution, one before I'd arrived there – in 1975 – and another subsequent to my arrival, in about 1976. By the time he'd arrived in '76, I had already been assigned to Pines A unit, under Bill Morris, so I'd avoided coming into direct contact with the man until much later, when I was transferred to a unit that adjoined Langshaw's. I was never under his care, except on the occasional weekend, when he'd provide cover, if my housemaster was off duty. I knew him, but not that well.

I remembered him being the only house parent at Greystone who didn't have a wife with him. He'd told us that his wife had 'died of cancer'. I assumed that's why he'd had a hiatus between his stints working at Greystone. I also recalled that he had been known to have favourites among the boys.

At the time, I guess I knew there was something not quite right about him, although at my young age, I couldn't say exactly what this was. The police asked me if Langshaw 'ever took anyone into his house' that adjoined the unit and I told them what I knew: that there were three boys, in particular, who would go into his house in the evenings, to watch telly. He even took them on holidays to London and when they came back they had brand-new football kits. The other kids used to call them 'Langshaw's bum chums', but until that day I'd never stopped to think what that phrase might actually have meant. The gravity of what was being revealed by the police visit started to sink in, and I suddenly felt physically sick. The police were digging to try to get me to recall even the smallest of details, but not having lived in his unit, I guess most of what I could tell them amounted to little more than hearsay – though it would no doubt corroborate the stories of others.

The policemen who came to see me that day had used a process that became known as 'trawling' – a policy by which they would contact anyone whose name was connected to an institution where someone was being investigated, and invite them to give testimony. Trawling was later banned because it led to a number of false claims of abuse, which undermined legitimate prosecutions.

But in truth, had it not been for that policy – flawed as it may have been – the true scope of abuse may never have been uncovered, in this and many other institutions that I'd had the misfortune to be interned within. I told the officers at my flat what I knew. I said that while I had not been sexually abused, I had been physically and racially abused at Greystone. I had also suffered what became known as 'pindown' (solitary confinement of children) at the Liverpool Children's Admission Unit when I was just nine years old. But the police were somewhat single-minded in their investigations at that time. They wanted to uncover sexual abuse at Greystone and since I was not a victim of this particular crime, they had no further use for me. After opening up a massive can of worms, they left me distraught and horrified.

I started to hyperventilate after they left and struggled to calm my breathing. The police had said that because my experiences were not part of their investigation, they couldn't help me, but they had given me an NSPCC helpline number to call. I phoned in an almost desperate manner, struggling even to form coherent sentences. After speaking to an advisor for about an hour, which was mostly spent trying to calm me down enough to understand why I was calling, they also told me that they couldn't help me. They advised me to 'call the Samaritans' if I 'felt suicidal' and to contact a solicitor – which I did.

The whole episode had hit me like a sledgehammer. I was in the middle of my first Ramadan – fasting as a fledgling Muslim. Everything in my life had been moving in a positive direction: my life had been totally transformed since meeting Gil in 1984, just as I had come into adulthood. I had travelled the world, found Islam, moved from menial labour to white-collar office work and I was looking into applying for university. Then the darkness of my childhood in care was suddenly thrust back into focus – centre stage – and it hurt, all over again. I was beside myself.

Initially, the lawyers didn't want to take my case because they were unsure if it would attract 'legal aid' funding from the government; also because it was historic and likely to be beyond the limitation period allowed by law to bring a claim – and because there was no sexual abuse in my case and that was what the police investigation was focused upon. The lawyers felt they would have a better chance of securing civil compensation for victims if there were criminal prosecutions to support the evidence. But then a slew of people came forward and most of the criminal and civil law firms in Liverpool were inundated with allegations from new claimants. Before long, a whole swathe of class actions was launched, relating to allegations of child abuse in almost every care home in North West England, in what became known as 'The North West Child Abuse Cases'.

Several years later, BBC *Panorama* did a programme about Langshaw's sexual abuse of children and used footage of Greystone

Heath. I called the BBC and had them mail me the transcript, which I gave to my lawyer. It turned out that Langshaw had been investigated previously in 1986 for sexually abusing boys in his care but the Tory politician Edwina Currie had chosen to exonerate him whilst she was Parliamentary Under-Secretary of State for Health with responsibility for the childcare system. At the time when they finally arrested Langshaw, after the initial aborted investigation, he was employed in a senior role with responsibility to write a policy review on child abuse for Southport Council. A 1997 BBC *Panorama* report, 'Hear No Evil', reported:

> In November 1994 Alan Langshaw pleaded guilty to thirty
> specimen charges of buggery, indecent assault and gross
> indecency. He confessed to abuse at Greystone Heath, St
> Vincent's and against teenagers with learning difficulties at
> Halton College in Widnes. He was jailed for ten years having
> admitted abusing boys in his care for twenty-two years.

I was twenty-six when the police had knocked on my door, investigating Langshaw, for what I came to understand later was in fact the second time. I had locked the whole care experience stuff away and now, as unwelcome as it was, all the details started coming back to me. I found myself reliving the whole experience in forensic detail.

It couldn't have come at a worse time for me. Later in 1992, after years of painstaking restoration of my failed childhood education, I was finally accepted at a university to do a degree course. I was due to start in September at Liverpool, but what should have been a triumphant time was tainted by this trauma.

Also, with Jalal and Bantu asking me to manage them, I'd taken a huge step forward in my music business career, from being a runner for Gil into real artist management.

It felt serendipitous, in a way, that Gil's career had started with him being influenced by Jalal and the Last Poets, and now I was using everything I'd learned with Gil to work so closely with them. He had given me the most rigorous training through sheer generosity, and now I could parse contracts and negotiate hard on terms, I could manage all the logistics with the band, I could run merchandising, touring and recordings in parallel. Everything was aligning, and the legal case was a distraction that I could have done without.

While Gil was on the road a lot in the early 1990s, Jalal and the Last Poets weren't touring that much at all. Gil managed himself as an artist. Jalal, by contrast, was badly in need of an advocate. Here was the man known around the world as the 'Grandfather of Rap' but he'd received hardly any financial reward for all his musical innovations. To understand why, you need to go back to the very beginning of the Last Poets.

Jalal was born in 1944 in New York, and grew up in Fort Greene in Brooklyn. His birth name was Lawrence Padilla but, like many black Americans during the civil rights era, he changed it to an African name and became known, for a time, as Alafia Pudim. This was his name when he cofounded the Last Poets with Umar Bin Hassan and Abiodun Oyewole, and percussionist Nilijah, in 1968. (Alafia Pudim changed his name again later to become Jalal Mansur Nuriddin, when he converted to Islam.)

The Last Poets took their name from a poem by a South African poet called Little Willie Kgositsile, who was a member of the African National Congress, but was living in exile in New York in the 1960s. He believed that he was living in the 'last age of poetry' and that guns would take the place of poems. The early members of the group would meet at the Harlem writers' workshop known as the East Wind Associates.

They started performing for the community, on the basketball courts in Harlem in 1968, with politically charged spoken word and percussive accompaniment from Nilijah's conga drum. They were considered – by many at that time – as 'the voice of the people' and Jalal and Umar would often tell me that becoming a 'hit act' in music business terms was never one of their intentions when they joined. 'We were just kids in the neighbourhood,' they said. 'We knew what was going on in society and on the streets – we just wanted to stand up and tell the people.'

With the murders of Dr King and Malcolm X and the jailing of the Black Panthers, and with so many other activists going into self-imposed exile from America, the civil rights movement shifted from politics to poetry. The political vacuum that was forming in the late 1960s left the people looking for a new movement to follow. Record producer, Alan Douglas – having worked with Jimi Hendrix and a number of jazz acts including Miles Davis and Art Blakey – sensed the mood of the people, and saw that there was a market for radical black activists or artists with a 'right on' message. When he heard of the Last Poets' performances, he reached out to Abiodun (aka Dun). He was shocked to hear Dun tell him: 'Nah, man, we ain't coming downtown, if you wanna hear us, you gotta come uptown, to Harlem.'

Douglas rode into Harlem in his Jaguar, pushed through the crowds on the basketball court, while Dun told him, 'You stand there?' Then they launched into their radical set of hard-hitting proto-rap rhymes and blew the whole court away. Douglas immediately signed them to his label – Douglas Records – and released their first album, the self-titled *The Last Poets*, in 1970. This record included the track 'Niggers Are Scared of Revolution', which established the Last Poets as principal exponents of the Black Arts Movement, and sold a reputed one million copies by word of mouth alone.

Gil wrote his early hit 'The Revolution Will Not Be Televised' as a response to the Last Poets' poem 'When the Revolution Comes' from that same album.

Jalal had learned to 'toast' – a form of bragging rhyme that started on death row in US prisons and grew to become part of prison culture – when he himself was in prison. This was different from the form of 'toasting' that had developed later in Jamaica, where singers freestyled patois lyrics over reggae instrumental tracks called 'dub plates'. Jamaican toasting was very melodic, often with singing as well as freestyling. American jail toasting was purely spoken word, often with no music at all, and there were no choruses, so it didn't have a conventional song structure. They were essentially epic stories told in poetic form but often recited rhythmically, with a discernible meter that you'd expect in poetry. Jalal had learned some classic 'jail toasts' such as 'The Titanic' and 'The Signifying Monkey' – which was later made famous by the comedian character Dolemite, played by Rudy Ray Moore.

While Douglas may have been astute in seeing the potential of the group's poetry, it is unlikely he would have foreseen exactly how much of an impact they would have on black music for the next fifty years, particularly the next project they embarked upon: a jail toast which Jalal had written, called *Hustlers Convention*.

When Douglas took Jalal to a place to record this new jail toast, there was a band rehearsing in the room below. Douglas thought the music would go well with Jalal's rhymes, so he went down and asked the band if he could put it together. That band was the up-and-coming jazz-funk act Kool & the Gang, and they agreed to allow their music to be used on three of the tracks. Unfortunately, Kool & the Gang failed to tell Douglas they were signed to a different label, so when *Hustlers Convention* (which listed Jalal's pseudonym, Lightnin' Rod, as the artist) was released, their label threatened Douglas's distributors – United Artists – with a lawsuit. United Artists promptly withdrew the record and it quickly died a commercial death. Only 20,000 copies were distributed before the record was deleted from the market.

But news of this fresh epic jail toast spread quickly in the ghettos, and the few people that had it started to promote it. It became something of an enigma across black America. People thought it was just another jail toast and memorised it and passed it on to others orally, which was how all jail toasts were learned at that time; so within a few short years, it was considered to have never been recorded, as most people had – by then – learned it orally on the streets. Despite its troubled start, *Hustlers Convention* went on to become one of the most influential records in hip-hop history. Melle Mel, the singer with one of the first hip-hop groups – Grandmaster Flash and the Furious Five – memorised it and then released it as his own, on his group's eponymous 1984 album. It has been sampled by hip-hop giants Nas, Wu Tang Clan and the Beastie Boys. Public Enemy's Chuck D described its importance by saying it is 'a verbal Bible for people trying to understand the streets. It posed the question: "What is this life that's ahead of me, and how can I actually figure out how to handle it?"'

But despite having so much influence, by the early 1990s Jalal was very suspicious of the industry, in particular the business side of things. He focused purely on being creative. The upshot of this was that by the time I met Jalal and started working with him, about twenty years after *Hustlers Convention*, the Last Poets had made seven albums, a number of singles and played on some collaborations but Jalal was not receiving a penny in royalties – from any of them. He wasn't even registered with any of the royalty collection societies.

I said to him: 'You need to get the business side sorted out.'

'Malik, I'm a poet,' Jalal told me. 'I can't be a poet and a businessman.'

That's how we started working together back in 1992. So while Jalal was teaching me about Islam, I started representing him, looking at how I could pull in the recognition and recompense he deserved.

It became evident that the Last Poets were so entangled in contracts with various record companies that had clearly ripped them off, that it would take a good lawyer a long time to get to the bottom of it of all. My primary objective was to get Jalal in a position where he could launch a legal challenge to these contracts, whilst also trying to get him in a situation where he could at least collect royalties from the music he was making now.

But even this was not easy. I'd tell him, 'Jalal, we need to fill out some forms', and he would say to me, 'Malik, man. I'm a poet.

You deal with that stuff.' So I would fill the forms in and tell Jalal to sign them. Eventually, Jalal started receiving his royalties, for the first time, in a recording career that began in 1968.

In my eyes, this was all about correcting an injustice. There was no money in it for me. From January through to September of 1992, I made about £500.

Trying to market Jalal as a solo project was difficult, too, because people knew him as a Last Poet and the industry wanted younger people. The Poets were not an easy sell anyway, as they had a reputation for being 'in your face' and confrontational and it scared music business people off. For me, working in music management for the first time, I suppose it was what you call 'a steep learning curve'. But it was worth it: with Jalal, I knew I was working with a significant figure in black music.

With Jalal at BBC Radio 5 promoting *Hustlers Convention*.

Aside from all the contractual problems, there were positive aspects to it all. A big opportunity arose while Jalal and Suliaman had begun to mix their latest Last Poets album – *Scatterap/Home* – in the studio in Paris with their vibraphonist Kenyatte Abdur-Rahman, for Bond-Age Records. A chance came up for a Last Poets reunion with former members and one of the group's former producers, Bill Laswell, in the US.

Two early members, Abiodun Oyewole and Umar Bin Hassan, both re-emerged and decided they wanted to rejoin the existing line-up with Jalal and Suliaman. The last piece in the jigsaw was a percussionist called Abu Mustapha – who had played with the group in the early days; he came out of jail and had also come over to live in Paris, as had the vibraphonist Kenyatte. Abu Mustapha also wanted to re-join the band, but this would involve making something happen business-wise so that they could be sustained.

All the poets had had some initial discussions with Laswell, and we were invited to go to New York where Jalal and Suliaman could record some demos for what was supposed to become a Last Poets' reunion album.

Laswell's studio was in a run-down area of Queens. When I'd set off for the US, I'd changed my cash into traveller's cheques in US dollar denominations, as a security measure, knowing how dodgy New York could be. At least if you got your traveller's cheques stolen, they could be cancelled, and you could have them replaced.

I tried to cash the cheques in a bank in Harlem first. They had the American Express sign in the window. I queued up, waited my turn and then presented it to the teller, who called the manager.

We had a lengthy discussion, where I reiterated that they advertised American Express, and this was an American Express traveller's cheque – in US dollars – so why couldn't they cash it? Neither the teller nor the manager had ever seen or even heard of a traveller's cheque. I guess Harlem wasn't a tourist destination. Finally the bank manager said, 'Look, I'm gonna cash a $20 for you, but only so I can find out what it is.' I was pretty shocked. I mean, I'd cashed traveller's cheques in Nigeria, Turkey and the Caribbean; this was the bastion of first-world economics, and they didn't even know what their own 'American Express' US dollar traveller's cheque was.

I had a similar experience in Queens, when we first visited Laswell's studio. Again I wandered into a bank with the American Express sticker in the window and queued up. I noticed that everyone was looking at me and it occurred to me that I was the only non-white person in the bank. Before I got to the teller, the manager walked up to me in the queue and asked, 'What do you want?' I said, 'To cash an American Express traveller's cheque.' He said, 'You can't.' 'Why not?' I asked. 'You don't have an account here,' he said. 'I asked him, 'How do you know I don't have an account here?' To which he replied, 'You're not Polish and this is a Polish bank.' At this point I was getting extremely pissed off with America. 'OK then, open me an account?' I retorted. 'I can't,' he said, 'you're not Polish.' I was about to say, 'How do you know I'm not Polish?' But then the absurdity of the situation overcame me, and I gave in and left.

Just as I arrived at the address of the studio, I made one last attempt to cash a traveller's cheque. I figured if I could buy something small in a store, they'd give me the change in cash and that would be as good as cashing one in a bank. So I went into a deli-catessen, which had lots of sandwiches and condiments laid out and a big spit roast, like you get in an Arab shop, for chicken shawarma or doner kebabs. I went to the counter and asked the Polish man behind it, 'Do you take traveller's cheques?' He walked over to the spit and drew a three-foot-long knife from behind the gas pipes, walked back to the counter, leant over it with the knife erect like a Cossack soldier with his sword drawn, which he held about six inches from my cheek. He said menac-ingly in a thick Polish accent: 'What did you say?'

Realising the imminent threat of the knife, the obvious hostility of the Polish kebab man and the now familiar absurdity of American city life, I held my ground and equally firmly restated – in an unequivocal manner – 'Do! You! Take! Traveller's! Cheques?' To which he snarled 'No!' I retreated cautiously, never taking my eye off the knife and being careful not to flinch or show any fear, in case he freaked out and decided to slice me like a kebab.

By the time I got to the studio, I was pretty traumatised and reassessing the country I was in. We introduced ourselves and I asked Laswell why it was so difficult to cash a traveller's cheque in America. He said, 'Oh man, you have to go to Manhattan to do that, where the tourists go. Check out one of those bureau de changes around Times Square, they'll cash it for you.' So the next day, that's what I did. I got on the subway all the way from 169th Street to 42nd Street, just to transfer my money into a spendable currency. It was a trip, all right: I noticed that the train started off a hundred per cent black in the Bronx, then as we passed 125th St in Harlem, it started to get a little whiter, until I reached 42nd street, and apart from Asian tourists it was almost entirely white.

That's when Jim Crow segregation and the whole apartheid racist ideology started to become clear to me. America was no better than South Africa. It was just as segregated and just as racist, and it made me feel sick.

Regardless, the whole Laswell album proposal was gearing up to be promising. It would be on the Axiom label, distributed by Island Records. Though we had no idea a feud was brewing behind closed doors.

I guess the fact that there were plans afoot for solo albums, on top of the band reunion, didn't help. I had started to talk to Jalal about the possibility of him making a solo record.

Meanwhile, Jalal and Suliaman were talking with former Last Poets Umar Bin Hassan and Abiodun Oyewole about how the Last Poets' reunion album might work. They may have been equal members back in the early 1970s but a lot of things had happened since then, a lot of records had been made. This left some questions. Who was going to be in charge? Also, who had the rights to the name the 'Last Poets'?

Soon after we arrived in New York, Umar brought in a black female lawyer from Connecticut, who suggested that they trade-mark the name – the Last Poets. The next step they'd planned was the new album with Bill Laswell. They'd cut the demos and were waiting on Laswell to decide what he wanted to do. Time was passing and Suliaman, Jalal and I eventually returned to France to finish mixing *Scatterap/Home* with Kenyatte, who was already back there.

We were all planning to go back to America, as soon as Laswell had talked to Chris Blackwell – the owner of Island Records, who distributed Laswell's Axiom label – to get a budget to do the album. But it never happened. Laswell stopped taking our calls. After talking to Blackwell, he decided to exclude Jalal, Suliaman and Abiodun – and make a solo album with Umar. That record, *Be Bop or Be Dead*, was subsequently released on Axiom and distributed by Island. Umar and Abiodun then registered the Last Poets as a trademark, excluding Suliaman and Jalal, who were then legally obliged to stop using the name. At the time, Jalal and Suliaman didn't have the money to challenge this, but they were pissed. Umar and Abiodun had left the band in 1976 after *Jazzoetry* and *At Last* were released, and Jalal and Suliaman had produced several albums and kept the band and the name alive since then. So now, sixteen years after they'd left, they had returned, convinced Jalal and Suliaman to let them back into the group, only to throw them both out of it.

Two years later, Suliaman passed away – and by then, Jalal decided there was no point in contesting it. *Scatterap/Home*, which was finally released in 1994 on Bond-Age Records in France, was to become the final studio album bearing the name the Last Poets and featuring Jalal and Suliaman.

After that, I helped Jalal pursue a solo career, acting as a consultant while I was still at university, advising him to set up his own label and put out his own albums. I gave him a list of things he needed to do to make this happen. Jalal eventually moved to France, took on a manager called Monty, and did set up his own label – called On the One – and released the records *Fruits of Rap*, *Science Friction* and *On the One* on that label, as well as two compilations entitled: *Prime Time Rhyme of The Last Poets, Vol. 1 & 2*.

Despite all the drama, there was something of a happy ending to the story of my management of Jalal many years later. While

I was proud to have helped him get his second solo career started, under his name 'Jalal', there remained some unfinished business and that was Jalal's epic masterpiece *Hustlers Convention*.

It had never been performed live since it was recorded in 1972, and released in 1973, so in 2014 I was commissioned by a film company in Manchester, called Riverhorse, to produce a live show of *Hustlers Convention* for its fortieth anniversary, for film director Mike Todd. I was also hired as the Associate Producer, and worked voluntarily as the publicist for the film. The Executive Producer was Public Enemy's Chuck D.

I put on the show in London with the help of musical director Orphy Robinson, who painstakingly deconstructed the original music and hired a stellar band of musicians to realise Jalal's vision of 'The Hustlers Convention Live' at the Jazz Café in London. It coincided with the long-awaited reissue of the album. Charly Records, who had, by various meandering legalities and some other irregularities, acquired the rights, rereleased the album and co-sponsored the event. Jalal agreed to perform on one condition – that my band, Malik & the O.G's would open the show.

Orphy had helped me put my live band together and produce our first live show for the inaugural LIMF (Liverpool International Music Festival) at Sefton Park in 2012, for curator Yaw Owusu. Simon Glinn had initially arranged for me to meet Orphy at Liverpool Philharmonic Hall and he went on to create the live band of Malik & the O.G's, who opened that night for Jalal's *Hustlers Convention* fortieth anniversary.

The event was organised in conjunction with the documentary film to facilitate the segment of the narrative that traced the record's origins and then brought it into the present. This set Jalal in his true context as the writer of *Hustlers Convention*, and cleared up any doubts as to who it was that released the first-ever gangster rap album. But more importantly, it gave Jalal a public platform to explain why he wrote it.

He'd characterised all the street hustlers and all the political and economic Wall Street hustlers, and put them in the same bag, making no distinction, other than to say: the politicians and bankers make more money from their hustle, and the black man on the street gets all the blame for his little hustle and fills up jail cells as a result. His intention was not to glamorise hustling, but to characterise it and set it into context so that people would understand its allure and see that all that glitters is not gold. The problem was that the album ran away with itself on the underground circuit, under a pseudonym. Without an artist laying claim to it, people were interpreting it for themselves. It was so slick; people took to copying it by glamorising their own hustles, and what we know as gangster rap today was born.

The show was attended by a whole host of music royalty: Alan Douglas himself came through, as did Gilles Peterson, cofounder of Acid Jazz Records. Actress Cathy Tyson was there, and rapper Longsy D. The high priest of funk, George Clinton, sat at my table and watched the whole show – including my set – having arrived with Jalal's former French manager Monty. The band consisted of Gil Scott-Heron's drummer Rod Youngs, Brand New Heavies' trombone player Dennis Rollins, jazz virtuoso vocalist Cleveland Watkiss, guitarist Mo Nazam, pianist Jonathan Idiagbonya, Gil Scott-Heron's percussionist and flautist Ebo Shakur, bassist Tiago Coimbra and backing vocalist Chantelle Nandi, with vibraphonist Orphy Robinson as the musical director.

The original engineer who'd recorded the album in 1972 – Ron St Germain – flew in and did a multi-track recording of the audio, with the help of my engineer Tom Parker, to be mixed at a later date for both the soundtrack to the film and a possible *Hustlers Convention* live album. The whole event oozed credibility. Prior to the show, I had decided to spin it as a news item, rather than a gig. It worked, and we were inundated with press.

I told reporters that this album was to hip-hop what the Rosetta Stone was to Egyptian hieroglyphics. It was the cipher to decode the whole thing, and make it all make sense. The press ate it up to such an extent that Jalal told me, 'Malik, if you book me one more interview, I'm not gonna do the show.' Then Monty arrived with George Clinton from Funkadelic and an offer of a BBC Radio 6 Music interview with Jalal and George Clinton, and I had to turn it down.

But that night, Jalal had his big moment where he was centre stage – and everyone who mattered was present, and he delivered his message, and introduced me and my band to his fan base. It was a huge endorsement for me, and a recognition of all the work I'd done over the years in the background with little or no remuneration. This was Jalal's way of paying me back – and I am, to this day, grateful for it. Jalal wanted to set the record straight, and this show in February of 2014 and the film the following year did just that. Finally, Jalal got a measure of closure and satisfaction from it, although he always claimed that he 'chose the message over the money' and for that, he earned everyone's respect.

CHAPTER 13

THE COURT CASE

My early work in music management took up much of my time and energy in 1992, but it didn't prevent me from pursuing my dream of going to university. I was studying at the Liverpool Institute of Higher Education, later renamed Liverpool Hope University.

I had to find subjects that required little or no prior experience, particularly those that did not require you to have an A-level qualification in the subject. I also had to rule out anything that had a significant science component, as I had studied hardly any science at all.

I told them that I was looking for an opportunity to do American studies, because if you decided to do it as a single honours degree, later you could spend a year in the USA on an exchange programme. This appealed to me, but I knew an American studies degree would be pretty useless for any career, so I decided to do a combined honours degree. For this, I'd have to choose three subjects initially, study them all for the foundation year, then choose two majors at the end of the first year and drop one subject.

They said that there was 'no prior experience required for sociology', and I figured that's what social workers study. Perhaps if I studied that, I could find out what they're teaching social workers that causes them to mess kids' lives up in the way they do? So I chose that as well. Finally, I needed one more subject. I'd travelled the world, and learned a lot about different countries, world affairs and geo politics from my time with Gil, as well as weather cycles and the natural environment from my time at sea. I'd also done almost five years of horticulture on the farm at Greystone Heath so I thought I'd try out for geography. I had a passion for the physical environment, and I had developed an understanding of the topography of places around the world and the political impact of environmental matters such as pollution. At Greystone Heath they also kept bees, they had a goat, and they produced crops. They had an orchard of apples and pears that we harvested and from which they produced cider. I hated the farmer, Jim Murray, who was bigoted and both a physically and verbally aggressive man, but I'd learned a lot about cultivating the land and growing produce while I was there.

As I didn't have the requisite qualifications to gain a place to study any of these subjects, it came down to convincing admissions tutors that I had what it took to become a serious student. My case was helped by my BTEC performance review for my first year at college, through Littlewoods. Though that course had no relevance to the ones I was applying for, I had achieved distinctions in four out of my five subjects, which showed that I had the capacity and diligence to succeed – if afforded an opportunity.

I also put forward strong arguments when I met the respective tutors for each subject. I told the sociology tutor, 'Well, I've spent most of my childhood in care and dealt with social workers, with heads full of sociology, so I've seen the perspectives these guys are taught from the recipient's side and I understand the system from within.'

There was no reason to meet the American studies tutor, because anyone could do that course. There were no A-levels in American studies, as it was something of a pseudo-subject that no one took that seriously.

Then I met the course leader for physical geography, a guy called Jim Moore. The name didn't ring any bells at that time, but the first thing he said when I walked into his office was, 'Don't I know you from somewhere?' 'No, I don't think so,' I replied. 'What school did you go to?' 'Several schools.' 'Ever gone to Gateacre Comprehensive?' This, of course, was the place where I'd had the fight with Floyd and been subsequently expelled. My face went as close to white as a black man's could ever get. I couldn't bring myself to tell him the truth, so I just said, 'No.' Thankfully, he bypassed that part of my history and asked if I had a geography background. I explained that I had a lot of experiences in farming as a child, doing horticulture for four and a half years, that I had travelled the world, by going to sea, and this had given me an understanding of the natural environment, as well as geo politics. It all came down to Jim Moore's decision. If he said yes, I was in, if he said no, I was fresh out of subjects, and would probably have had to throw in the towel and try something else.

'I shouldn't really do this,' he said, 'but I'm going to give you a chance. I believe everybody deserves a chance.' I was elated, this pushed me over the line. I was finally going to university. On the basis of that decision, I was accepted into LIHE (Liverpool Institute of Higher Education) and I began my studies there in September 1992. In the foundation year, all you were required to do was pass, and the pass mark was forty per cent. So assuming I passed the Year 1 exams, I'd get to choose one subject to drop and then I would spend the two subsequent years of the actual degree studying my two elective subjects.

The university was an amalgam of three Christian teacher-training colleges: two were Catholic – Notre Dame and Christ's – the other one, St Katherine's, was Protestant. Both St Katherine's and Notre Dame had been female-only, with Notre Dame originally run by nuns. St Katherine's had once trained female missionaries and was run by an order of monks from St Joseph's monastery which was across the road.

Students were still divided into houses – Catholics would register at the Christ's–Notre Dame site, and Protestants registered at the St Katherine's site. I'd already parted ways with the entire Catholic faith of my childhood, along with the whole drinking blood and eating flesh under the idols thing when I attended Catholic church at Greystone, so I registered at St Katherine's. Those of other faiths could choose either, and you would have lectures in both. For the purposes of the degree, all your studies would be consolidated and issued by your college as 'an accredited institute of the University of Liverpool', who were at time the awarding body.

My first thought as a fledgling Muslim was that this place was very hostile to Islam. My second thought was that seventy-five per cent of the students were women, and my third thought was that there were no black teachers and almost no black students. They were clearly averse to admitting black students, men and Muslims.

I was still feeling somewhat humbled to have been offered a place there at all, but it soon dawned upon me that I might not be wholly welcome. The university described itself as an 'Ecumenical University', which sent missionaries to Africa to convert Muslims to Christianity. When they realised that I had gone the other way, their hostility towards me was palpable in class, and doing my undergraduate degree in a university run by nuns and monks became a battle of wills. It wasn't helped by the fact that the university was in Woolton – a predominantly white suburb of Liverpool, which held so many difficult memories for me, from Menlove to the Liverpool Children's Admission Unit on Acrefield Road.

I remember walking out of there on the first day and feeling alone and out of my depth. I walked up to the bus stop and there were two black women standing there. Though I didn't know them, I couldn't help myself – perhaps they thought I was a bit crazy – but instinctively I opened my arms, raised them to the skies and declared: 'Black people!' They looked at me and said, in American accents, 'You know what, brother, we was thinking the same damn thing!'

Tonya Leslie and Claudine Fong were exchange students from SUNY Plattsburgh, a state college in upstate New York. They were studying English and had come over to Liverpool for a couple of semesters. 'We've only just arrived in the city, we don't know where we're going,' they told me. 'We don't know anywhere. We're staying in the halls of residence and we're the only black people there – can you show us where to go?'

This chance meeting was the start of a great friendship. For those six months Tonya and Claudine made my experience at the university bearable. In the lecture halls and seminar rooms, I would sit down, and the white students would get up to sit somewhere else. I remember going on a field trip and talking to a girl from North Liverpool with a similar background to myself. Later the other students would go up to her and ask, 'Why are you talking to him?' They would threaten to ostracise her, just for talking to me. So I realised early on that I wasn't going to make many friends in this place. On top of getting my degree, I formed an objective to find out what it was that caused people who were intelligent enough to get university degrees to be so ignorant about other people?

I also soon discovered that the American studies course at the university wasn't going to suit me either. When discussing the plight of slaves, post-emancipation, the tutor – who was a middle-class white woman from the Midwest – told us things like, black people 'were better off under slavery, because at least they had a place to live and weren't homeless and had work'. She'd also make comments like: 'The Indians had it coming, because they were so hostile.' She was a believer in 'manifest destiny'. That it was the colonists' Christian duty, to 'guide the heathens' and 'tame the natives'. She'd use quotes like, 'It is no sin to appropriate the land over which the heathen savage roams but which he never cultivates.' I was so upset after one of these lectures that she had to take me back to her office to calm me down with a cup of tea. She really didn't see a problem with what she was saying, and neither did anyone else.

To my mind, this was propaganda and bigotry dressed up as facts and it was being pumped out into fertile young minds, who would go on to become the thinkers, the movers and the shakers – the social policy makers – for the next generation. Stating that 'black people were better off as slaves' wasn't such a big leap from thinking that 'slavery wasn't a crime'. I had one lecturer who described the Cree Indians in Canada – who were fighting for land rights from the French Canadians – as 'a burden on society', who 'didn't make proper contributions to the tax system'. The lecturer talked of how 'they were always arguing about land rights' and 'getting in the way' of mining and mineral extraction. As we were being taught all of this, I was thinking, these guys have become like guests in their own land and you want to take away their last vestiges of freedom, like the freedom to fish in their own waters and farm their own lands – in their traditional way? I thought: you want to pollute their land, for energy independence, and you expect them to stop shooting walrus? As I saw it, this was not knowledge, it was the propagation of the system of hegemony that was the residue from the days of slavery and colonialism.

As you might have gathered, I didn't much enjoy my first year at university – socially or academically. In fact, had it not been for Tonya and Claudine, my first year would have been a total nightmare. I passed – but I needed some time to adjust to the new reality, and some space to develop the basic tenets of my new-found faith of Islam. My unhappiness there, coupled with my now tentative work in music management, were key in my decision to take a year out in 1993 – a year I spent mainly working with Jalal but also taking lessons at the local mosque with one of the imams, who taught me the rudiments of the religion and the basics of reading and writing in Arabic – the language of the Quran.

When I returned to university in 1994, I was no longer Mark Watson. By now, I was a lot further along my road to enlightenment as a Muslim and had become Abdul Malik Al Nasir. I continued my studies with a new cohort, whom I did not know – nor did I try to get to know them. I'd already had time to process the pro-Christian, anti-Muslim racist sentiment that prevailed in that institution and by now, like I'd done on the ships, I was ready to go in and get what I wanted out of the experience, with little regard for their opinions of me, and defiantly on my own terms. This brought me into conflict on more than one occasion, as I decided that whenever some racist, Islamophobic, white-supremacist, Judeo-Christian colonialist bullshit was being taught, I would challenge it openly and with facts.

I became the nemesis of many teachers there and they gave me no leniency. In 1995, I'd spent three days in hospital without sleep when my first child was born and as such delivered a key essay a day late. It was marked at seventy per cent, a first-class mark, but due to it being a day late, my tutor reduced it to half marks – awarding it a mere thirty-five per cent – which was below the forty per cent pass mark – from a first to a fail.

I'd been asking the university to assess me for dyslexia since 1992. I finally got my assessment and was diagnosed as both dyslexic and dyspraxic in 1996, while in my final year of study. It was too late to get any reconsideration for any mark-downs that had occurred before, but typical of my treatment at that institution, which couldn't abide the fact that a Christian could ever convert to Islam. Despite it all, I graduated in 1996, with honours.

That boy with dyslexia, who was taken into care at nine, thrown into a variety of cruel institutions – none of which showed any interest in his progress – the boy who had pretty much taught himself to read, was now armed with a BA honours degree.

Meanwhile, my legal case against Liverpool City Council Social Services – and at that time, Manchester Social Services (in respect of my time at Mobberley Hall in Knutsford) – still had a long way to go when I finally graduated. First, I'd had to wait for the conclusions of a slew of criminal cases that arose from a raft of allegations of abuse at six care homes, including Greystone Heath, Mobberley, Dyson Hall and Woolton Vale, all of which were being investigated in what was initially called 'Operation Granite'. Granite was later consolidated into what came to be known as 'Operation Care' as other cases in the North West of England began to emerge. Successful prosecutions in these cases were seen as necessary to provide a sound basis for the civil cases to proceed – or so the lawyers had said.

The other claimants and I still had the huge hurdle of getting legal aid in order to fight our cases in court. To obtain this, we needed to get past the problem of what they call 'statute limitation'. Under this statute, or act of Parliament, we needed to have brought our cases within three years of the offences being committed. But of course, at the time, we were children and thought what was happening was normal; after all, the people perpetuating these crimes were the social workers, the police and the courts. We didn't know they were offences then, since the brutality was normalised to such an extent that everyone accepted it. Of course, there were also cases of abuse where victims knew the horror of what had been done to them, but were so scared that they dared not divulge what went on. Even the few that did were not believed. If the likes of Langshaw were being protected to the hilt by people like Edwina Currie, then Home Secretary, then what could children in care, or the traumatised and maligned adults many of them grew up to be, do about it?

Eventually, we were able to argue that it was unreasonable to expect a minor to bring a lawsuit within three years of an offence, so this became three years from when you cease to be a minor – eighteen in the UK – meaning you should bring your case by the age of twenty-one. But most of us were already much older than that, so this didn't address our concerns fully either. So it went back to court, and it was argued successfully that where abuse is systemic and normalised to the extent that the victim is not aware that they have, in fact, been the victim of a crime, then the limitation period should flow from three years after they have knowledge that what took place was indeed a crime. So, if they had told someone like a doctor, or a counsellor or their parents, and had thus became aware that they had been a victim of a crime, then limitation should flow from that 'date of knowledge'. This ruling allowed most of us to bring historic claims, provided only that our solicitors filed suit at court within three years of that established 'date of knowledge'. Unfortunately, in my case, they did not.

There was also the matter of gaining access to our social services files, locked in their archives at Hatton Garden in Liverpool. I had to get hold of all the details of my history in care, before they realised that I wanted to sue. Many of the criminal files had been butchered by their archivists, and any incriminating materials had often been removed or redacted, making it very difficult for the criminal prosecutions. I wasn't a part of the criminal cases, so I simply made a freedom of information request to have access to my file, without alerting the authorities to any impending lawsuit. They agreed to allow 'limited access'. Before the authorities disclosed any file, they had it reviewed internally. They would then often black out (or redact) certain details – unless you had a court order for full disclosure.

The difficulty for many people who had suffered terribly in care was that when they finally got their hands on the disclosed files, all the key documents proving their claims were often missing. This frustrated the lawyers – to the point where they had to look at each claim on the basis of what was missing from the file, rather than what was there. They then reverse-engineered their arguments, to demonstrate that these files had been tampered with to escape liability. I doubt anyone ever proved who had removed what documents – but all of us fighting cases knew that a number of social workers who had been responsible for our care had later been promoted to positions of influence that permitted them access to these files. This included, in my case, Sydney House's former deputy warden, Bill Crabb – the man I'd walked in on in a tent once, receiving an oil massage from sixteen-year-old Stephen. After fighting off abuse allegations at Sydney

House, Bill was promoted to a desk job at Hatton Garden – social services' head office. It turned out he had never qualified as a social worker, and before coming to Sydney House he had worked as a bus driver. Now, just like Langshaw, he was an accused abuser working in the head office with access to the files of those who were claiming abuse.

When my request for access to my file was granted, I was told that it would be 'reviewed by a social worker' and I could then 'come in and ask her questions', but that I couldn't have the actual file. I prepared a list of questions for her in advance, to ensure I'd get the key info I needed. I wanted the details: which homes I was in and when, what my leave entitlements were, any sanctions on home leave entitlement, my medical records, assessments, my court dates and a copy of my actual care order from the juvenile court in 1975.

I went to the headquarters in Hatton Garden, Liverpool, and met a middle-class white woman there, called Janet Lenehan. She had prepared a summary with a chronology of my key comings and goings, along with a copy of my original care order, and the rationale for taking me into care in the first place. I immediately found her condescending and judgemental, acting as if she knew me, just because she'd read my file. I guess it never crossed her mind to question the people who had written it? 'I'm glad you were not one of my kids!' she said cheerily. 'You were a little bugger!' I guess she didn't know at the time how utterly inappropriate that comment was.

I knew social services wouldn't admit to anything that might constitute an admission of liability, so just to be on the safe side, I recorded the conversation and used the transcript in my evidence. Ms Lenehan unwittingly disclosed failings verbally, which she would never have put in writing, and this would later prove valuable in strengthening my case.

Of what was disclosed initially, the most useful, unedited information was simply the timeline of events. One of the hardest things to assemble, when bringing a case, is a record of precise times, dates, locations and names – which are all vital. I was nine years old when this all started and was totally unaware of the formalities and legalities in the background. All I knew was the results of them – what was actually happening to me. The timeline they provided proved a great aide-memoire for me to fill out all the blanks when I prepared my evidence.

Later, after I issued a suit against Liverpool and Manchester City Council Social Services and the court ordered full disclosure of my file, my lawyer was surprised at how intact my records were, compared to others whose files had many key documents missing. This, I was told, was because I was never abused sexually.

As I started to scour the documents in my full file, I came across a batch of handwritten letters. They were in a script that I immediately recognised for its scruffy scribble and its spelling errors; they were addressed to the social worker, between 1974 and 1975, by Flo'.

She was demanding that the social worker 'get this woman and her kids out of my house'. She also had letters petitioning for her by Councillor Margaret Delaney on behalf of the 'Pensioners Union' claiming: 'The stress of this woman and her kids has been the likely cause of Reginald's stroke.' I was horrified and took the letters to my mum. She was hurt and angry. For decades, whenever I had bumped into Flo' and on a few occasions when I'd visited her over the years since leaving care, I'd always asked her what had happened, why I was taken away. And Flo' would always say, 'Oh, it was your mother's fault.'

Just before I got disclosure of the full file from social services, I'd made another such visit to Flo' and informed her that I was 'getting the file' imminently. The next time I came, she banged on the wall and her neighbour came in. I didn't know the woman but I sensed Flo' had brought her in because she was scared of what I might do if I'd discovered the letters. I enquired, 'Can I help you?' The neighbour said, 'I'm just here for Flo', in case she needs me.' She'd never been there before when I visited so I asked: 'Needs you for what? I'm here to have a private family conversation if you don't mind?' Flo' looked unnerved but said to the neighbour, 'It's OK, we're just talking.' The neighbour started out of the door saying, 'Just knock on the wall if you need me, Flo'.' I recall thinking this was adding insult to injury. When I was an innocent eight-year-old child and you had the power, look what you did to me? And now you're an eighty-odd-year-old woman, you still paint me as the villain.

As soon as the neighbour left, I said to Flo', 'I got the file and I saw the letters from you, from Margaret Delaney and the Pensioners Union.' She paused and then look shyly at me and said, 'Sorry for that.' Three words! My entire childhood, my trauma, my family being ripped apart, years of childhood imprisonment, beatings, solitary confinement, soul-destroying racism, all reduced to three words – reluctantly offered by way of mitigation – after thirty years of denial and casting blame onto my mother, and that's all she had to say to me? In that moment, I put my arms around her wizened old frame, hugged her sincerely, kissed her on the forehead and gave her three words of my own: 'I forgive you!'

She seemed startled and said the final three words that we'd ever exchange: 'Thanks for that.'

I turned and walked out and we never saw each other again. A few months later, I heard she'd died and one of her friends had cleared out her house. I went to see them and she gave me some pictures of us as children, some of my old toy cars and my father's seaman's discharge book and death certificate. I wondered why Flo' kept childhood pictures of us, and why would she keep my toy cars for thirty years, if she wanted us gone so badly? I never found out and now it was too late. But I realised at that moment that she'd lived long enough to face the truth of what she'd done to me, to my mum and siblings – and despite all that I'd been through, I possessed something that she never did: compassion. She'd had to live and die with the knowledge of her guilt, but for me, I'd found the truth and got some closure, at least on that part of my life, and I found a measure of solace in that.

The file yielded many truths. One such revelation was that the social workers suspected that 'Reginald might be the father'. This meant that none of the adults had told the social services who our father was and the assumption was that my mum and her kids were simply lodgers, and therefore had no rights as tenants. This was the core argument being used by Flo' to evict my mum. They'd never admitted that he was my father, but we all called him Dad and he was one of only a handful of black men for miles around, so it wasn't rocket science.

The file did, however, have several specific documents missing, which related to the social worker Colin Derby's removal of me from Mobberley after I got stabbed and had a tooth knocked out, and also Bill Crabb sending me back to Greystone after the Lake District incident with him and the self-professed rent boy, Stephen, in the tent.

The lawyers were issuing so many other abuse cases at the same time that there was a preoccupation, of both the police and the lawyers, with the sexual abuse victims. The police would not even consider my case for criminal proceedings, even though there was evidence showing a victim and several perpetrators of violent assaults, some with severe physical consequences. At that time, they considered my case to be weak. However, after they started to assemble the whole picture of abuse at Greystone Heath School, the evidence of others would later shed more light on the significance of my own case.

It wasn't just the police who initially showed a lack of interest in my story. At first, lawyers didn't want to take on my case, because it didn't fit in with the two hundred or so other claimants involved. However, when a series of group action cases against alleged perpetrators of abuse at Greystone Heath and other institutions got close to court, my evidence was seen by the QC representing the victims as highly significant. I would later discover that the violent beatings I arbitrarily received at Greystone Heath and Mobberley were not actually random, as I'd always thought, but part of a sinister ploy by the abusers. What the lawyers argued was that I was used, literally, as a 'whipping boy'. I was a big lad for my age and being from the streets and pretty tough – even at nine years old – I was known as someone who could take a beating and not hang himself. This apparently, made me the perfect fit for this role.

The social workers, who were raping and sexually abusing specific individuals in Greystone in particular, wanted compliance. In order to scare potential victims into submission and keep the other children silent about their own abuse, the social workers would beat the crap out of me in front of everyone. I was being used as a tool to keep everyone else in line.

Suddenly, everyone cared about what had happened to me and my case became desirable for the group action – but by this time, I'd lost faith in the lawyers and had moved my case out of Liverpool to Manchester, and out of the group so I could go solo.

It had become obvious to me that the legal scene in Liverpool was a very tight network, with all manner of allegiances. There were care workers being indicted who had close relationships with people in the judiciary, as they'd been working alongside them in the courts for years. Some solicitors even hired former social workers to look over their abuse files and paid them as consultants. Most shocking was the revelation that my lawyer appeared to be deliberately slowing down my case so it would pass the statute of limitation (now set from my date of knowledge). She was also making overt efforts to cancel my legal aid, which would have closed the book on my case for good, but I contacted the legal aid board and demanded a change of solicitor, arguing that mine had been negligent and was abetting those trying to cover this whole scandal up.

I took on another firm, who were leading another of the group actions, and they essentially carried on where the previous firm had left off, trying to suppress my evidence and undermine my case. I spent six months in the city archives and extrapolated every set of minutes from every council meeting in chambers, every committee or subcommittee or juvenile panel that I could find, and went through them with a fine-tooth comb, extrapolating any detail at all relating to any home or person I'd come into contact with during my time in care. Accounts, budgets, floor plans, disciplinaries, hirings, firings, legislative changes, statutory instruments, policy documents, whatever – and I made copies. Then I sat down with a highlighter pen for three months making a note of any correlations between details and writing a report as an addendum to my statement of evidence. When I completed it and showed it to my solicitor, it was 46,000 words long. Each document referred to within it was duly cited using the Harvard method that I'd learned at university. My own solicitor did everything in his power to tell me that it was inadmissible.

I demanded a change of barrister and a specialist QC, which was eventually granted. My choice was the eminent recorder Judge Allan Levy, QC, who had chaired the Staffordshire PinDown public inquiry. There was no one more qualified than him for a case like mine. My solicitor and I attended his chambers in London. I asked him – in front of my lawyer: 'Is the appendix to my statement admissible?' He drew a breath, leaned back and then said purposefully, 'Do you know what you've done here?' My bowels started to stir, as I immediately thought I'd unwittingly done something to undermine the whole case, due to my lack of legal training. 'I have no idea, Mr Levy, what have I done?' He said, 'I chair public inquiries, and what you have produced here, single-handedly, is a competent public inquiry.' He then proceeded to offer me a pupillage in his chambers, if I ever decided to be a barrister. The look on my lawyer's face said it all.

He had clearly been acting against his own client and the QC had flushed him out – he had to go.

Shortly after returning from the meeting in chambers with the QC, I sacked the second law firm. Predictably, they also tried – and almost succeeded – in getting my legal aid cancelled. I short-circuited their plans by putting in a complaint to the legal services commission, arguing that 'the guy at their high-cost case unit', who approved or rejected applications for legal aid in these cases, was 'colluding with my solicitors, to cover up their negligence'.

I also invited them to independently audit my file – which they did – and they simultaneously removed that legal aid guy from my case – as I had an active complaint against him – and assigned me someone else, who approved my legal aid, so I could still bring my case to court. But now having potentially fallen foul of the 'date of knowledge' in the limitation period, due to my solicitor's failure to issue proceedings in a timely manner, I could get to court and have my case collapse on that technicality alone. I didn't have a choice. The last opportunity I had for justice was a provision in the statute limitation, which gave the sitting judge a 'wide discretion to disallow the limitation period, if not doing so would be prejudicial to the plaintiff' – in this case, me.

My reputation with local lawyers now preceded me and no one would take my case on. In the end, I went through the Legal Services Commission's entire list of lawyers in the North West and contacted them all. The very last one – Hugh Potter in Manchester – returned my call. I told him I had a hearing in court to have my case – now detached from the group action – moved from Liverpool to Manchester, and I needed a lawyer. I said that if he didn't represent me, I would have to represent myself. At that stage, Hugh would only agree to attend this hearing as an observer. The district judge at the hearing agreed to allow the case to proceed in Manchester; and Hugh said he would take on the case, if legal aid was willing to approve a further change of solicitor, which they did. When Hugh looked through my files, he said that in the twenty or so years he'd practised as a solicitor, he had never seen a case 'so deliberately mismanaged'. That was the beginning of the end of the whole long battle against my own lawyers. With Hugh's perseverance and legal know-how, we started making rapid progress.

Liverpool City Council Social Services, sensing that the game was now entering the final stages, started making offers to settle the case out of court. The first offer was a laughable £8,000. Then it became £35,000. Then £80,000. I never responded to any of them. I wanted my day in court, and that was it. However, at this stage, Hugh advised me, that this could be considered by some as a 'reasonable offer' – and that if I turned it down and it went to trial, it would be on record that a 'reasonable offer' had been made – and if I lost, I would be exposed to costs in the region of £500,000. Effectively, it would have bankrupted me. There was a big risk involved, but I had a sense of responsibility – if I won the case at the high court, it would set a precedent – and there were other people whose cases would be affected. Two guys who had been in the homes had already committed suicide, before their cases were settled.

On the day before the trial was due to begin, Liverpool City Council Social Services raised the offer to £120,000 with a public apology from the City Solicitor. I again refused; I wanted a public apology from the Lord Mayor of Liverpool on paper with a Town Hall letterhead. But the Lord Mayor of Liverpool had never made a public apology before, and I was told he wasn't going to be making one now. Then at 10 a.m., on the day of the trial, and with the court sitting, Liverpool City Council Social Services agreed to my demand – £120,000 and a public apology from the Lord Mayor with the Town Hall letterhead. Even better, it was not going to be an 'out-of-court settlement', with all the secrecy that shrouds the details. This was to be what is called an 'in-court settlement', so I would get an actual legal judgement. This was the best victory I could have hoped for.

My long and torturous battle to get justice for my time in care was finally won. Over the years that I'd fought the case, I'd often spoken to Gil about it. He would listen intently – for hours on end. He wanted to know all the twists and turns – I think he was fascinated, particularly, by the strange behaviour of my lawyers in Liverpool. He wrapped his head around all the complexities and legalities easily and invariably summed up several hours of my descriptions of the events and arguments in a few short sentences. His advice was invaluable, and I always followed it. He even went so far as to write a statement of evidence by way of a character witness for the judge.

I had obviously showed an aptitude for law during the long fight for justice, as Hugh Potter offered to take me on as a trainee if I did a GDL (Graduate Diploma in Law), and my barrister, who was also a pupil master and head of chambers, offered me a pupillage too. So now I had a degree that could be converted into a law degree with a one-year conversion course at Chester College of Law, after which I could either take a training contract with Hugh and become a solicitor or do a further two-year BVQ (Bar Vocational Qualification) and then take a one-year pupillage under my barrister at his chambers, or at the chambers of Allan Levy, QC.

I decided to apply, and was accepted into, the prestigious College of Law in Chester and started attending – with an offer of a training contract and two pupillages on day one.

I used some of my settlement money from the case to finance my learning. But a couple of months into the course, someone close to me could see something stirring inside me. She asked: 'If you could do whatever you wanted right now, what would it be?' I paused and said I'd sit down and write a book of poetry. The next day, I withdrew from the law school. I'd won my case, I had never intended to be a lawyer, I did what I did because my own lawyers (prior to Hugh Potter) were crap and working against – rather than for – their client. But Hugh had restored my faith that there were some good lawyers out there, and I could now see that my true vocation lay elsewhere. I formed my own publishing company, compiled my poetry and published it in 2004. The book was called *Ordinary Guy*, by Mark T. Watson, dedicated to Gil Scott-Heron and the Last Poets.

CHAPTER 14

A TRIP UPSTATE

I was heartbroken in 2001 when it was brought to my attention that Gil had been sent to jail. Our fortunes had switched: as my career was rising, Gil's was in a state of decline and it was a painful pill to swallow.

In July of 2001, Gil had initially avoided going to jail by accepting a plea deal, after admitting possession of half a gram of cocaine. He'd agreed to do a stretch of rehab on the condition he could do a tour of Europe before the rehab began. But he was arrested after the tour for failing to turn up for a court appearance.

It was around this point that the press started sniffing about, looking for a story. I took a call from a reporter at the *New York Times*. I asked them how they got my number? They said, a woman called Monique de Latour had given it to them. Monique was a girlfriend of Gil's, whom he had met a few years before. As soon as they mentioned her name, I knew what their game was.

It was Monique who had got Gil arrested and it seemed that she was trying to make a name for herself. She was hoping to drag us all in it with her, but my loyalty was to Gil and I knew what she was trying to do. The New York Times said they wanted to do a 'balanced piece about Gil', but I had never spoken to the media at all about Gil up to that point, and I certainly wasn't going to start by supporting the person who'd put him in prison. They were following her angle on the story and I wanted nothing to do with it.

I told them: 'If you want to do an article about why I'm doing a master's degree at university, under the mentoring of Gil Scott-Heron, then fine', but if their story was about bringing down the man who'd raised me up, then I wanted nothing to do with it – and with that, I hung up the phone. The New Yorker also contacted me, again saying that Monique had given them my number. I told them the same thing I'd told the New York Times. I have never spoken to Monique since.

When the New York Times article came out, its headline described 'a ravaged musical prodigy at a crossroads with drugs' and it painted a picture of a genius who began his career 'with an explosive brilliance', who had reached a point where a reviewer had described him as 'a raggedy old man'. Monique's description in the New Yorker was even worse. You don't speak about someone like that in the newspapers, to the cops and the District Attorney, and then claim you're supposedly 'trying to help' them. She destroyed the man she claimed to care about, someone who took her in when she was destitute, and I could never understand that.

At the end of a BBC documentary about Gil – which was broadcast in 2003, the year that Gil was released from that first term in prison – Gil says: 'I don't know who else I could have been, and I don't who else I'd rather have been.' But Gil hated that documentary – made by British filmmaker, DJ and musician Don Letts (of Big Audio Dynamite fame) – and he refused all requests from the BBC after that, relenting only once on the condition that he could choose the presenter. He chose the poet Lemn Sissay, and they did a final radio documentary for BBC Radio 4.

In fact, much was written about Gil around this time – and the theme was almost always his 'descent into drug addiction and poverty'. But this was a distortion of the truth. Journalists used the fact that he lived in a small flat in Harlem as a sign that by the end, he was impoverished. He was not impoverished. He could have had seven figures in the bank, but that wouldn't have stopped him living in a single room in Harlem. He was a humble man. He didn't like the trappings of wealth. His motivations were his generosity and kindness.

People knew he had his demons, but it was his courage that always grabbed their attention. In any case, if he'd sat in judgement over me when I was eighteen, and left me where he found me, I'd probably be dead now, so I would never profess to have the right to judge him either.

But it is hard to understand how a man of his talent and stature had ended up in jail.

He was incredibly resilient and resourceful, but he was by no means perfect. Jalal once described him as 'a victim of his own poetry'. The truth is, when you take on the system, the system hits back. Gil was outing the plots and schemes of presidents, CIA directors, FBI and COINTELPRO (Counter Intelligence Program) operatives, military contractors, despotic regimes, the KKK, apartheid South Africa, nuclear energy corporations; these were powerful and dangerous adversaries to have – and to be uncovering their crimes and indiscretions publicly was bound to have repercussions. It is therefore not surprising that Gil became a victim of drugs, and eventually ended up in the prison industrial complex, as that too was part of the 'Man's' plan for black Americans in the post-civil rights era. It was, after all, on George Bush Senior's watch – as Director of the CIA from 1976 – that the Colombian Medellín cartels of Pablo Escobar et al. flooded the black communities of America with cocaine, to ensure that there would be no resurgence of the civil rights movement, which had ended some eight years before. So yes, Gil was a victim. But compare the half gram of cocaine he was convicted for against the tons of cocaine that the CIA shipped into the black ghettos of America – on Bush's watch – and consider how Gil ends up in prison, having disclosed the corruption of government. Now consider that Bush goes on to become the president of the United States? There's a lot of irony there, but not so many surprises.

So in May of 2002, I flew to New York, hired a car and embarked upon a long drive northbound, to upstate New York, to visit Gil. He was being held at Watertown Correctional Facility, a medium-security jail just south of the Canadian border, near Buffalo. On that trip with me, was Gil's percussionist Larry McDonald, his bass player Robbie Gordon, and his US tour manager Melvin. Rob and Melvin had driven up the night before from DC, and met Larry and me in New York.

I don't think any of us on that trip found it easy to see Gil in jail. He was someone we all looked up to, as a close friend, an employer and, in my case, a mentor. Watertown Correctional – like most prisons – looked brutal, bleak, and far distant from anything remotely resembling a place where you'd want to be. How had it come to this? We were used to seeing Gil being idolised on stage, with hundreds and sometimes thousands of fans hanging on to his every word. Now here we were, heading inside a vast, isolated compound that was ringed by a perimeter fence, laced with barbed wire and patrolled by armed guards, to see him escorted into a visitors' room by men in grey uniforms.

Inside the prison complex that day in 2002, after we'd gone through all the security checks, they told us to take a seat in the visiting room while they fetched 'the prisoner' – even them referring to him as 'the prisoner' incensed me to my core. It took away not only his dignity, but his very humanity. A guard muttered as he walked in the room: 'Ah, the famous Gil Scott-Heron.' That was a taste of the sort of provocation he was being subjected to.

As Gil started towards us, another one of the guards called at him: 'Heron, come here!' Gil didn't have a choice but to go over to see what he wanted, and the guard waited until he was stood in front of him, then just pointed downwards and said, 'Tuck your shirt in.' I was raging inside at this point and wanted to rip into this guy but I had to remind myself he was a prison guard. I told myself you can't do that – if you say anything, he's going to take it out on Gil after you've gone, you just need to bite your tongue. Then I consoled myself by remembering that when Gil would eventually leave this place, he'd be Gil Scott-Heron, a superstar musician, respected globally, while this guy would always be some little prison guard, stuck in some backwater detention centre in the middle of nowhere. No one was going to know anything about him, other than the fact that he had once had the privilege of telling the mighty Gil Scott-Heron to 'tuck his shirt in'. At that thought, I smiled and let it go.

Gil hadn't been told who his visitors were, and when he saw us a huge grin broke out on his face. We all embraced each other. But despite this feeling of happiness, I think seeing Gil in this place – for myself, Larry, Robbie and Melvin – was a huge jolt. The reality of Gil being there hit us all very hard. It was like looking at a lion in a cage. You can confine someone and put them in prison fatigues, but you can never mask their true character. This sense of a 'lion in a cage' was amplified by the reality that the people running this institution really didn't understand just how globally influential Gil was.

What did come as a relief, though, was that Gil looked really healthy. He'd been pumping iron, eating three square meals a day – which he rarely got when we were on the road – and he looked more relaxed and fit than I'd seen him in years. Still, leaving him was the toughest part of the trip. Melvin drove Larry back to New York, before returning home to DC. Rob and I booked in a local hotel for the night and returned to visit Gil again the next day. I can't begin to say how hard it was to leave. I put $100 on Gil's tab, so he'd have some petty cash to get small things he might need inside. It was heartbreaking, and that long journey back to New York was daunting. Leaving Gil so far away in that desolate place reminded me of being institutionalised myself. I knew how much of an anti climax it was when everyone left, and you were the one who had to remain.

As it turned out, Gil clearly had the mental strength to withstand the negative psychical effects of incarceration. He would say to friends that he never complained in prison – 'If you complain, then no one wants to hang out with you,' he said to them. He also told me that he was writing new material. I asked if they gave him writing materials and he said, 'I don't need them.' He pointed to his head, 'I'm writing them here! I don't want these fuckers to see them.' I had no idea that he was – in fact – writing a new album, which would turn out to be his last.

Monique wrote loads of letters to Gil when he was in prison. He never opened a single one. I asked him why, and he said, 'I can't stop people writing to me in prison, but I don't have to read their letters. That way, they can't get to me, in a place where I can't do nothing about how it would make me feel. If I don't read it, it can't affect me.'

A year after his release from his first jail term, I produced the first tangible product of the years of help and mentoring I'd had from Gil and Jalal – my first book of poetry.

In 2004, after I'd received the cash from my settlement in 2002 from Liverpool City Council, I decided to publish a book of my poetry. I never sat down to write poetry, in order to become a poet. I had no desire to ever publish my poetry when I was writing it. Writing poetry was simply my way of resolving the dilemmas inside my soul, the issues within myself.

When I had started writing, I was semi-literate, and had a lot of angst built up inside me. I was angry at a system that had taken away my father's house in a mostly black but cosmopolitan area, and thrust us into a white, concrete ghetto miles away. They had taken me into the care system when I was a young child, and then seriously racially and physically abused me until I was eighteen;

then, they'd just thrown me out onto the streets with £100 and nothing else to my name.

I hadn't had a way to articulate my anger until I met Gil, and started travelling the world with him and also writing at sea. The anger had started fuelling my creativity, and it carried on for years.

But in 1992, I suddenly stopped writing. With the healthy scepticism that I'd developed working with Gil as my benchmark, I'd already started to question all I'd been taught growing up. But after becoming a Muslim and discovering the Quran, I started thinking that all this old knowledge and information I had been brought up to believe – via society and the care system and the schools – wasn't true. I had been misinformed by everyone and everything in my life; by teachers, by social workers, the media and by the Christian church. Almost everything I'd learned had been taught from perspectives I could no longer trust. I wasn't prepared to take anything I was told as fact, until I'd scrutinised it myself and measured it against what I now knew from reading the Quran. I was also getting first-hand accounts from people in the Caribbean and Africa about their history. Theirs was the take on history that white people hadn't written and would never admit to, like the barbarity of slavery and colonialism.

When I started reading the Quran, I began to resolve things in my head and discovered perspectives on life and religion that rang true in my heart and soul, despite my scepticism and general mistrust of people and religion up to that point.

I took a hiatus from writing in 1992 for a few years whilst I re-examined all that I knew in light of my new knowledge from the Quran. When I returned to poetry some years later I found that much of my work was actually in accord with Islam, which I'd now come to understand a lot better – and that was a factor in my deciding to publish my poems in 2004, after I'd won the case.

There was a big body of work I'd written from 1986 to 1992 that had been stored away for many years. I initially had no intention of ever returning to it. For me, it had already served its purpose, in developing my literacy, so that I could go to college and university. It had also acted as a catharsis for me – a way of excising the demons from my abusive upbringing, in the white ghettos and the brutal care system.

I'd never thought about returning to the verses, about changing or updating them, even though I was reading the work of a much younger me. But now, I decided that if I was to give them a new purpose and share them with others, I should stay as true to the original poetry, in the context in which I wrote it, as was possible. These poems were effectively a written testament to what Gil had taught me – and they represented a snapshot in time, encapsulated in rhyme. I had seen how Gil used poetry to uplift people but also to enlighten them, and – where necessary – to indict the system.

It was this aspect of Gil's work that had most impressed me. I had the same objectives: to seek justice and hold the system to account, for what it had done to me and my contemporaries. Soon poetry became more than just a tool to learn the skills to hold them to account; inadvertently, it became the most potent and enduring way of indicting them all.

I used to write prose and then try to find a meter in it, a rhythm to explore different lyrical structures or song arrangements.

Sometimes, what started as an anecdote, became a poem; what started as a poem, became a song; and what started as a song, became a story.

I also decided to use the pen name 'Mark T. Watson', rather than Malik Al Nasir, as the author of the book. The reason for this is crucial – and integral to what Ordinary Guy is about. It's explained by Jalal but in a nutshell the poetry is about my transition – going from one person to another person, from Mark to Malik – and my journey to finding the truth about myself and my life.

I spoke to Jamie Byng about getting the book published. Jamie had republished Gil's early novels in the 1990s with his imprint Payback Press, an offshoot of his bigger publishing company, Canongate. Jamie told me that Canongate didn't generally publish poetry – it wasn't that profitable. They had published some of Gil's, but that was because it was part of a bigger body of work. He did say, however, that he would be happy to help me self-publish it, and I was grateful for that.

I was also not without experience of desktop publishing; from the years I'd spent in advertising and PR with Ramona and later at Littlewoods, I knew all about typesetting, colour correction, reprographics, image manipulation, lithographic printing and magazine production – so I knew how to produce a few proto-type copies of the book. On Jamie's advice, I then went to the Frankfurt International Book Fair in Germany. Jamie introduced me to a guy who agreed to be my distributor and Ordinary Guy was no longer a pipe dream, it was becoming a reality. Jamie's team at Canongate got me set up with a printer, and handled the initial print run for me as a favour.

Gil was elated when I sent him a copy. This was not simply because it was dedicated to him but also because he knew that without his mentoring I wouldn't have been able to read or write fluently. And now here I was, with my own publishing company, publishing my own book of poetry – poems that he had appraised over the years. It was like everything had come full circle. It also demonstrates what you can bring out of a person, if you just give them the space and the context within which to develop their potential.

The launch event for *Ordinary Guy* was held at Borders bookshop in Speke, Liverpool, in December of 2004. By now, I already had plans for more than a book – I wanted to make a film and an audiobook to accompany the physical text. The idea for the audiobook was to record the narrative from start to finish. But that evolved into setting the poetry to a drumbeat – which was Robbie Gordon's idea. In the style of the original Last Poets' work and Gil's early output – such as his first recording of 'The Revolution Will Not Be Televised' – that became the next logical step.

A friend of Gil's called Shirani Sabaratnam – who was a film producer, married to Channel 4's then Head of Programmes, Stuart Cosgrove – agreed to direct and produce the film, if I could put up the budget. I arranged to have the launch filmed, so the footage could be used for the documentary later and Shirani attended the launch and agreed subsequently to help.

To get the audiobook started, I also hired Robbie Gordon, Gil's bass player – who was also a music producer – to come and record the recitals at the launch. I booked him a flight from DC and put him up at the Alicia Hotel in Sefton Park – where I'd once worked as the kitchen porter – and we stayed up most of the first night recording the entire book from start to finish with his recording equipment that he'd brought with him (to record the audio at the book launch).

Things really began to take off when Gil and Jalal both agreed to come on board too. Gil offered to record one of my poems to demonstrate how appreciative he was of my dedication to him in the book. After his release from prison, I made arrangements for him to go to Robbie's home studio in DC, where they recorded a vocal track for my poem 'Black & Blue'.

Then I flew to the States to film Gil talking about my work, in a TV studio in DC which Robbie had set up. Part of the film shows me interviewing Gil about the origins of rap in the spoken word genre, where my work fits into that, my book's significance and Gil's influence from the Last Poets. I also went into BBC Radio Merseyside and filmed an interview with veteran talk show host Roger Phillips: we spoke about my relationship with Gil and how he'd mentored me. That became the main narrative thread for the whole film. A friend in London, Steve Carney, who I'd lived with when I was down there, had a sister Anne who ran a production house, training women as camera crew and filmmakers. I called Anne and she and one of her students, Bev Le'Roc, came with two cameras and filmed the first Liverpool elements of the documentary for me. That ended up forming the main narrative of the documentary entitled *Word-Up – From Ghetto to Mecca*. To give it some black British input, I also went to London and filmed dub poet Benjamin Zephaniah, talking about the significance of my work and how it fits in to the political spoken word continuum, coming out of the Black Arts Movement. We also shot Gil's drummer Rod Youngs and me reciting poetry around the streets of London.

Jalal was living in Paris at the time we were making the film, so I made two trips there to film the sections in which he appears. I hired an English cameraman in Paris, called Stuart Nimmo, through a fixer. It was a memorable trip. I remember asking Stuart to take me to the Middle Eastern area of Barbes in Northern Paris that evening. He was reluctant – I think he thought he would stand out and they might steal his £50,000 camera – but when we went there, we were made welcome and he loved it. I could speak a little Arabic and wanted to eat halal food, so I fitted right in. Stuart seeing this relaxed a bit. I don't think ghetto shooting was his forte, but he was a great cameraman and a lovely bloke, and we got on really well.

Stuart took Jalal and I to his apartment, to film the interview and he captured Jalal reading 'Malik's Mode', the foreword that he had written about me – in rhyme. I also hired a recording studio called 'Mercredi 9' near the Rue des Pyrénées and I flew Rod Youngs in from London, and laid down some drum tracks for the audio book and filmed all that too. When I got back to London, Shirani had booked an edit suite at TV Soho with veteran TV editor Dani Jacobs and spent the best part of a week editing the film *Word Up – From Ghetto to Mecca*. I missed the start of the edit, as I was on a trip to Dubai for another project, but Shirani shipped all the rushes to me on VHS, and I sat up in a Dubai hotel watching the rushes and logging the time code of the key shots that I wanted to include. When I got back to London, I went to the edit suite and sat through the final edit. At last, the film was finished and as well as producing and publishing my first book, I had now produced my first film. It eventually premiered (in 2011) at the Phoenix Cinema in Leicester, as part of Black History Season. It was dedicated to Gil and went on to be shown in cinemas in the UK and Canada.

All that remained was to finish my audiobook. But that project was also evolving, and what was supposed to be the audiobook ended up becoming a full-on double album project.

By the mid 1990s my music management career had taken me far beyond untangling Jalal's back catalogue – though Jalal's influence remained as large as ever. I had begun working on a major music and media project with investment from the Middle East. Part of this project involved setting up a record label called MCPR, with the intention of producing Islam-friendly 'clean' music. This meant making music to promote 'harmony and understanding between the West and the Islamic world'. The musicians involved did not need to be Muslim, but the work would be produced in ways conducive to Islam – with no instruments except percussive ones and just voices and sampled sounds of nature, applied to various different genres, with clean lyrical content that you could play to kids. The music videos were made with no alcohol, or nudity or profanity on-set – very challenging when making hip-hop or reggae videos.

With the investment behind me I could start looking at acts to sign. One was the Liverpool producer Lloyd Massett – with some grime artists – called Raw Unltd. Lloyd had had success with OMD and had also worked out of Pink Studios with Andy McCluskey and Hambi Haralambous, during the Jalal and Bantu period. Indeed, it was Lloyd who'd introduced me to Jalal.

We recorded Lloyd's album at SARM West – or Hook End

Manor Studio – in Reading. The day we arrived at SARM West, Madonna and Justin Timberlake had just left. But when the album was finished, we took it to New York and hired ex-Hit Factory engineer Andy Grassi to mix the whole album, at Wyclef Jean's Platinum Sound studio. We needed to put up some cash to block the studio time. I wanted 'Clef and Jerry to know that I was serious, and I'd bring him more business, so I paid them $20,000 upfront.

People like the legendary bass player Stanley Clarke and the rapper LL Cool J were at the studio around the same time as us, also rapper and actor Lil' Bow Wow (*Like Mike/The Fast and the Furious*) came through. Shakira was making her biggest-ever hit record 'Hips Don't Lie', engineered by Grammy Award-winning engineer 'Super' Dave Clauss. For our money, we got a phenomenal team of engineers, including a young guy called Serge Tsai. Serge was from Surinam, on the Caribbean coast of South America, and he immediately got the idea of what we were trying to do with this percussion-only production. His colleagues Mike DeSalvo and 'Super' Dave Clauss had done all the recording on the Raw Unltd album and I'd started developing my album on the back of that project, using the downtime in the studio – through the night – after Lloyd's album wrapped for the day. We'd even flown Mike DeSalvo over to England to do the vocal recording with Raw Unltd's rappers at SARM Studios before Andy Grassi had mixed that album.

But for mixing black music, with drum ensembles, like what I was doing on my album, Serge Tsai was the man. He told us that in Surinam people were so poor they didn't have electricity for 'plug-in' instruments, so plenty of music was made using just drums and percussion.

As we had block-booked the studio, we had access for twenty-four hours a day. The way it would work is that in the daytime we would work on the MCPR acts (10 a.m.–10 p.m.) and then at night (10 p.m.–6 a.m.) I worked on my own album in what studios call the 'downtime', when they can't rent it to anyone else. Dave Clauss wanted to get experience (this was before he won the Grammy) so he was more than happy to work with us through the night. This arrangement also worked when we went back to the UK and recorded at SARM West. We brought Mike DeSalvo and worked with the same routine; days on the MCPR acts and SARM's in-house engineer Graham Archer did the nights on my album. It meant very long days – I remember staying at the Marriott Hotel in Manhattan while we worked at Platinum Sound studios, and doing twenty-hour days before crashing back at the hotel for less than four hours a night.

Working at Wyclef and Jerry Wonda's (the Fugees) studio had so many benefits. They put their whole production team to work on my albums. It was great to have that expertise on tap, and they added a lot to the process with advice, guidance and a fantastic set of production skills. Serge Tsai – Wyclef's senior engineer – mixed my album for me, and Rod Youngs and Larry McDonald (both from Gil's Amnesia Express tour) provided most of the drumming and percussion. In fact it was Rod Youngs who first coined the phrase 'Rhythms of the Diaspora'.

Working with their team at Platinum was an amazing break, and it brought some real talent to my records. My own album *Rhythms of the Diaspora, Vol. 1 & 2* featured Gil Scott-Heron – who recorded one of the poems from my book entitled 'Black & Blue' – and the Last Poets (Jalal Nuriddin and Kenyatte Abdur-

Rahman). It was released on my own label, Mentis Records, in 2015. Vol. 1 contained songs from my book *Ordinary Guy* and was introduced by rapper and actor LL Cool J, and Vol 2 also contained poems from the book and was introduced by bassist and producer Stanley Clarke.

CHAPTER 15

THE DRESSING ROOM

On September 18th, 2007, I was working on my song 'Innervisions' – a tribute to Stevie Wonder – at Wyclef's studio in New York. Wyclef asked me if I was working that evening? He said he was playing at the 'Dream Concert' at Radio City Music Hall, a 6,000-seater, art deco venue, with a vast music hall that used to stage a lot of film premieres – by 2007 it had become a major music venue, in the Rockefeller Centre, on the Avenue of the Americas in midtown Manhattan. To say this was a 'hot ticket' would be an understatement. The Dream Concert was staged as a memorial to Dr Martin Luther King Jr ('Dream' refers to King's famous 'I have a dream' speech from 1963). It was a fundraiser for the Martin Luther King Memorial Foundation in Washington DC.

Stevie Wonder was top of the bill. Stevie had not toured for a decade and the Radio City show was his only New York date that year. 'The Queen of Soul', Aretha Franklin, was also playing – as were Carlos Santana, John Legend, Usher, Ludacris, BeBe and

CeCe Winans, Kenny 'Babyface' Edmonds, Talib Kweli, Robin Thicke, Joss Stone, the country star Garth Brooks and, of course, Wyclef Jean. The great and good of American black talent – Halle Berry, Morgan Freeman, Russell Simmons were all there …

There was no way I was missing this show, so I let Serge carry on with the mixing, but asked him to print me a rough mix of 'Innervisions' to take with me, in case I got to meet Stevie. What seemed strange, though, was that Gil hadn't been invited. If you knew Gil's role in creating Martin Luther King Day in America – the first and only national holiday named after a black man and held every year on Dr King's birthday, January 15 – you would understand why it was strange.

In 1979 Stevie joined members of the Black Caucus in the US Congress to call for a national holiday to honour Dr King. A bill with this motion had just failed to pass in the House of Representatives, but momentum was gathering to honour Dr King with a holiday. In July of that year Stevie played at a big rally in Atlanta, and a year later a tour got underway in support of the campaign.

Stevie was going to do the tour with Bob Marley. Stevie was very close to Bob. His album *Hotter than July*, which he released in September of 1980, in particular the reggae song 'Master Blaster (Jammin')', was basically a tribute to Bob Marley and was written for that tour. But Bob was suffering from cancer and by then could no longer go on the road. So Stevie asked Bob who he should get to do the tour instead. Bob said, 'Gil Scott-Heron!'

I know that the cause was hugely important to Gil, having grown up with Jim Crow segregation laws in Jackson, Tennessee, one of the states where civil rights battles were still being fought.

Having had to run the gauntlet attending a white school, after the landmark Supreme Court case ruled that 'racial segregation was unconstitutional', Gil had himself suffered, first-hand, the racism and discrimination which Dr King had fought against and ultimately died for. Dr King was also murdered in Memphis, which is not far from where Gil grew up as a child – so the issue was very close to Gil's heart. He agreed to go on the tour.

Gil joined Stevie's tour in Houston, Texas, at the end of October 1980. On January 15th, 1981, Martin Luther King's birthday, the first half of the dates climaxed with a massive rally in Washington DC. I knew that being part of this musical campaign meant everything to Gil, and he had massive respect for Stevie for organising it and funding it. One of the reasons I know this is because Gil wrote a book about the tour called *The Last Holiday*. He was writing this book in the 1980s and 90s – I remember him giving me pages to read back in 1988. But he still hadn't finished it when he died. Jamie Byng, who published it posthumously with Canongate, had to get someone in to finish the last chapters.

Gil recalled one memory of going on the road with Stevie: a night in December 1980, when they played at the Oakland Coliseum and John Lennon had just been shot in New York. I guess it is hard today to remember – if you are old enough – or imagine what it was like when news didn't travel around the world as fast as it does today. Back then you relied on newspapers and radio bulletins to find stuff out. Stevie had heard the news after leaving the stage, before an encore. Gil writes very movingly about how when they both went out to address the crowd, all of the people there had no idea what had happened.

Gil also talked a lot in the book about how – unlike many – Stevie never forgot about what Dr King achieved – and how we should never forget what Stevie did to remember him.

When Wyclef asked me to go the Dream Concert, that September day in 2007, I agreed. I quickly got myself back to the Marriott Hotel in Times Square to freshen up. I dashed back to the studio to collect Serge's mix of my Stevie tribute, and headed over the few blocks to get to the show with Sharmont – Wyclef's road manager – who'd hooked me up with a ticket and a back-stage pass. When we arrived at Radio City, Wyclef was sharing a dressing room with John Legend. Next door was Robin Thicke – who one of the crew described as the 'blackest white man in America'. 'Clef said: 'Hey, Malik, did they hook you up?' I said: 'Yeh, man, thanks – I got access all areas.' 'Clef said: 'You know Stevie Wonder's on the next floor down?' He knew I was doing a Stevie tribute at the studio. 'You should go check him out, you got the pass?' I didn't need prompting. I headed for the service elevators and called the lift. When the lift opened, Aretha Franklin was in it, with two men – one on either side of her. I totally lost my shit! In that instant, I froze like a deer in the headlights and didn't know what to do. It was one of those moments in time when you feel like you are stepping out of your own reality, levi-tating and looking down on yourself. But I just couldn't countenance getting in the lift. I had every right to get into the lift – but this was 'the Queen of Soul'. I was star-struck and waited for the next one.

I'd rung Gil to tell him that Stevie was doing a Martin Luther King concert at Radio City and he said, 'Give Stevie a message from me?' I'd assured him, that if I could, I would.

I took the next lift down a floor and found Stevie Wonder's dressing room. I knocked on the door. His security guard, a Muslim brother, answered. I told him that I had a message for Stevie from Gil Scott-Heron. The door closed, and a few seconds later, it was flung open and I was ushered in and sitting next to Stevie Wonder. Despite their close friendship forged during that tour, Stevie and Gil had lost touch.

I sat down with Stevie and told him all about my relationship with Gil. He asked me if Gil was out of prison. I told him that he was, and then I gave him Gil's message. Stevie asked, 'Are you in touch with Gil right now, can you get him in here?' I said, 'Sure, man.' So I called Gil up and told him, 'Look, man, I'm with Stevie Wonder right now, he wants to see you. Can you come down?'

'Yeah, I can do that. Can I bring my lady?' 'Sure, I'll hook up two tickets.' 'OK, I'll be down,' came Gil's reply.

Stevie called his bodyguard – I think his name was Hakim – and asked him to hook me up with two tickets for Gil. So Gil and his girlfriend took the subway downtown from Harlem, and forty-five minutes later, he was at the stage entrance at Radio City. I headed down to the auditorium, and as I came out of the back-stage area Cuba Gooding Jr was standing there, right by me. Now, he is a major hero of mine, but I didn't have time to even think about trying to talk to him – I had to get to Gil.

At the entrance area of Radio City, I began to get a measure of the scale of this event. One side of the street alongside Radio City was filled with black stretch limousines – each one with the name of the artist in the window. Inside, there was just this frenzied energy you get when there are so many top acts about to perform. This crowd was thick with adrenaline. Eventually I found Gil, and the three of us headed through the auditorium. The atmosphere, by now, was electric, with the performances having just started. I struggled to get Gil to the backstage area. I flashed my pass, but the security man stood in front of us, and refused to let Gil and his girlfriend go any further. I said to the guy: 'Man! Do you know who this is?' He replied, 'I don't care who this is – he doesn't have a pass.' I said: 'This is Gil Scott-Heron. He is Stevie Wonder's guest. He is one of the reasons there is a Martin Luther King Day. This concert probably wouldn't be happening without this man. Now let him in!'

At this, the security guy put his hand in the air and just said: 'OK, go on, brother ...' Gil muttered sarcastically, 'Yeh. They got short memories.' But we passed unhindered after that. As we walked past, Gil started chuckling. He told me, 'I taught you well.' I guess he was laughing because he saw that same cheek that I had shown back in 1984, when I was trying to get backstage to meet him for the first time. Now, twenty-three years or so later, I was using that same front to get him backstage. The tables had been turned all right, and there was irony in that moment.

When we reached the dressing room where Stevie and his entourage were sitting, I opened the door and Stevie announced, 'Gil Scott-Heron y'all.' The whole dressing room with over thirty people in it all stood up and erupted into applause as Gil walked in. I was astounded. Gil Scott-Heron was getting a standing ovation in Stevie Wonder's dressing room: it was a precious moment and one that I will forever cherish. Then Gil and Stevie just sat there reminiscing about that tour in 1980–81. There were TV monitors in the dressing room, so we could see the show. When Ludacris came on stage, launching into some profanity with one of his raps, I remember saying, 'Does this guy even know why we're here, or what this represents?' Gil asked, 'Who is he?' I replied, 'He's called Ludacris,' Gil retorted, 'There it is! The answer's in the name.' And Stevie and Gil burst out laughing. They were laughing and joking so much they looked like a pair of schoolboys. Gil was saying, 'I am writing a new song, I got the verse, I just need the hook ...'; then Stevie said, 'Well, I've got the hook' and Gil repeated, 'I got the verse ...' It was something to see and went back and forth a few times before they moved on to other topics.

Witnessing Gil getting that kind of reception in that room, and then sitting there joking with Stevie, made a real statement for anyone present about his importance and place in black American musical history. In many ways he was a link between the past and the future. It came as no surprise years later when Gil received a posthumous 'Lifetime Achievement Award' at the Grammys and was also inducted into the Rock & Roll Hall of Fame. It would have been nicer, though, if he'd got that recognition in his lifetime.

Gil always described himself as a 'bluesologist', which he defined as 'a scientist of the blues'. His voice and music encapsulated the spirit of the blues tradition. He could be singing about pain, but he did it in such a way that he could make anyone listening feel really happy. I guess he had a way of finding a connection with people – through his music – which lifted their spirits. He was more than just a troubadour telling stories; he was one of the great sages of our time, who imparted profound wisdom through his literary canon as well as his extensive musical catalogue.

His importance shouldn't be considered only in the context of history though – his influence on later music is huge and far-reaching. Although he saw himself as belonging within the blues and jazz traditions, both he and the Last Poets are credited with being the founders or 'godfathers' of rap.

There was a long-standing rift that emerged between Gil and some of the Last Poets – mostly Jalal – about who founded what. When Gil first came on the scene, reporters used to ask him if he was a Last Poet. Gil would neither confirm nor deny it. Jalal in particular was incensed because when Gil brought out 'The Revolution Will Not be Televised', it felt like it sat in conversation with the Last Poets' record 'When the Revolution Comes' – except that Gil contradicted it.

Jalal took 'The Revolution Will Not be Televised' as Gil breaking ranks. At that time, the Last Poets were considered the vanguard of the cultural revolution, with the Black Arts Movement stepping in to fill the void left by Malcolm, Martin and the Panthers. The Last Poets were touring extensively on the college circuit while Gil was a student at Lincoln University. Gil had approached them after the show with a multitude of questions, and soon thereafter he'd emerged with this seemingly contradictory statement, in a format which was identical to theirs, all while allowing the press to assume that he was a Last Poet, thus capitalising on their platform. But what really pissed Jalal off was the fame that Gil went on to accrue, particularly after the success of 'The Bottle' on the Strata-East label.

At this time, there was a feeling that the FBI were targeting the Last Poets and trying to suppress their careers, fearing a second civil rights movement. Jalal felt that Gil was a sort of 'Last Poets lite' that was more palatable to America than the raw uncensored material that the Last Poets had become known for, after the underground success of their reputedly million-volume selling, 1968 classic, 'Niggers Are Scared of Revolution', which Alan Douglas released in 1970. So this rift evolved between Gil and the Last Poets, which was exacerbated when rap grew as a genre, directly from what they'd produced. The block parties that the Last Poets started in 1968 on the basketball courts had also evolved. By the mid 1970s, we'd see Jamaican DJ Kool Herc starting a new kind of block party, plugging his turntables into the lamp posts in the street for power – with the advent of hip-hop culture, spoken word and percussive break beats at its core.

Rap and hip-hop were now considered identifiable genres, and the accolade of 'Godfather of Rap' was given to Gil – and not Jalal or the Last Poets.

There were other claimants, too, O.Gs of the style that would become known as rap. The Watts Prophets, a west coast spoken-word outfit from California, were formed in 1967 after the Watts Riots of 1965; and their works were as unfiltered as that of the Last Poets, so there was a similar FBI effort to suppress them, as they were operating in the territory that spawned the Black Panthers. The US government was petrified of a resurgence of black power.

Some of the performers at the Dream Concert that night in 2007 wouldn't have been there if it hadn't been for Gil, the Last Poets and the Watts Prophets. But the difference between Gil and the Last Poets et al. and a lot of younger hip-hop stars – like Ludacris, for example – is that for them, when they started out, it wasn't about attaining wealth or fame. It was all about the Black Arts Movement, dedicated to keeping black consciousness alive, after Malcolm X and Martin Luther King were assassinated.

Jalal's motivation for rapping was about encouraging black self-determination. Gil's was – at first – about black southern voter registration. Jalal was waking people up to the real hustlers on Wall Street and Gil was talking about the hustle in Congress and the White House. But they were both trying to encourage black people and poor people, more generally, to stand up and claim their equal rights. However, that message got skewed and took off in another direction with a lot of hip-hop. Rap came from the same root but branched out in a different direction – some of it is now called 'conscious rap' but mostly it's what they regarded as 'unconscious rap'. Jalal would often say, 'We was rapping, whilst they was napping' – suggesting that rappers had produced nothing more than a parody of the real thing, considering the difference between the conscious and the unconscious. A lot of the performers took the music but left the message. They never took the time to understand what Gil and the Last Poets were really all about. They chased the bling and glorified the hustle and basically missed the point.

But in respect of the rift between Gil and the Last Poets and who copied whom, I was somehow caught in the middle. I loved and respected all of them, so when I started working with Jalal and he told me of the rift, I felt compelled to raise the issue with Gil. It was very uncomfortable for both of us, because Jalal was quite hostile about it, feeling that Gil had taken credit for what the Last Poets had started. Added to this was the notion of Gil being raised up, as the Last Poets were being pushed down. But I think, while there may have been some truth in that, there was also the fact that Gil took care of his business side of things and the Last Poets really didn't. Jalal could also be quite a jealous person and resented Gil's success. I spent years trying to get Jalal to see that they were to rap what Malcolm and Martin were to civil rights – both necessary, both influential in their own ways, but both pitching to a different segment of the same audience. He did eventually come round to this way of thinking and cooled out somewhat but it took me years.

At first, Gil had been slightly reticent and appeared not to want to go there with the discussion. I told him how Jalal felt about it and what his problem was, and he listened intently, but didn't really say much. But later he did an interview and the reporter asked him, 'What do you think about being called the "Godfather of Rap"?' Gil glanced at me, then looked back at the reporter and said, 'That title belongs to the Last Poets.' From then on, whenever Gil was faced with the question, he would either dodge it or credit the Last Poets. Later articles about Gil reference him as being 'reluctant' to accept that accolade – well this is the backstory to that reluctance.

Gil's prominence did enable him to influence hip-hop performers across the US and internationally. In New York, one of the first hip-hop groups, Public Enemy, often acknowledge Gil's influence on them and their cofounder Chuck D once said: 'From his voice and cadence to his wit and punchlines, the first hip-hop artists were able to take their style and attitude from Gil Scott-Heron.'

In Chicago, two of the biggest names in hip-hop acknowledge how he helped shape their sound – Kanye West and Common (who Gil described as 'a fine young man'). Kanye sampled Gil's

'Home is Where the Hatred Is' for his hit 'My Way Home'; and Gil repaid the compliment. On Gil's last tour in 2010, he spoke every night about Kanye sampling him and how on his last album, *I'm New Here*, he'd sampled Kanye. Gil neatly described this as a 'natural exchange that exists between artists'.

LA rappers Kendrick Lamar and Warren G, Philadelphia's Schoolly D – in fact, artists from all over the US and the world – have sampled Gil's music. This stretches back to the 1980s, and still goes on today.

CHAPTER 16

THE LAST TOUR

Though Gil took a hiatus from recording, due to the Arista case, his work was constantly being reinterpreted by a host of hip-hop artists, with samples and covers. His back catalogue was providing a seemingly endless source of inspiration for a new generation of artists, seeking to bless their own tracks with some of Gil's highly credible source material.

But Gil wasn't done. In 1994, I arrived in London to start the tour, and Gil was playing at the Jazz Café in Camden town (which at that time was owned by the Mean Fiddler group); however, instead of our normal soundcheck, MTV had set up some sort of a promo event. There were cameras and journalists everywhere, and this is where I encountered Gil's first post-Arista release, of the album called *Spirits*. Gil was back, and I had new merchandise to sell again. Gil told me that he'd made a deal with this record company called TVT, but if the record didn't sell a certain number of copies, they would own a piece of Gil's publishing. I asked,

'Wasn't that a bit risky, bearing in mind what you just went through with Arista?' 'No!' he replied, 'cause it's gonna sell' – and it did.

I think the threshold was about 25,000 copies, if memory serves me right? They hit that figure in the first week. See, what I learned from merchandising at the shows was that Gil's fans were hungry for any product he was associated with. By not producing an album for so long, but continuing to tour incessantly, what he was inadvertently doing – in marketing terms – was creating what they call 'a latent demand for the product'. People want it, but it's not available. As soon as it becomes available, there's a rush on the product. You'll see the same thing these days when Sony bring out the new PlayStation, or when Apple launch the next-generation iPhone. There'll always be more people wanting it than the market can supply. So the *Spirits* album was an instant success.

Gil also made a deal with TVT Records, to reissue some of his returned masters from Arista. Under this deal, I recall three albums being reissued, they were *Winter in America*, *The First Minute of a New Day* and *From South Africa to South Carolina*. The albums were originally released in 1974 and 1975, so by 1998 they were already more than twenty years old, meaning some of the crowd weren't even born when they came out. When people would heckle and say, 'When are you going to release a new album?' Gil used to joke and fire back: 'When y'all buy up all them old ones.'

In 1996, Gil had reissued *The Vulture* and *The Nigger Factory* through Payback Press; and in 2001, Gil had also reissued the poetry from *So Far, So Good* as part of a new anthology, under the new title *Now and Then*, a reference to his new material being packaged with his old stuff. Gil dedicated it to his mother, Bobbie Scott-Heron.

But despite the books, there were no new records forthcoming. After *Spirits* nothing new was released for some sixteen years. A slew of live albums and *Best of Gil Scott-Heron* compilations came out, but from what I could see Gil didn't have a lot to do with promoting them.

There was also the period where Gil was in and out of prison, between 2001 and 2007, where many people in the industry appeared to have written Gil off. But anyone who knew Gil, knew well that 'down' did not necessarily mean 'out'. I wasn't the only one who visited Gil in prison; Jamie Byng visited around the same time I did and was working with Gil on his long-in-the-making memoir *The Last Holiday*. But Gil was also receiving another key visitor, whom I knew absolutely nothing about at that time, a young producer and record company executive called Richard Russell.

Richard wanted to make a record with Gil, which meant heading off to the States. You could say the story of how this record came about started in New York's notorious Rikers Island prison – or you could say it all began in a teenager's house, in north-west London, in the 1980s. It depends on how you wanna look at it.

Richard started vibing to Gil's music as a kid. He had got a taste for American soul music from hanging out in 'rare groove' clubs in London as a teenager. Tracks like Gil's 'The Bottle' and 'It's Your World' would get played, and Richard picked up on the intelligence in the lyrics. Soon, he was listening to all his albums at home; LPs like *Pieces of a Man* – right through to the last Arista records – and TVT's *Spirits*.

Twenty-five years or so later, Richard was to have a major impact on Gil's career. In the early 1990s, during the rave scene in the UK, Richard released his own hit record, 'The Bouncer', and started working as an A&R scout for a record company called XL Recordings. The label signed loads of successful acts, people like the Prodigy, Adele, and Dizzee Rascal. By the mid-noughties, Richard was the chairman of XL – but despite being a successful music executive, I guess he still had a real desire to get back in the studio and make music.

Having been so into Gil's music as a teenager, Richard felt a big responsibility to bring Gil's music to a new, younger audience; and by 2006, he had the resources to be able to make a record with him – if he could find him, and then persuade him to do it.

Finding Gil was not as easy as he'd thought it might be. Richard didn't know me at that stage – if he had, I could have helped. As it was, he started by calling his friend Jez Nelson, a radio DJ at Kiss FM. He put him in touch with the documentary maker Don Letts – who made the BBC film about Gil in 2003 (which, of course, Gil hated). Don suggested he get in touch with Larry Gold, who owns the famous New York jazz club S.O.B.'s (Sounds of Brazil – not, as some thought, Son of a Bitch) where Gil used to play regularly. But no one seemed to know where Gil was, until eventually Richard spoke to Jamie Byng, Gil's publisher. It was Jamie who told Richard that Gil was in jail.

Richard then started writing letters to Gil in prison – and to his surprise, he started getting letters in reply. Eventually Richard went to see Gil in Rikers Island, and talked him into making a record. They immediately had a good connection. Gil realised

Richard wanted to make music that was truthful and good – not something purely for commercial gain. Gil had been asked to do other stuff and had turned it down, but I think he saw that Richard had the right motivation.

You see, if Gil didn't want to do something, he just wouldn't do it. He was quite stubborn like that. Big media outlets with millions of viewers would ask me for interviews and I'd put it to Gil and sometimes he'd just say, 'I ain't doing it.' I'd be like, 'But Gil, they have a twenty-million audience.' Gil would say, 'I don't care, I ain't doing it!' And that would be that. Soon after Gil got out of prison, they were in a studio and got under way with what would be Gil's last studio album.

Gil was considered a pioneer throughout his recording career – from his first record, *Small Talk at 125th and Lenox* (for Bob Theile's Flying Dutchman label), to 1994's *Spirits*. *I'm New Here* was also pioneering in a lot of ways. Gil went back to his roots in the blues, covering Robert Johnson's 'Me and the Devil' and transforming John Lee Hooker's 'T.B. Is Killing Me' to 'New York Is Killing Me', while Richard introduced the trip-hop, electronica and dubstep to the mix, which would take Gil to a whole new audience.

Of course, no one knew this was to be Gil's last record when they were making it, but there is something poignant for me in the fact that it starts with a version of Gil's 'On Coming from a Broken Home' – the poem he wrote in 1988, when I toured with him in the States, and when he reminisced on his childhood as I was telling him about my own.

In 2010, Richard Russell released *I'm New Here* on his XL Recordings label and what would be Gil's final album was born.

Richard told me of a moment during the making of that record that summed up what Gil was like. It captures his powers of perception. Richard is somewhat unique in the UK music industry, because he is both an artist and an executive. He said that one day, when they were working in the studio, Gil said to him, 'So is this what you do now? You do realise this is a demotion?'

What Gil was saying – or asking – is what did Richard want to do? Did he want to become a music maker, or just work as a music executive? Richard said that this was the dilemma he had faced almost all the way through his professional life, until Gil's question forced him to face it head-on. He decided that he couldn't be properly happy unless he was making music. And that's what he has been doing ever since. He's made about eight or nine albums since that record with Gil.

I'm New Here went on to be remixed in 2011 by the DJ and musician Jamie xx, who only used Gil's vocals from the original album and underlaid them with a heavy bass-driven sound. This remix, entitled *We're New Here*, and a later further remix by Chicago-based jazz musician Makaya McCraven, *We're New Again*, introduced Gil to new dance music orientated audiences, helping to preserve his legacy.

I'm New Here was Gil's first record for sixteen years, but it also put him right back in the spotlight. After that long hiatus, many people had forgotten about him. Others had been born and grew up without knowing him. Now, with a new album to promote, Gil went back on the road. To do a sell-out European tour.

*

You never think that your best friend is not going to be there one day. We just went to work as always. The tour was incredibly gruelling, and it was my job to ensure that Gil got to where he needed to be, show by show. I also acted as the liaison between Gil, Richard and the team at XL.

Richard contacted me with the two further remix singles that had been done of the track 'New York is Killing Me'. One was by Mos Def and the other was by Nas. Richard asked me to get Gil to listen to them, and ask him to approve them for release. It was a task, as the tour schedule was packed, and Gil took every spare moment to rest. But I eventually got him to sit down and played them to him. He asked me what I thought of them. I told him, 'Both of these artists are credible in the hip-hop world and do conscious rap. They have large followings and can expose you to a wider young audience.' He said, 'Yeh, but what do you think of the songs?' I said, 'They're both dope.' He said, 'OK, call Richard and tell them they're approved.' Which I promptly did. I think XL released them the next day. Looking back, it is insane to think of the trust that Gil vested in me and my opinion. I'm sure that if I'd have said I didn't like the remix tracks, he would have said 'no' to them. That's how tight we were, after twenty-seven years working together.

After all of Gil's problems, I believed fans needed to hear that voice again: that 'blend of mahogany, sunshine and tears' to remind themselves that he was not just a genius but a bluesologist who encapsulated the pain of our people and enunciated it for us with a noble elegance that was both soothing and inspiring.

The album made me think of the importance of giving people a chance to redeem themselves, but it also reminded me how fallible we all are, and why we need to be forgiving to our fellow human beings. One of the songs – the title track in fact – went: 'No matter how far wrong you've gone, you can always come around.' ('I'm New Here', XL Recordings, 2010)

It reminded me of the time when I met Gil, and I was down and out – in the homeless hostel – the black sheep of my family. I'd looked in the mirror at eighteen years old, just after I'd met Gil, and I'd said to myself: 'It's never too late to clean up your name.' That moment was a pivotal point in my life, when I turned my back on the streets, and embraced the opportunity that Gil was then offering me back in 1984. Here I was, all these years later, and this time it's Gil trying to turn his life around, and I'm helping him.

It occurred to me. That that's what human beings are supposed to do. If one of us falls, another should pick them up. When we stand tall and another needs our support, we should return the favour. This is the cycle of life – and in that moment, a whole life

On tour with Gil in 2010.

cycle had occurred and was about to conclude. But as George Clinton of Funkadelic reminds us: 'Every ending is a new beginning; life is an endless unfoldment.' I did the whole European leg of that tour and he sold out venues from London to Hungary. I feel so blessed that we had that precious time together.

The band was like a big family, both on and off the road. In many respects we still are. But like in any relationship, the dynamic evolves over time, as do the people. My relationship with Gil was different in 2010 from how it was in the early days of the mid 1980s. We'd often have heated discussions, which occasionally digressed into arguments. As anyone who met him would testify, Gil was an intellectual. People said he had a 'hyper-intelligence' and a perception so acute the word 'direct' doesn't begin to describe it. It felt like he could peer into your soul. People always said he had a deep spirituality and at the same time both a softness and a hardness to his aura. But he was also a very proud man.

When it came to proving a point, even if he knew deep down that he was wrong, he rarely backed down. Yes, he was extremely compassionate and sensitive but when things got serious he would argue a point as if he was arguing for his life. In the face of this, most people would just back down.

When you're talking about an artist who has had a certain degree of commercial success, people around them don't want to get fired. But my relationship with Gil was completely different. It wasn't a commercial arrangement as such. I was there because Gil wanted me to be there. I was his protégé. And without a proper employer–employee thing between us, it meant we sometimes had arguments. I rarely got the sense that he was reprimanding me. I think he enjoyed having an adversary, someone who didn't care if they would get fired. He respected that because he saw potential in me to speak on the issues that he was speaking on, without fear or favour. I never pandered to his whims or tried to flatter him. I never behaved like a sycophant. I kept it real from the day I met him, to the last time I saw him.

On one occasion on a tour, we were on our way to Modena in Italy, via the Swiss Alps. We were passing log cabins, covered in what looked like one-foot-thick pristine marzipan on the snowy rooftops. It was like a scene from 'Hansel and Gretel'. But inside the tour bus, Gil and I were engaged in a heated discussion. Everyone else was silent. I was at the front, navigating the driver, and Gil was in the middle – with his then girlfriend Aggidio – who'd joined us on that leg of the tour.

Our angry words were flying back and forth, the length of the Mercedes Splitter, as the bemused band sat in silence. Neither of us was backing down, and no one else wanted to get involved.

There came a point where Gil suggested to me that I didn't know what I was talking about. But we were arguing about the care system, and I obviously had substantial insight into the matter. That's when I became vociferous, shared some irrefutable facts and – as I think anyone present would agree – won an argument with Gil – for the first time. In fact, he swallowed his immense pride and actually conceded. He'd taken into account, on reflection, the dozens of in-depth conversations we'd had over the years about the care system. He knew that my insight was not gained from news media or other secondary sources, but from my own experience in the system, with all its horrors, and that I had spent years fighting legal cases around this issue. He knew that I knew what I was talking about, and he knew why I couldn't let it go.

All through this episode I got a feeling that Gil was trying to force the argument out of me. I remember Larry McDonald, with his flowing dreadlocks and a deep Jamaican patois, telling me: 'Gil like to test people, ya know? He always testing people to know if they for real or not.' In other words, Gil was getting me to substantiate my views, just as he himself had done many times over the years, and in the face of great opposition. He'd stood up before the world, knowing that he had lots of powerful people against him. Given the opposition, he knew that if I couldn't defend my point of view, I'd be ineffective in the struggle for our people's human rights. I'll never know for sure what exactly he was thinking that time in the Alps, or on similar occasions, but he made no secret of the fact to others that he was training me.

He wanted to know that one day, when I stood up on a stage doing what I do, I'd be prepared to share my worldview and back it up with evidence. I now realise that there's only one way to learn how to successfully argue your point – and that's to actually argue your point.

On Gil's last tour, however, he started being argumentative for a different reason. He had been frail – he had a number of health problems by this stage – and had started having me call people on his behalf but then forgetting about it. Generally, Gil didn't call people, you called him, so this was all a bit different. He was also starting to get things mixed up – even though he was totally sober.

As a result of his confusion, he would start shouting at me about who had sanctioned making certain calls and I'd have to remind him. One time, he called me up yelling, forgetting that he'd given me the very set of instructions that I'd executed. I basically gave him a piece of my mind. He hung up on me but called back a few days later.

I didn't pick up. I was seriously upset with him because it all seemed so irrational. I still hadn't known the extent of his illness.

When he rang again I thought to myself, Gil doesn't ring that many people that often, so I picked up and the conversation was different. He was still Gil, assertive and in charge, but he wanted to make sure there was no ill will between us.

A few weeks later it became clear why I got that call. He was putting his affairs in order. He must have known that he was dying, that his prognosis was not good.

At the start of that last tour, Jamie Byng had turned up at the Royal Festival Hall on the South Bank of the Thames in London with a film crew. Gil was playing a show at the venue, but Jamie wanted some footage for a project of his about Gil.

I'd driven down from Liverpool that day in my brand-new silver Mercedes C180 saloon and parked up outside the Royal Festival Hall. I caught sight of Gil's keyboard player Kim Jordan. She was doing a photoshoot for a Gospel magazine and when she saw me getting out of my Merc she gave me a hug, then she got right back to work – incorporating my car into her shoot!

I went inside the venue and saw Gil and Jamie and the band with some old friends; it was like a family reunion.

Jamie's crew interviewed everyone who was there, including me – and took Gil off to a studio to shoot him doing some solo performances on his Fender Rhodes piano. Jamie also filmed himself in conversation with Gil, discussing some of Gil's childhood memories and reflections on some of the most pivotal moments in his life and career. Gil decided that he didn't want to fly to the next show, he wanted to drive with me. So the band and the tour manager – Walter Laurer from Vienna – flew ahead, and Gil and I drove in my new Merc.

I ended up driving Gil across England and Scotland for most of the remaining dates of the tour. It was great to spend so much quality time with him, just the two of us. One of my fondest memories was driving through the Highlands of Scotland and arriving at a small roadside cafe run by two old Scottish women, who made their own cakes and jams. We stopped for refreshments and sat eating the most delicious apple pie and custard, and I remember thinking that I was the most privileged guy in the world, to be having this experience, with this great man, in this remote place.

As we drove off, I put on Corinne Bailey Rae's debut album, and we started to listen. It got Gil's attention. He was like, 'Who's this?'

'It's Corinne Bailey Rae,' I replied. I told him I'd read an article about her, and that she was just an 'ordinary girl from Leeds who got a music deal, having recorded most of the first album in a basement at home'.

'Fuck that!' Gil said. 'She ain't ordinary – find out who's handling her? I want to write a song for her.'

I did find out and it turns out that they'd be sharing a bill at Somerset House in London a few weeks later. I got Walter to reach out to her people but for one reason or another, it never happened. I couldn't make that gig – it was a 'mop-up' show a few weeks after the official tour ended, so I never got to speak to Corinne's people, and that was a missed opportunity. It is my hope that one day she'll hear about this and if she's so minded she might fulfil the last wish that Gil expressed to me in some form, perhaps by recording one of his songs or writing one about him – who knows.

After the UK leg was finished, we all flew to the continent for a gruelling European tour. On the last day there, we were in Rome, about to perform at a dance festival. Richard Russell had tapped into the dance world and Gil's new tracks were catching on in the club scene. The local Italian promoter, asked us if Gil would appear for an unscheduled impromptu pop-up performance, in a venue where no one knew who he was? Gil chuckled and said 'cool', so a little later me, Gil and the promoter left to do this mystery pop-up show.

With its ancient alleyways and buildings that date back to the days of the Caesars, visiting Rome – as anyone who has been there will tell you – is like stepping back in time. Just before we arrived at the venue, amid all this ancient splendour, I saw Jamie Byng coming from the opposite direction. We all greeted and hugged, walked a few yards and then arrived at this great doorway, where we had been told to meet. As we passed through it, I realised that we were in some sort of ancient monastery. We all looked at each other, somewhat bemused as to what was going on.

Beyond the gateway was a square enclosed courtyard, surrounded by a building several storeys high with balconies all round. People were milling about but no one knew who we were.

There was a PA system, a small stage with a microphone and a Fender Rhodes piano set up on it, and a couple of stage lights, but that was it. The promoter ushered Gil to the piano.

I noticed some Roman numerals on the wall, etched into the ancient marble with gold writing: 'MDLXVIII'. I looked at it, and then pointed to it and said to Jamie, '1568'. Jamie looked perplexed. He and I had discussed my lack of education in the past, and he'd always remarked how difficult it must have been, and how incredibly privileged he himself had been to have had a private school education. He hadn't expected me to have a working grasp of Roman numerals.

The irony was, though we were from opposite ends of the social spectrum, Gil had mentored and nurtured us both. We had the incredible privilege that afternoon to be the only English fans at the exclusive pop-up Gil concert, in a sixteenth-century monastery in Rome. Jamie and I sat through the whole thing, vibing off the music, cracking jokes and chucking like two schoolboys, while our teacher played the piano and sang some of our favourite tunes. These were magical moments that I will cherish forever.

That night, after this mini concert and the main show, which was staged on a marble rooftop built by Mussolini – of all people – Jamie, Gil and I all went back to our hotel.

I showed them some of the music videos I'd been producing in South Africa, Jamaica and New York, for the songs we'd recorded at Wyclef Jean's studio and then it was Jamie's turn. He had all the footage edited from the interviews he'd done with Gil in London, together with some intimate piano sessions Gil had played at the studio, on the day he arrived to do the show at Royal Festival Hall. In one of the interviews, Gil talked about his childhood and recalled the time he'd spent with his grandmother in Jackson, Tennessee. He talked about how his grandma had instilled a set of values in him, and repeated the mantra she'd taught him: 'If you could help someone, why wouldn't you?'

When I heard those words, I burst into tears. Gil and Jamie both moved to comfort me, they knew much of what I'd been through. But I was now so far removed from that homeless guy with holes in his shoes, who had snuck his way backstage in 1984, with nothing more to offer than a compliment. It was a sort of graduation from the faculty of Gil Scott-Heron. It was a sombre but somehow beautiful moment, and it was also to be the last time I would ever see him.

Gil had once said about me: 'When you see someone take the opportunity, take the chance that you're offering them, and run with it, and become a full-fledged adult, and an artist, and a gentleman, and a father and a husband, and a brother of peace and generosity, you feel as though the spirits have touched you in a special way, because they have seen one of your dreams fulfilled.'

A few days later, Bilal Sunni Ali, the saxophonist from the Midnight Band, Gil's first touring outfit – who'd written the horn parts on Gil's biggest hit 'The Bottle' – sent me a message on Facebook to say that 'Gil was ill', and that he'd been in hospital and some dates he was supposed to be playing in the US had been cancelled. I was worried. You see, the trouble with Gil was that he internalised his problems. He would never say if he was going into hospital, he wasn't that kind of guy; he would listen to all your problems, but he wouldn't burden you with his own.

I ended up phoning him and when I called his apartment number, I got his answer machine, so I left a message saying:

'Look, I really need to know that you're OK, can you give me a call.' A day or so passed and he didn't call back, so I called his cell phone; that was on the Friday. It went straight to voicemail and I left a message again, saying: 'Gil, I'm really concerned now, can you just please call me, just let me know you're OK, I really need to know you're OK.' But there was no response.

EPILOGUE

On Sunday morning, I was lying in bed in my apartment in Liverpool when the phone rang. It was Mick Ord, the editor of BBC Radio Merseyside. He was someone I'd worked with briefly a couple of years earlier, when I'd done an internship to get a bit more insight into radio. Mick had since been very supportive of me and had advocated for me as a referee, having been impressed with my work at the station. Mick said, 'I am really sorry to hear about Gil.'

I couldn't figure out what he meant.

'You haven't heard then?' I was a bit disorientated and quite bemused by the call.

'Mick, I've just woken up, what is it?' I asked.

There was a pause and a moment of awkward silence. 'I'm really sorry to be the one to break this to you, but Gil's passed away.'

I felt physically sick, I couldn't speak for a moment, my head was still waking up and simultaneously trying to process the words coming out of Mick's mouth. Mick carried on speaking, but I really had no clue what he was saying at that point, as my mind just went blank. Then tears started to roll down my face.

Later, I came to know that two days before, on Friday at 2 p.m. Eastern Standard Time – the same time that I'd been calling and leaving messages – Gil had been pronounced dead at St Luke's Hospital in New York City.

Mick had heard the news overnight and wanted a comment for the Upfront show, which was the only black segment they had on the station and which was due to go out that evening. His was to be the first of a barrage of press enquiries I'd receive. I told Mick I'd get back to him. I needed to make some calls, but people in the States would still be asleep due to the time difference. I felt helpless in that moment, so I called Jamie Byng. Jamie picked up straight away and confirmed the tragic news. We were both in a state of shock. Jamie advised me to speak to Richard Russell, since Gil had been touring what was to be his last album, *I'm New Here*, for Richard's XL Recordings label at the time of his passing.

Richard Russell and Jamie Byng were also being besieged by the media. When I spoke to Richard I got a bit more clarity on what was happening, but everyone was being asked for comment and no one knew quite what to say. Richard said to me, 'Gil told me about how he met you and a bit of your story and it sounded amazing. Can you just tell me – in your words – how it all came about between you and Gil?'

I had only ever had a professional relationship with Richard, but I found myself pouring my heart out to him.

Richard listened without saying a word while I spoke for about half an hour, and at the end he simply said, 'That's a powerful story. Would you be willing to tell that to the press?' I'd never spoken to the press about Gil, especially when they'd contacted me previously trying to dig up dirt on him. My immediate instinct was to feel uncomfortable about what Richard proposed, and I refused. But Richard said: 'Look, I've got people coming at me from all sides for a statement or a story on Gil and if I don't give them one, they'll likely just make one up. Your story is really powerful and it shows Gil's kindness – the likes of which the media and the fans would never see. I think if you tell them that story, they'll remember Gil in a positive light and not focus on his more recent difficulties with prison and drugs. The question is, how would you want him to be remembered?'

We needed to show the public the Gil whom we knew – the kind-hearted, super-intelligent man, who had changed our lives. So I agreed, and Richard directed his press enquiries to me.

That night I went into BBC Radio Merseyside and spoke of my heartfelt thanks to Gil for all that he'd done for me. It was important to me that his legacy lived on, and that people outside his fan base knew of his body of work, which had so inspired me. That was to be the first of my many interviews about Gil and how he had changed my life.

I also did an interview with the *Independent* newspaper, then *Mojo Magazine*, followed by *Rolling Stone* in the US, all referred from Richard Russell. Then the *Guardian* journalist Simon Hattenstone rang me.

By this time, a few days had passed and we had still not heard what arrangements were being made for Gil's funeral. I'd flown to Spain for a week's holiday with the family, which had been booked months before, and I was trying to mask my grief for the sake of everyone else, while simultaneously trying to work out how I could get to the US on short notice when the funeral arrangements would be announced.

I was in a park when Simon's call came through. He said he wanted just four hundred words for a piece to go in the *Guardian*. I began to tell the story and Simon took notes. After about half an hour, he stopped me and said, 'Malik, I can't write anymore, my hand has seized up, can I call you back in an hour?' 'Yes, that's fine,' I said – and an hour later when he called back I did the rest of the interview. What came next, I did not expect. The *Guardian* printed the interview verbatim over two double-page spreads. When it hit the news-stands, my phone and inbox started blowing up with requests from journalists in the UK and the USA. Then the radio stations started calling. I was trying to grieve but with all the attention given to my story, I had been tossed into what was fast becoming a media storm. I had worked in PR and knew about handling a story – but I had never before *been* the story.

I turned to my friend, the poet and broadcaster Lemn Sissay for advice. Lemn understood me better than most. He'd been through the care system and had had a horrific time of it. He too had become a poet, and he used his poetry to turn his pain into positive energy. He'd grappled with being a black kid, who'd been left behind by the state, but he had found his way and was one of my respected peers. I knew he would guide me right, and help me navigate this storm. When I called him and explained what had happened, he took such a cool approach to it. 'Ah!, he declared, 'they're having a feeding frenzy. Don't worry, brother, this will be very intense for a few weeks, but then it will die down and the news agenda will shift to other things. You just have to be organised. Take all their details, and then schedule things in a timeframe that fits for you. Don't let them push you around. They need your story, they will wait if they have to. Don't get crushed under the weight of it all.'

That was a pivotal moment for me. Lemn had not only reassured me that I could handle this as a professional, but he'd also given me cause to put my feelings and emotions aside, so that I could deal with the matter at hand without completely falling apart. I needed something to hold me together, I needed to feel that I had some purpose left. All my adult life I'd worked to improve myself with the hope that when I next saw Gil, I could show him how I'd progressed, so he could be proud of my development and inspire me to do even better. But that was all gone now. Gil was never going to be there to do that anymore. My teacher was gone forever. I thought, school's out! It was time to emerge, and put everything Gil taught me to good use. It was time to make an impact of my own.

Richard Russell rang again and said, 'The funeral arrangements have been made and I assume you'll be wanting to go?' 'Yes, I do but …' 'Don't worry about it,' he said, anticipating my concerns. He booked me a flight to New York, and he assured me that I didn't need to worry about anything. A few days later his assistant called me and booked me a hotel in Harlem, close to where the funeral would take place.

When I arrived in New York, I headed for the hotel. The first time I'd been in Harlem with the Last Poets in the early 1990s, Harlem was a ghetto – one hundred per cent black, the only white people I'd seen there were cops. But in recent years there'd been a gradual gentrification creeping uptown, and I was shocked now to see so many white people and boutique hotels and bars when I arrived at 125th Street in the heart of Harlem.

The next day I headed for the church on the East Side Highway where the ceremony was being held. For a brief moment, I was stopped by a family member, who wondered who I was. That was a gut-wrenching moment for me but fortunately the next person I saw was the saxophonist from the Midnight Band, Bilal Sunni Ali. Bilal and I had done several tours together with Gil, and were very close. Bilal said, 'Don't worry about that, brother, they don't know you. I've got you.' Everyone knew Bilal, he was there with Gil right from the start of his career and everyone respected him. I had a momentary flashback of trying to get backstage at the Royal Court Theatre in 1984, the very night I met Gil. And here I was again almost twenty-seven years later trying to get into his funeral; it was the completion of a cycle which was ending how it had begun.

There were many celebrities and high-profile music business people at the ceremony, which was broadcast nationwide on the black TV channel BET. After the funeral I approached Kanye West, who had performed, and told him I had a plan to stage a memorial concert for Gil in the UK. I wanted to know if he would be willing to perform. He said he was coming to the UK in November and that if I could get the concert arranged for then, then sure, he would be more than happy to perform.

As it turned out, my tribute concert to Gil did not take place until long after Kanye's visit to the UK that autumn. But while I never managed to get Kanye involved, the idea of a tribute to Gil began to expand into more than a single show – it became a programme of events in Liverpool that reflected the city's respect and love for an artist whose bravery, honesty, integrity, wit and inspirational qualities struck a chord with its people.

The strength of Liverpool's affection for Gil was certainly something I felt deeply, with everyone who was involved in getting the programme off the ground.

In another neat kind of symmetry, these events also showcased all the knowledge, skills and education Gil had given me – poetry, performance, management, promotion, political awareness.

And fittingly, what I organised to commemorate Gil ran in conjunction with the city's annual UNESCO International Slavery Remembrance Day. In honour of Gil, I curated a spoken word event 'Poets Against Apartheid – The Legacy of Gil Scott-Heron' at the city's International Slavery Museum.

There was a screening of my film *Word Up – From Ghetto to Mecca* and then of a documentary made by Iain Forsyth and Jane Pollard called *Who is Gil Scott-Heron?*, featuring interviews about Gil's life and work with a number of people who were close to him including myself, Jamie Byng and Richard Russell – who had commissioned it.

The programme also included a formal civic reception and dinner at Liverpool Town Hall, hosted by the Lord Mayor of Liverpool, with the climax of events being a tribute concert titled 'The Revolution Will Be Live!' at St George's Hall. I opened with my band Malik & the O.G's to a packed house, and we made the front pages of national and music press alike.

I released my album *Rhythms of the Diaspora, Vol. 1 & 2* to coincide with 'The Revolution Will Be Live!' tribute events that I co-produced, in honour of Gil Scott-Heron.

The tribute that I'd discussed with Kanye West at Gil's funeral had taken me four years to put together. However, with the help of Simon Glinn, who'd promoted Gil's last Liverpool gig in 2010 at the Liverpool Philharmonic, and the people he introduced me to – Yaw Owusu, curator of Liverpool International Music Festival, who commissioned this event, and Rich McGinnis, founder of the club night Chibuku in Liverpool, who partnered with me to create the production company Yesternight Productions – we would put on an evening that truly honoured Gil. With a packed house and a six-hour showcase, I got some closure on the loss of my dear friend and mentor.

For me, it was the final chapter of an amazing journey. I had come full circle – from a homeless, semi-literate teen, who'd snuck backstage at Gil's show, decades before, to having accomplished what I never thought possible. With my city rallying behind me to help pay homage to the man who'd turned my life around, I couldn't imagine a more fitting way there could be to say: 'Thank you, Gil. You saved my life!'

ACKNOWLEDGEMENTS

There are many people I would like to thank, and people without whom I would not have been able to write this book. In brief, and with acknowledgement that I am indebted to far more friends, family, mentors and colleagues than are listed below, I would like to extend my gratitude to:

Gil Scott-Heron

Jalal Mansur Nuriddin

Oli Wadeson

Simon Hattenstone

Simon Glinn

Rich McGinnis

Lemn Sissay

Michelle Anita Cowan

Reynold Parry

Ramona Da Gama

Richard Haswell

Guy Morley

Orphy Robinson

Wanjeri Gakuru

Sergio Elmir

Mahlikah Aweri

David Olusoga

Charles Walker

Olivia Martin

Indy Vidyalankara

Richard Russell

Bilal Sunni Ali

Kim Jordan

Larry McDonald

Phil Marshall

Tiago Coimbra

Julie Coimbra

Makhou N'Diaye

Mo Nazzam

Tom Parker

Nambuusi Kyeyune

Veslemøy Rustad Holseter

Paislie Reid

Sophia Ben Yousef

Michelle Parry

Cleveland Watkiss

Chantelle Nandi

Anton Brooks

Tim Harvey

Rory Brett

Carl Hyde

Michael Edwards

Jamaal Jackson Rogers

Bobby Davis

Sumita Bidaye

Katharine Patrick

JD Smoothe

Sidney Mills

Wyclef Jean

Stanley Clarke

LL Cool J

Marie Labropoulos

Phil Rainford

Pete Hooker

Mike Cave

Chris Gehringer

Marivaldo Dos Santos

Jonathan Idiagbonya

Ruari Frew

Elec Simon

Jerry Wonda Duplessis

Michael DeSalvo

Dave Clauss

Serge Tsai

Tonya Leslie

Matthew Hamilton

Karl French

Jamie Byng

Arabella Pike

Jo Thompson

Saba Ahmed

Ebo Shakur

Tusdiq Din

John Henry (Hank) Gonzalez

Sabine Cadeau

Jaqueline Parry

Ed Thomas

Henry Lord